D1604829

The Economics and Politics of High-Speed Rail

The Economics and Politics of High-Speed Rail

Lessons from
Experiences Abroad

Daniel Albalate and Germà Bel

LEXINGTON BOOKS
Lanham • Boulder • New York • Toronto • Plymouth, UK

Published by Lexington Books
A wholly owned subsidiary of The Rowman & Littlefield Publishing Group, Inc.
4501 Forbes Boulevard, Suite 200, Lanham, Maryland 20706
www.rowman.com

10 Thornbury Road, Plymouth PL6 7PP, United Kingdom

British Library Cataloguing in Publication Information Available

Library of Congress Cataloging-in-Publication Data

Albalate, Daniel, 1980–
  The economics and politics of high-speed rail : lessons from experiences
abroad / Daniel Albalate and Germà Bel.
     p. cm.
  Includes bibliographical references and index.
  ISBN 978-0-7391-7123-3 (cloth : alk. paper) ISBN 978-0-7391-7124-0
(electronic)
  1. High-speed trains—Economic aspects. 2. Railroads and state. I. Bel, Germà.
II. Title.
  HE1051.A33 2012
  385—dc23   2012013843

∞™ The paper used in this publication meets the minimum requirements of
American National Standard for Information Sciences—Permanence of Paper
for Printed Library Materials, ANSI/NISO Z39.48-1992.

Printed in the United States of America

To Aida and to my parents.
—Daniel Albalate

To Milagros and Anton.
—Germà Bel

Contents

Acknowledgments   ix

Preface   xi

Part I. Introduction

1   Development of High-Speed Rail in the World   3

2   High-Speed Rail in the United States:
    An Overview of the Debate   9

3   High-Speed Rail: The Analytical Framework   21

Part II. Case Studies Worldwide

4   Japan: *Shinkansen*   35

5   France: *Train à Grande Vitesse* (TGV)   57

6   Germany: *Neubaustrecken*   79

7   Spain: *Alta Velocidad Española* (AVE)   95

8   China: *'Zhōngguó gāosù tiělù*   113

9   Other Experiences: Italy, Korea, and Taiwan   129

Part III. An Evaluation of High-Speed Rail

10 Lessons from International Experiences   157

11 Conclusion: Desires, Beliefs, and Reality   175

Contents

Bibliography	181
Index	189
About the Authors	193

Acknowledgments

This book has benefited from comments and suggestions by a good many friends and colleagues from different areas. Although it is impossible to mention them all, we do not want to overlook some of them. We have profited from our discussions on different aspects of high-speed rail and infrastructure policy in the United States with John Foote, Rick Geddes, Tony Gómez-Ibáñez, Mildred Warner, and Viktor Chiyuan. Robert Poole and Samuel Staley offered us very useful suggestions on how to orient the publication of this work. We received valuable research assistance from Guillem Carrès and Anastasiya Yarygina. We are thankful to William Truini for his great contribution to the quality of the English language in this book. We are grateful to the International Union of Railways for the authorization to reproduce various high-speed rail maps from around the world. Lastly, we are grateful to Lenore Lautigar for all the facilities provided through the editorial process.

Preface

> Despite its dramatically rapid and massive growth over a period of a half century, despite its eventual ubiquity in inland transportation, despite its devouring appetite for capital, despite its power to determine the outcome of commercial (and sometimes political) competition, the railroad did not make an overwhelming contribution to the production potential of the economy.
>
> —Robert W. Fogel, 1964, 235

Robert W. Fogel is an American economist who was awarded in 1993 the Nobel Prize in Economics Sciences. The book *Railroads and American Economic Growth: Essays in Econometric History* (1964) is one of his most important contributions to the economic literature. Fogel greatly improved the empirical analysis of the effect the railway had on the US economy in the second half of the 1800s, and his main conclusion was that railroads were not indispensable in economic development. Therefore, Fogel showed that, contrary to previous historical arguments, the onset of the railroad was not the most important technological revolution in history.

The high-speed rail (HSR hereinafter) has been seen as a contemporary revolution in transportation technology. The concept of the high-speed train is generally used to designate a railway capable of reaching speeds higher than 250 kph (155 mph), which involves the construction of its own specific track. The entry into service of high-speed rail (*Shinkansen*) between Tokyo and Osaka in 1964 was a landmark in passenger rail transportation. Indeed, it was a true modernization in rail transportation, which was later imported to Europe with the Paris-Lyon line of the French *Train à Grande Vitesse* whose commercial operation began in 1981. Both lines were soon highly successful, both commercially and financially, and paved the way for the progressive extension of the respective high-speed rail networks in Japan and France. Later, the implementation of high-speed rail began in other countries, such as Germany, Spain, and Italy. . . . This transformation of ground transportation infrastructure has become the symbol of modernity in many countries, and, from the financial perspective, high-speed rail lines have become the most important projects in those countries where this innovation has been implemented.

The expansion of high-speed rail has been promoted with great enthusiasm and optimism by its supporters. This is so despite the widely recognized fact that only two lines in the world, the Tokyo–Osaka and the Paris–Lyon, have been able to fully recover the costs of both their construction and operation, as even the president of the International Union of Railways has pointed out.[1] Growing financial and economic problems, however, caused by the expansion of high-speed rail, have hindered arguments in favor of its extension. A recent pamphlet published by PWC[2] states that high-speed rail networks in Japan, France, and Spain are profitable "according to their respective companies" (Smith, 2011, p.8). Nonetheless, in reality only the first two lines (Tokyo–Osaka and Paris–Lyon) have been profitable, as mentioned above. A good deal of space in the same publication is dedicated to praising the benefits and, in particular, the financial profitability of the extension of the *Shinkansen* network in Japan, only to go on and state without missing a beat that:

> The government privatized the system in 1987 after the debt that had built up after three decades of continuous HSR construction reached ¥37.1 trillion, or some 10 percent of GNP. About 30 percent of the debt was assumed by the newly privatized companies, while the other 70 percent was transferred to a government agency, which recouped more than a third by selling surplus JNR land. Ultimately, however, JNR's outstanding debts passed into the government's balance sheet. (Noda, 2011, p. 20)

As clear as clear can be. The *Shinkansen* network had to be privatized because of financial problems caused by its extension, and a financial burden equivalent to 7 percent of GDP was assumed as public debt by the government, a small part of which was compensated for by the sale of public assets. While privatization has been used as extreme policy in Japan, the recourse to private sector through Public-Private-Partnerships (PPP) has not been an effective tool to extend HSR networks in the world. Examples of PPP failures are presented in the experiences of Italy and Taiwan.

In the case of Spain, the cost of the investment is not recoverable—the funds are non-recoverable—and it's very debatable whether the service will recoup all of its operating costs, there being a lack of information on individual lines. Despite this, the extension of the high-speed rail network continues in Spain, which now has the longest network in Europe. On February 3, 2012, the government of Spain announced the adjudication of different works on the Madrid to Galicia high-speed rail line, for a sum of $1.3 billion. This line, which extends from the center of the Iberian Peninsula to the northwest, and on which work is already under way, will have a total cost of more than $20 billion, for a total trajectory of somewhat more than 400 miles. The demand estimates for when the line enters fully into service are between one and two million passengers a year, although it is calculated that a volume of traffic several times higher is needed to recoup the operating costs alone. At the same time, Spain is cutting back on public funds for basic services such as health and education because of the present budget crisis.

This seems particularly serious to us, if we keep in mind that the public resources used for high-speed rail imply a regressive transfer of income, in that taxpayers are subsidizing journeys realized above all by users belonging to upper-middle and upper income brackets, who usually travel for business reasons and whose ticket (the amount of which is far from covering the total cost of the service) is paid for by their employers.

The implementation of high-speed rail caused a veritable revolution in rail transportation. Its process of extension, however, has descended a slippery slope that has made it a nightmare for the taxpayer. This dynamic can be seen both in the process of extension that occurred in the pioneering countries, Japan and France, as well as in the process of extension in other countries that have taken this path.

We are convinced that deep reflection is needed in respect to high-speed rail. And such reflection is also very opportune in the case of countries such as the United States and the United Kingdom, which are currently immersed in a process of public and institutional deliberation over the advisability of implementing high-speed rail. The debate on this transportation innovation suffers from too much voluntarism and too little use of the available data and qualitative analyses. For this reason, it seems to us that a review and analysis of the most significant experiences in countries that have implemented high-speed rail networks can be a useful contribution.

Our approach is that of economists. In general, we are quite concerned with the relation between what a public policy accomplishes and what it costs; that is to say, between the results it achieves and the use of resources it demands. In economic analysis, these questions are summarized in the comparison between benefits and costs. Our analysis doesn't solely examine financial benefits and costs, however, but also looks at factors such as territorial and environmental issues, among others, that transcend strictly financial aspects. In this sense, our work has multidisciplinary characteristics. We believe this enriches the analysis and gives it greater social usefulness.

The scheme followed in this book begins with a very brief review of the present state of high-speed rail in the world, where we describe both the networks in service in different countries, as well as the most important recent decisions made in relation to HSR.

Next, we review the nature of the debate on high-speed rail in the United States, which is centered above all on plans to create this infrastructure in California.

We also dedicate a chapter within this introductory section to analyzing what seem to us the most important issues observable in the experiences of high-speed rail. We use a methodological structure that permits a systematic analysis of the important questions relating to the financial and economic costs involved. This, however, is not all: we also address questions relating to the structure of the network, its impacts on mobility, its territorial effects, and its environmental effects.

The central section of the book contains chapters on the different national experiences, presented in chronological order according to seniority in the process of implementing high-speed rail and the size attained by it. The order of the cases thus runs: Japan, France, Germany, Spain, and China. The cases of Italy, Korea, and Taiwan are also included in a final chapter. The experiences of these latter three countries offer features of great interest, although because the information available is more limited than in the case of the previously mentioned countries, we have been forced to relax the structure of the analysis.

The work closes with a final section dedicated to extracting the lessons offered by the analysis of the different national experiences, and ends with a summary of the principal conclusions. We hope these will be useful as much to economists, geographers, and planners of transportation and mobility, as to those policymakers with responsibilities and decision-making capacities in relation to these subjects. We hope as well they will be of use to the interested general public.

A last reflection seems pertinent to us: the concept of opportunity cost occupies a central place in economic analysis. When all is said and done, public policy, and life in general, takes place within a context of limited resources that can be put to alternative uses. This was often overlooked in the preceding period of economic expansion, so abruptly interrupted by the crisis that has affected the most developed countries in recent years. In many countries, economic expansion was fueled by the availability of abundant financing at low prices (interest rates). As a consequence, the high level of indebtedness, both public and private, is one of the primary problems both at the present moment and in upcoming years.

In this context of severe budgetary restrictions, there is a growing need to carefully consider the existing alternatives in the use of public resources. Almost half a century of high-speed rail experience leads us to suggest that restraint, so often absent in the decisions made in so many countries, must recover a primary role in the decisions made in relation to projects that can so seriously affect taxpayers.

Barcelona
February 15, 2012

NOTES

1. See Victoria Burnett, "Spain's High-Speed Rail Offers Guideposts for U.S.," *New York Times* (May 29, 2009), www.nytimes.com/2009/05/30/business/energy -environment/30trains.html, accessed on February 12, 2012. It is worth noting that the fact that Société National des Chemins de Fer Français (SNCF) financial records do not segregate the Paris–Lyon line from other lines makes difficult to prove that full construction costs of the Paris–Lyon line have been recovered.

2. PWC, *Gridlines* (2011), kc3.pwc.es/local/es/kc3/publicaciones.nsf/V1/96A0A 717BE20B7AFC12579910038AED9/$FILE/Gridlines.pdf, accessed on February 12, 2012.

I

INTRODUCTION

1

Development of High-Speed Rail in the World

Almost half a century has passed since the first high-speed rail line went into service in Japan between Tokyo and Osaka in 1964. The great success of this line of the *Shinkansen* was followed by successive expansions of new lines in Japan, and in 1981 high-speed rail arrived in Europe with the opening of the *Train à Grande Vitesse* line between Paris and Lyon. The extension of high-speed rail in Europe accelerated beginning in the late 1980s with lines opening in Germany and Spain over the following years, while the network in France continued to expand. In the 2000s, a more accelerated expansion of high-speed rail networks occurred in Spain, China, and Italy, while lines on the principal routes in Korea and Taiwan also entered into service. Additionally, HSR sections of limited length entered into service in countries such as Holland, Belgium, and the United Kingdom to connect with the international network at different points.

Table 1.1 presents detailed information on the miles of high-speed rail service that are in operation in the world, as well as the miles under construction in countries that already have HSR service. The table only includes lines that are strictly high speed, that is to say, lines on which trains can surpass a speed of 155 mph. Background information has been obtained from the International Union of Railways, which presents data up to November 1, 2011, and lines whose maximum speed does not surpass 155 mph have been excluded. Furthermore, the Ourense–Santiago–A Coruña line in Spain and the Dijon–Mulhouse line in France, which both entered into service in December 2011, have been taken into account.

China has the world's most extensive network, with more than 2,000 miles in service and almost 2,000 miles under construction. It is followed by Spain, whose more than 1,300 miles of HSR make it Europe's leading

3

Table 1.1.   Miles in Operation and under Construction in Countries with HSR already in Service

Country	Miles in Operation	Miles under Construction	Total Miles in Country	Operation Miles/ Million Pop.	Total Miles/ Million Pop.
China	2064	1997	4061	1.5	3.0
Spain	1319	1043	2362	28.6	51.2
Japan	1297	235	1532	10.2	12.0
France	1265	43	1308	19.4	20.1
Germany	641	127	768	7.8	9.4
Italy	419	0	419	6.9	6.9
South Korea	256	116	372	0.5	0.8
Taiwan	214	0	214	9.3	9.3
Belgium	130	0	130	11.9	11.9
The Netherlands	75	0	75	4.5	4.5
United Kingdom	70	0	70	1.1	1.1
Switzerland	22	45	67	2.8	8.5
Total World	7772	3606	12296		

country, slightly ahead of France, which has almost 1,300 miles. If we include the lines under construction in Spain, amounting to more than 1,000 miles, Spain's leadership in Europe is secure, given the little construction activity currently taking place in France. Japan is the third country with the most extensive network, with almost 1,300 miles in service, and somewhat more than 200 under construction. Germany and Italy have more reduced extensions, while those of Korea and Taiwan are on an even smaller scale. As mentioned, Belgium, Holland, and the United Kingdom have lines of limited length that are used for their international connections.

The nominal comparison of the number of miles in service or under construction in each country offers only limited information given the significant differences existing between these countries in territorial and demographic terms. Perhaps the best way to compare the extension of the different networks is to relate it to the population of each country. Table 1.1 also presents (1) the number of miles in service per million inhabitants of each country, and (2) the number of total miles (in service and under construction) per million inhabitants. This makes it possible to relate, albeit in a somewhat generic way, the offer that exists and is under construction with the potential demand, which is based on population (in addition to other characteristics such as population density, wealth, etc.).

Spain's leadership is quite notable, with almost thirty miles in service per million inhabitants, very far ahead of France, which has less than twenty miles. If we also include lines under construction, the case of Spain assumes truly striking characteristics: with her more than fifty miles per million inhabitants it will multiply by 2.5 the ratio of France, which remains in second place. Belgium, Japan, Taiwan, Germany, and Italy present very similar ratios. Figure 1.1 shows in an ordered way the relative extension of the network in each of the countries with functioning high-speed rail service.

Although they have not been included in table 1.1, it should be pointed out that some countries without high-speed rail (strictly speaking) in operation are at present building lines that will offer this service in the near future. Such is the case with Russia, Turkey, Saudi Arabia, and Morocco. In all of these countries lines are currently being built that connect the principal cities.

Recently, the principal news regarding decisions for new lines has come from Brazil and the United Kingdom. In Brazil, there is a project being promoted to build a 322-mile line between the cities of São Paulo and Río de Janeiro. A great number of difficulties, however, are keeping the project from becoming a reality. In July 2011, the Brazilian government suspended bidding for the third time on a contract to build this high-speed railway because of a continued lack of interest from construction firms. The primary reason for the lack of interest by international companies is the view that the costs of the project estimated by the Brazilian government, $20 billion, are far below what the definitive cost of construction could reach, given the technical characteristics of the project and the orographical features of the territory through which the line would run. On January 10, 2012, the Brazilian government filed a new invitation to bids, and it is hoped that the bidding process will end in the fall of 2012. It is difficult to predict if this time it will be definitive and if construction on the new high-speed line can thus definitively begin.

The other important decision in respect to high-speed rail was made by the government of the United Kingdom, which proposes building an HSR line between London and Birmingham, with an extension to Manchester and Leeds. According to the announcement by the Secretary of Transportation of the British government on January 10, 2012, the first phase will see construction of a new 140-mile line between London and Birmingham by 2026. The second phase will see lines built from Birmingham to Leeds and Manchester by 2033. A formal consultation on second phase routes will begin in early 2014 with a final route chosen by the end of 2014.[1] The British government has delivered information on its decision, praising the beneficial effects of the project. It is interesting to observe that the government's informative material makes no mention of the economic costs of the project.[2] On the other hand, this information is indeed included in other, more detailed reports, such as *High Speed Rail: Investing in Britain's Future—Decisions and Next Steps*, presented by the British government to the Parliament in January 2012, which makes the following estimates on costs: "A high speed rail network of this kind will cost approximately £32.7

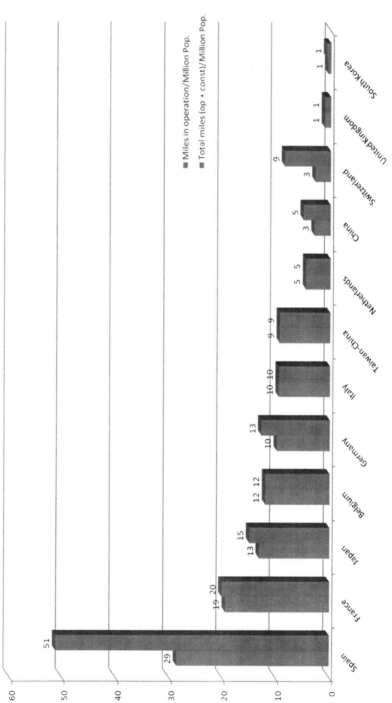

Figure 1.1. Miles per Million Inhabitants. In Operation and Total (Operation + Under Construction)

Legend:
- Miles in operation/Million Pop.
- Total miles (op + const)/Million Pop.

Data by country:
- South Korea: 1, 1
- United Kingdom: 1, 1
- Switzerland: 3, 9
- China: 3, 5
- Netherlands: 5, 5
- Taiwan-China: 9, 9
- Italy: 10, 10
- Germany: 10, 13
- Belgium: 12, 12
- Japan: 13, 15
- France: 19, 20
- Spain: 29, 51

billion [$51.8 billion] in 2011 prices over two decades to develop and construct, a total which includes significant allowances for risk and optimism bias. In addition, there will be rolling stock costs of around £8.2 billion in 2011 prices" (UKDfT, 2012, p. 26).[3]

Although the details of phase two are still unknown, the 140 miles of the phase one London–Birmingham line are expected to cost £16.3 billion ($25.8 billion). This means a cost per mile of $185 million in 2011 prices. This is indeed a huge cost per mile, even if no cost overruns occur in the future. According to the British government, benefits from the project are higher than costs. Only the future will tell, however, whether this project suffers from cost underestimations and benefit overestimations,[4] as is the norm for projects of this magnitude, above all when governments have political interests in advancing them. We should keep in mind the argument offered by the government in the report presented to Parliament, which stated that, "The Government believes strongly that the time has come to act with the same boldness as our Victorian predecessors" (UKDfT, 2002, p. 18). It is worth recalling that being brave in politics is often very expensive for taxpayers.

Probably for these reasons, the HSR project in the United Kingdom has met with strong opposition, both from analysis by prestigious research centers, such as the Institute of Economic Affairs and the Adam Smith Institute (see Hawkins, 2011), and from the influential weekly *The Economist*, which published on September 3, 2011, an article with the expressive title, "The Great Train Robbery," the subheading of which stated, "High-speed rail lines rarely pay their way. Britain's government should ditch its plan to build one."[5] In the same issue, *The Economist* published another piece titled "High Speed Rail: Railroad to Nowhere," in which it was stated that, "Plans for a new high-speed rail link rest on mistaken assumptions about economic geography."

A detailed debate on the HSR project in the United Kingdom is outside the scope of this work. We feel it is fitting to mention, however, that the report made by the British government to the Parliament in January 2012 refers to the fact that, "While other countries, such as France, Germany, and Japan, have already invested heavily in new high-speed links and networks to enhance capacity and performance on key interurban routes, the UK has focused on incremental improvements to existing lines" (UKDfT, 2012, p. 16). It is interesting to note that among the precedents cited in the report, Spain is not mentioned, a country that has developed its high-speed rail network more aggressively than France, Germany, and Japan, as we have seen.

In contrast, in the case of the United States, and more specifically in the case of California's HSR, emphasis has been placed on what a comparison with the Spanish case can offer to the debate in California, given the existing similarities in terms of population, area, population density, and distance between principal Spanish cities (Madrid and Barcelona, 428 miles) and California (Los Angeles and San Francisco, 432 miles).[6] The comparison between the cases of Spain and California has been the subject of other studies, such as one by Zhong, Bel, and Warner (2012). In later chapters, the Spanish experience will be examined in greater detail, as will be the experiences of other countries that have most ambitiously developed HSR networks. Before this, however, it is appropriate to look at the debate concerning the development of HSR in the United States, which we shall examine next.

NOTES

1. See the British Department of Transports' press release of January 10, 2012. www.dft.gov.uk/news/press-releases/dft-news-20120110, accessed 9 February 2012.

2. See decision on assets.dft.gov.uk/publications/hs2-governments-decisions/ hs2-governments-decisions.pdf, accessed 9 February 2012.

3. See assets.dft.gov.uk/publications/hs2-decisions-and-next-steps/hs2-decisions -and-next-steps.pdf, accessed 9 February 2012.

4. A good review of the systematic functioning of this type of bias can be seen in Flyvbjerg (2009).

5. This can be found at: www.economist.com/node/21528263, accessed 9 February 2012.

6. Comparative data on Spain and California can be found on the web page of *The Sacramento Bee*, www.sacbee.com/2012/01/15/4188592_a4188891/spains-high-speed-rail-system-offers.html, accessed 10 February 2012.

2

High-Speed Rail in the United States

An Overview of the Debate

The discussion of the prospects for high-speed rail in the United States has a long history.[1] A relatively recent, significant landmark in this process was the passing of the Intermodal Surface Transportation Efficiency Act in 1991, by which the US Congress mandated the Federal Railroad Administration (FRA) to select not more than five corridors as HSR corridors. In 1998, the Transportation Equity Act for the Twenty-First Century authorized the selection of six additional corridors, thus increasing the total number to eleven. These corridors were chosen in the following years.

An important step was made on February 17, 2009, when President Obama signed the American Recovery and Reinvestment Act, which provided funds (US $8 billion and US $1 billion yearly for at least five years) for the Federal Railroad Administration to assign to intercity and high-speed rail projects. Two months later, on April 16, 2009, the president unveiled his administration's blueprint for a national network of high-speed passenger rail lines. The purpose of this plan, as the president stated, is to reduce traffic congestion, cut dependence on foreign oil, and foster livable urban and rural communities.[2] Indeed, the existing infrastructure is deemed to be insufficient to handle the nation's future passenger and freight mobility demands (FRA, 2009).

Official reports have considered ten high-speed rail corridors, of different lengths, as potential recipients (see table 2.1 and figure 2.1),[3] although the Federal Railroad Administration received demands from forty states totaling more than US $100 billion. On March 14, 2011, Transportation Secretary Ray LaHood announced the designation of the Northeast Corridor (NEC), which includes the existing NEC main rail line and any alternative

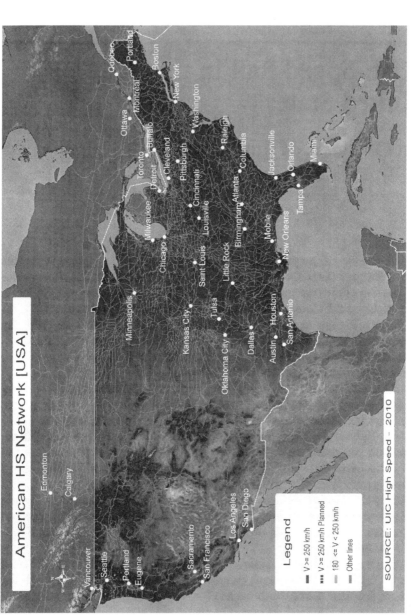

Figure 2.1. United States: HSR Lines. Source: UIC (International Union of Railways)

Table 2.1. United States Designated High-Speed Rail Corridors

Corridor	Major Cities	Characteristics	Miles
California	San Francisco, San Jose, Oakland, Sacramento, Merced, Bakersfield, Los Angeles, Anaheim, San Diego.	The new HSR system being developed in California is electrically powered. Such a system would operate at sustained speeds of 220 mph over much of its length on dedicated rights-of-way except for access to certain urban areas (e.g., San Francisco–San Jose). Phase 1 involves San Francisco to Los Angeles and Anaheim.	800
Pacific Northwest	Vancouver, Seattle, Tacoma, Portland, Eugene.	Designated in 1992. Incremental improvements planned to support 110-mph service with greater frequencies on the Portland–Seattle–Vancouver portion of the corridor.	466
South Central	San Antonio, Austin, Dallas, Little Rock, Oklahoma City, Tulsa.	The corridor consists of a hub at Dallas-Fort Worth, Texas, with spokes extending to (a) Oklahoma City and Tulsa to the north; (b) Texarkana, Texas/Arkansas, Little Rock, Arkansas, to the east and northeast; and (c) Austin and San Antonio to the southwest. The Texas Department of Transportation plans to connect the state's population centers on designated freight, intercity passenger, and high-speed rail corridors.	465
Gulf Coast	Houston, New Orleans, Mobile, Meridian, Birmingham, Atlanta.	This corridor would use New Orleans as its hub, with three spokes reaching (1) Houston, (2) Mobile, and (3) Birmingham and Atlanta. At Atlanta, the Gulf Coast Corridor would connect with the Southeast Corridor to Charlotte, Richmond, Washington, and Northeast Corridor points. At present, no corridor-type intercity rail service operates in this corridor.	940
Chicago Hub Network	Chicago, Minneapolis–St. Paul, St. Louis, Kansas City, Detroit, Cleveland, Columbus, Cincinnati, Louisville, Indianapolis.	This corridor includes spokes to St. Louis/Kansas City, Milwaukee/Twin Cities, Detroit, Cleveland, and Cincinnati/Louisville, with a link between Cincinnati and Cleveland via Columbus. In 2000, capital costs for the States' entire Midwest Regional Rail Initiative system (MWRRI, a plan advanced by nine Midwestern states) were estimated at $7.7 billion, for a ten-year program to achieve 110-mph service on many of the lines.	2,200

(continued)

Table 2.1. **(continued)**

Corridor	Major Cities	Characteristics	Miles
Florida	Orlando, Tampa, Miami.	The state of Florida has attempted more than once to develop the entire designated corridor (or portions of it) to support very high-speed (over 150 mph) intercity rail service but has not succeeded thus far in doing so. Tampa to Orlando HSR was most recently advanced as the first leg of a statewide system at an approximate cost of $2.5 billion on a dedicated infrastructure using the Interstate 4 right-of-way. The peak speed would be 150 mph with adoption of the electric power option. On 2011 the state of Florida rejected federal subsidies for HSR.	355
Southeast	Washington, Richmond, Raleigh, Charlotte, Atlanta, Columbia, Macon, Savannah, Birmingham, Jacksonville.	Plans show that with up to 110-mph speeds, trip times of two hours (Washington–Richmond) and four and one-half hours (Richmond–Charlotte) would be feasible.	1,490
Keystone	Philadelphia, Harrisburg, Pittsburgh.	The corridor consists of two different segments: Harrisburg–Philadelphia (Amtrak owned) and Harrisburg–Pittsburgh (Norfolk Southern owned). **East of Harrisburg:** The Philadelphia–Harrisburg segment is a mature passenger corridor, with frequent intercity trains. Speed on the line is now up to 110 mph. **West of Harrisburg:** The segment Harrisburg–Pittsburgh is a heavy-duty freight railroad, with only one passenger train round-trip per day. Significant infrastructure improvements would be needed to integrate additional passenger trains with the dense and growing freight traffic.	350
Empire	New York City, Albany, Buffalo.	The corridor extends from NYC through the Hudson Valley to Albany/Rensselaer and west across the spine of New York to Buffalo. In 2005, the NY State Senate set a Task Force to make	462

Corridor	Major Cities	Characteristics	Miles
		recommendations to continue the development of HSR throughout the State.	
Northern New England	Portland, Boston, Montreal.	With Boston as its hub, the corridor would serve destinations in Maine, Massachusetts, Connecticut, New Hampshire, Vermont, and the Canadian province of Quebec. The corridor currently includes routes from Boston to (a) Portland, Maine; (b) Montreal, Canada; and (c) Albany, New York, via Springfield, Massachusetts, with an extension from Springfield to New Haven, Connecticut. Frequent passenger service currently links Boston with Portland, and New Haven with Springfield. Less-frequent service connects Boston with Springfield and Albany.	705
Northeast Corridor	Washington, DC; Philadelphia; New York; Boston.	Designated on March 2011. America's most highly developed rail corridor. By 1992 the NEC had already undergone extensive renewal and upgrading and was already free of grade crossings south of New York and largely free of them to the north. Portions of it are capable of speeds of 150 mph.	456

Source: Adapted from www.fra.dot.gov/Pages/203.shtml. Info on miles completed with data from O'Toole (2009).

service routings for intercity passenger train service between the metropolitan areas of Washington, DC; Philadelphia; New York; and Boston.

Two types of project are included: one devoted to building world-class HSR corridors, as in Europe, and another aimed at making conventional services faster. Consequently, different investment strategies are envisaged: the promotion of new express services (on dedicated track operating at speeds over 150 mph), the development of emerging and regional services (operating at up to 150 mph on shared and dedicated track), and the upgrading of reliability and service on conventional rail services (operating at speeds up to 90 mph).

The United States has a rather *sui generis* conception of HSR. In the rest of the world, the term is generally used to designate a railway capable of reaching speeds of around 155 mph or more, which requires the construction of its own specific track (de Rus and Nash, 2007, p. 2). In the United

Table 2.2. Definitions: High-Speed Rail (HSR) and Intercity Passenger Rail (IPR)

Type	Definition
HSR-Express	Frequent, express service between major population centers 200–600 miles apart, with few intermediate stops. Top speeds of at least 150 mph on completely grade-separated, dedicated rights-of-way (with the possible exception of some shared track in terminal areas). Intended to relieve air and highway capacity constraints.
HSR-Regional	Relatively frequent service between major and moderate population centers 100–500 miles apart, with some intermediate stops. Top speeds of 110–150 mph, grade-separated, with some dedicated and some shared track (using positive train control technology). Intended to relieve highway and, to some extent, air capacity constraints.
Emerging HSR	Developing corridors of 100–500 miles, with strong potential for future HSR Regional and/or Express service. Top speeds of up to 90–110 mph on primarily shared track (eventually using positive train control technology), with advanced grade crossing protection or separation. Intended to develop the passenger rail market and provide some relief to other modes.
Conventional Rail	Traditional intercity passenger rail services of more than 100 miles with as little as one to as many as 7–12 daily frequencies; may or may not have strong potential for future high-speed rail service. Top speeds of up to 79 mph to as high as 90 mph generally on shared track. Intended to provide travel options and to develop the passenger rail market for further development in the future.

Source: DOT (2009, p. 2)
Note: Corridor lengths are approximate; slightly shorter or longer intercity services may still help meet strategic goals in a cost-effective manner.

States, on the other hand, HSR has been given a much wider meaning. Precise definitions for HSR in the United States have been provided by the Federal Railroad Administration–US Department of Transportation, as shown in table 2.2.

The definitions in this table show that only HSR-Express is strictly comparable with what is usually understood as high-speed rail in most countries, and particularly in those countries with the longest tradition and experience in building HSR networks, such as Japan, France, Germany, Spain, and Italy, whose experience we review and analyze throughout this book. In fact, among US programs, only the California High-Speed Rail project would clearly fit within the standard conception of HSR. It is worth keeping this in mind when drawing lessons from existing experiences.

The US Conference of Mayors produced an interesting study on the prospects for the development of HSR in the United States (USCM, 2010). The study was sponsored by the multinational company Siemens (in fact, one

Table 2.3.   Expected Demand for the Four First Routes of US High-Speed Rail

Route P2P	Maximum Speed	Miles	Million Passengers (One-Way Trips Only)	Year Forecast
San Francisco–Los Angeles	220 mph	500	7.2	2035
Chicago–St. Louis	220 mph	297	2.1	2035
Orlando–Tampa	186 mph	85	1.6	2035
Albany–New York	220 mph	142	2.3	2035

Source: Authors' own, based on info in USCM (2010)

of Siemens's major lines of business is the selling of rolling material and information technologies for high-speed rail) and analyzes the economic impact of the four routes where HSR development is expected to begin in the cities of Los Angeles, Chicago, Orlando, and Albany. The study predicts enormous economic benefits for these cities: in fact, the increases forecast are much higher than the typical 10 percent to 20 percent of usually accepted wider benefits in transportation studies (SACTRA, 1999), a range which is commonly used as the maximum threshold when wider benefits of transport projects are accounted for.

Particularly relevant to our current purposes are the forecasts on ridership provided by the study, which are displayed in table 2.3. The demand estimates suggest that the HSR in California is the only one likely to obtain volumes close to those in the most successful corridors elsewhere, such as Paris–Lyon, with twenty-five million passengers in 2008 (though far behind Tokyo–Osaka, the world's most successful with its 130 million passengers). Hence, it is worth turning our attention to the discussion on the California HSR.

CALIFORNIA HIGH-SPEED RAIL

The debate regarding the costs and benefits of building a high-speed rail system in the United States is a long-running affair, and the most intense analysis has been devoted to the California High-Speed Rail. In fact, this is by far the most important HSR project currently under consideration in the United States, and hundreds of millions of US dollars have already been spent on preliminary analysis and studies.[4]

An early cost estimate for the California HSR was provided by Levinson et al. (1997), which examined the full costs of an HSR system projected for a corridor connecting Los Angeles and San Francisco. The study concluded that it would be more costly than expanding the existing air service and marginally more expensive than expanding auto travel. The infrastructure costs alone were estimated at more than US $9.5 billion in 1994 (Leavitt et al., 1994), which is more than $22.5 million per mile.

The cost estimates have risen steadily ever since. An independent estimation made in late 2008 suggested that total HSR costs could reach $37 billion (assuming no overrun on any cost items), i.e., about $50 million per mile (O'Toole, 2008). Estimates conducted in December 2009 by the California High-Speed Rail Authority (CHSRA, 2009) as part of its Business Plan for the California HSR (San Francisco–Anaheim system, or Phase 1), put the costs at US $42.6 billion in the year of expenditure (2009 US $35.7 billion), an increase of 7.2 percent in real US $ over the California High-Speed Rail Authority's 2008 estimate.

These cost estimates were soon heavily criticized by independent evaluations. A report issued in February 2011 by Californians Advocating Responsible Rail Design (CARRD, 2011) estimated the real cost to be US $65.4 billion, based on information from official and publicly available documents produced by the CHSRA. In a report issued a few months previously, in October 2010, Enthoven, Grindley, and Warren (2010) had estimated the total cost of phase one to be US $80 billion. With time, these estimates have proved to be quite reliable.

In fact, the most recent official estimates, conducted in December 2011 by the CHSRA (CHSRA, 2011) as part of its 2012 Business Plan for the California HSR (Phase 1), predicted an enormous increase in costs: between 2010 US $65.4 billion (lowest cost feasible options) and 74.5 billion (highest cost feasible options), which represents an increase of between 80 percent and 105 percent with respect to the cost estimate of 2010 US $36.4 billion in the 2009 Business Plan.[5] According to the updated estimates, average cost per mile will be between 2010 US $126 million and 143 million. It is worth noting that the minimum cost is similar to the figure estimated by CARRD (2011), and the maximum cost is only slightly below the cost predicted by Enthoven et al. (2010). Indeed, the most recent official cost estimates are in line with the highest costs in Europe, those of the most expensive Italian lines, as shown in the corresponding chapter below.

In contrast, ridership forecasts have been reduced. The 2009 Business Plan forecasted forty-one million riders per year in 2035. However, the way in which the modeling was performed was heavily criticized by several technical reports.[6] Because of its robustness, it is worth mentioning the technical report issued in June 2010 by the Institute of Transportation Studies–University of California at Berkeley (Brownstone, Hansen, and Madanat, 2010, pp. 9–10). These authors state that "Our main conclusion is that the true confidence bands around the estimates from these models must be very wide. They are probably wide enough to include demand scenarios where HSR will lose substantial amounts of money as well as those where it will make a healthy profit." The 2012 Business Plan projected between twenty-three million (low ridership) and thirty-four million (high ridership) in 2035.

In conclusion, the projected costs of the California HSR have risen continuously, and ridership forecasts have decreased. Given these figures, it is doubtful that a high-speed rail link could be constructed in California without a considerable subsidy and that profitability is out of the question. In fact, considerations of this kind led the states of Wisconsin and Ohio to reject federal subsidies for HSR in 2010 and the state of Florida to do the same in 2011.

HSR'S ENVIRONMENTAL EFFECTS

The potential environmental benefits have been one of the recurring justifications put forward for promoting HSR in the United States. The US Department of Transportation emphasizes the contribution of HSR to energy efficiency and environmental quality, considered as one of the strategic transportation goals. Based on the view that rail is among the cleanest and most energy-efficient passenger transportation modes, DOT (2009, p. 3) states that "A future HSR/IPR network using new clean diesel or electric power can further enhance rail's advantage. According to a joint 2006 study conducted by the Center for Clean Air Policy and Center for Neighborhood Technology, implementation of pending plans for the federally designated HSR corridors could result in an annual reduction of six billion pounds of CO_2."

In fact, the California High-Speed Rail Authority expects major environmental benefits from the introduction of the HSR, among them, cutting air pollution and smog throughout the state (provided the electric power required by the trains can be produced by sustainable and renewable sources like wind and solar power), improved air quality, improved air energy (since high-speed rail uses only one-third of the energy of airplanes and one-fifth of the energy of the family car), reduced dependence on foreign oil, and large reductions in greenhouse gas emissions.[7]

However, a great deal of discussion has been devoted to the potential environmental benefits of HSR in the United States. Criticisms have been raised, particularly with regard to the energy consumption forecasts published, which are extremely favorable for HSR and excessively negative for other modes of transport. Most studies on HSR environmental efficiency in Europe find substantial advantages with respect to air travel, but less so with respect to car trips (van Wee, van den Brink, and Nijland, 2003; Lukaszewicz and Andersson, 2006).

O'Toole (2009) strongly criticizes the estimates of large energy savings and reductions of greenhouse gas emissions in the United States. On the one side, he notes that most estimates of HSR's comparative energy efficiency assume a car occupancy factor of 1.6 people, while in fact for intercity auto trips occupancy factors of 2.4 have been found in California. The difference is important, because an auto occupancy of 1.6 makes car trips less efficient than train, but an occupancy of 2.4 yields the opposite result. Regarding air trips, while acknowledging the higher efficiency of the train, O'Toole stresses that the airlines have achieved major improvements in energy efficiency due to technological change in recent decades—much greater than the improvements achieved by trains. The same applies to changes in auto energy efficiency. O'Toole also notes that official evaluations of environmental effects disregard the energy consumption and greenhouse emissions caused by the construction of the HSR. In general, then, he criticizes the CHSRA forecasts of environmental effects because they are based on highly optimistic assumptions for rail and pessimistic assumptions for autos and airlines.

Chester and Horvath (2010) made an important contribution to the analysis of potential environmental effects of HSR in the United States with their life-cycle assessment of the California HSR. This analysis takes into account the complete life cycle, thus considering infrastructure creation or expansion in HSR and all competing modes. Among the most interesting insights provided by this study is the fact that Sulfur Dioxide (SO_2) emissions are highest for HSR, because the primary fuel input is electricity. Levels of other pollutants such as Carbon Monoxide (CO), Nitrogen Oxide (NOx), Volatile Organic Compounds (VOC), and particles measuring 10Âμm or less (PM_{10}) are also high in the construction phase of HSR, underlining the importance of life-cycle considerations (Chester and Horvath, 2010, p. 5).

After a sophisticated computational exercise, and considering different assumptions of occupancy factor in all modes, Chester and Horvath determine the time of environmental payback of HSR investment and operation (Energy ROI). The payback of energy utilization and greenhouse gas (GHG) emissions is shown in table 2.4. In scenario 1, with high CSHR loading, small Air and Heavy Rail Transit (HRT) loading, and low auto occupancy, payback occurs in eight years for energy utilization and in six years for GHG. With average loading assumptions, payback takes twenty-eight years for energy and seventy-one years for GHG. For small HSR loading, high Air and HRT loading and relatively high auto occupancy, payback never occurs. Note that scenario 1, the most favorable to HSR payback, is not likely to occur, because airlines do not maintain operations on routes with this loading factor, and the auto occupancy factor is well below the actual auto occupancy in intercity trips in California. Therefore, the prospects for obtaining significantly lower energy and emission levels with HSR are bleak and extremely costly should they materialize.

There is a clear need for further analysis and discussion of HSR plans in the United States. Careful consideration of all the costs and benefits is re-

Table 2.4.   Energy Return on Investment Modal Utilization. Assumptions and Results

	Automobiles, HRT, and Air at Low Occupancy, CAHSR at High Occupancy	Automobiles, HRT, and Air at High Occupancy, CAHSR at Low Occupancy	Automobiles, HRT, and Air at Mid-Level Occupancy, CAHSR at Mid-Level Occupancy
CAHSR loading	75 %	25 %	50 %
Automobile passengers	2	2.5	2.25
HRT loading	25 %	75 %	40 %
Air loading	50 %	90 %	85 %
CAHSR energy ROI	8 years	Never	28 years
CAHSR GHG ROI	6 years	Never	71 years

Source: Chester and Horvath (2010, p. 7)
Note: Loading denotes the percentage of seats filled. HRT stands for "Heavy Rail Transit"; GHG stands for Greenhouse Gas.

quired, because the proposed project involves a considerable financial outlay. A detailed review of international experience would be helpful, and in fact the long-term experience with HSR in countries such as Japan, France, Germany, and Spain makes it possible to conduct evaluations of the different aspects of HSR results and impacts. This is the approach we take in this book, after providing a structured analytical framework that highlights the main issues that should be taken into account when reviewing international experiences.

NOTES

1. Details can be found in Schwieterman and Scheidt (2007).
2. See the official report DOT 51-09 on Thursday, April 16, 2009, at the Federal Railroad Administration website, www.fra.dot.com.
3. The length of these corridors is justified by the potential competitiveness and comparative advantage of HSR versus other transportation modes.
4. Some sources suggest that CHSRA had spent up to US $800 million by the end of 2011. See, for instance, Rail Passenger Association of California & Nevada: www.railpac.org/2012/01/12/railpac-writes-brown-feinstein-and-boxer-peer-review-committee-is-right-on-high-speed-rail.
5. Recall that the latest official estimate is given here in US $2010. If we take into account expected inflation during the years in which construction would take place, the nominal inflated range of costs would be US $98 to US $117 billion.
6. A brief explanation of several critical reviews of the CHSRA ridership forecast can be found in Enthoven, Grindley, and Warren (2010).
7. This estimate of reduced greenhouse gas emissions is twelve billion pounds per year. This seems slightly overoptimistic. The government-sponsored environmental analysis for the Madrid–Valencia HSR in Spain estimated a reduction of greenhouse

gas emissions of 0.265 billion pounds per year (see Bel, 2010). Expected ridership is about ten times that in the Madrid–Valencia HSR line; perhaps slightly more if we consider passenger-km, instead of absolute number of passengers. However, the estimation of greenhouse gas emission reduction for the CHSR is forty-five times the estimate for the Madrid–Valencia line.

3

High-Speed Rail

The Analytical Framework

This chapter examines the factors that must be considered in an analysis of the suitability of high-speed rail projects. This analysis must include multiple perspectives: (1) the objectives pursued (or why HSR is developed); (2) the design and structure of the network (or how HSR is developed); (3) the economic cost and its social return (or how much it costs and how much we get); and finally (4) mobility and environmental impacts (or what happens to mobility, cities served, and to the environment once HSR is in place). This structure of analysis will be used—whenever data and studies are available—in the review of international experiences, allowing a homogeneous dissection of each case study and facilitating the necessary comparisons in order to draw generalized lessons and conclusions regarding the role of HSR as a transportation alternative.

THE OBJECTIVES OF HSR AND
THE ARGUMENTS USED TO SUPPORT IT

A wide variety of arguments have been used to justify the construction of a high-speed rail network. An analysis of the literature on international experience serves to identify four main objectives: (a) alleviating problems of congestion as an efficiency objective; (b) connecting high-speed industrial areas with distribution centers and international transport as a logistics objective; (c) promoting regional equity and regional development; and (d) providing an alternative to air transportation in countries where geography allows competitive advantages for the railway.

Efficiency

(a) Eliminating bottlenecks in rail corridors with very high passenger volume is the main reason for the construction of a high-speed network. This motivation is related to the mitigation of congestion and is, therefore, an efficiency objective. Under this reasoning one would expect the first high-speed corridors to be operated to be precisely the most congested ones, where the potential demand for high speed—and therefore aggregate savings in time—is the highest possible. Even in experiences where targets other than efficiency have also been considered, the choice of highly traveled corridors is recurrent and normal because it allows commercial exploitation. This objective can be applied to both passengers and freight, depending where and how the bottleneck is created.

This was clearly the motivation for Japan and France, the two pioneers in the construction of high-speed networks. Germany and other countries also created HSR networks in high-density corridors.

Logistics

(b) The connection between large industrial areas and major international distribution centers is a key and necessary condition for an efficient distribution and commercial chain, and as consequence, for ensuring the access of national products to international markets in a competitive global market. Transport infrastructure, particularly an efficient railway network, is crucial for this purpose. HSR can offer significant time savings when industrial centers and international ports are far from each other. This industrial policy aims to promote productivity gains and increased efficiency in access both to final markets and to intermediate goods from the industrial zones.

This objective is similar to the previous one, as it considers the corridor of highest transport volume and specifically solves congestion problems for both freight and passengers. However, this policy has the specific objective of promoting logistic improvements. Therefore, in this setting, it is natural to expect complementarities between passenger and freight services.

The best example of this situation is Germany, given the east–west orientation of the rail network before the Second World War and the subsequent industrial mobility patterns generated between the southern industrial areas and the northern ports, which required the construction of a north–south connection, particularly for freight. This explains why the first two Neubaustrecken lines—Hannover to Fulda and Würzburg (opened in 1988 and completed in 1994) and Mannheim to Stuttgart (completed in 1991)—were selected to solve problems of north–south access for freight and congestion in existing routes.

Equity and Regional Cohesion

(c) Alternatively, HSR programs may ignore the priority of efficiency factors and start their projects in corridors with relatively low traffic volumes, pursuing goals of equity and cohesion and the promotion of regional development. Spain is probably the only example of a high-speed network of this kind; it prioritized the Madrid–Seville corridor over other congested routes such as those along the Mediterranean coast and the Ebro River Valley.

This approach responds to the belief that HSR can connect cities on the periphery to large nodes of activity and thus foster economic dynamism. From this perspective equality in access is viewed as promoting equal opportunities for low income regions and allowing them to enjoy the prosperity brought by the HSR. This vision can be justified from the supply side, with the government declaring the need to invest in HSR to promote the spread of economic development, and equally from the demand side—particularly if the belief of the prosperity attached to HSR has been used to justify investments—because, as has happened in several contexts, no important city wants to be left out of HSR investment programs.

Mode Substitution

(d) Finally, there is a fourth motivation—to provide a more efficient transportation alternative in areas where major cities are located at distances that give high-speed rail connection a competitive advantage over air transportation. Mode substitution makes sense in countries where the short distances between major cities make air transportation inefficient. In Italy, for example, the distances between cities are too short for the development of domestic air transport but too long for road alternatives. In this situation, high-speed rail has a competitive advantage that can result in higher time savings than in other regions with different geographical features (Catalani, 2006). Moreover, energy per mile flown is much higher in most of the journeys between Italian cities, because a disproportionately high amount of fuel is consumed in the maneuvers of taking off and landing.

So the motivation underpinning the plan is decisive as it directly affects the route selection, the network design, the characteristics of the infrastructure, and the profitability of investments. All these variables depend on the objective pursued by the government. The suitability of the objective in a particular context will have a definitive impact on the financial and social results of the implementation of HSR.

STRUCTURE: RAILS, FUNCTIONS, AND GEOGRAPHY

Urban structure and mobility patterns are the leading determinants for any transportation infrastructure: on the demand side, because transport must respond to mobility needs, and on the supply side, because geography and urbanization also limit its design. Although the function carried out by the infrastructure is always considered, other aspects influencing the design must not be ignored. In this respect, the economic policy perspective, political considerations, and regional development strategies can also play a relevant role in the design of the HSR network.

A first decision is whether HSR should specialize in passenger services or should complement them with freight services. Governments must also evaluate whether HSR lines are constructed from scratch or are just an upgrading of the current railway system. In some instances, countries have chosen to construct new HSR lines exclusively for passengers, while others have promoted more efficient freight mobility by upgrading the existing infrastructure, albeit at lower speeds and incurring higher costs. Therefore, the decision regarding the object of mobility has major consequences for the design of the network—particularly as regards the technical attributes of the infrastructure—and for its cost.

A further decision regarding network design concerns the technical properties of the infrastructure. On the one hand, planners have to decide whether conventional lines should be used in order to access city centers. By making this choice, construction costs can be substantially reduced because of savings on expropriation costs in populated areas, although there is a parallel fall in commercial speed. The experiences described in this book show different responses to this dilemma. On the other hand, the function of the service shapes infrastructure requirements. Freight services, for instance, require tracks that are able to resist heavy weights, and also need smooth slopes. These factors are obviously crucial when decisions regarding investment are taken.

The common pursuit of efficiency targets means that congested routes are usually chosen for establishing HSR services. In contrast, the pursuit of other objectives makes the selection of routes and stations connected to the network a more random process and more vulnerable to pressure from politicians and from private interests. Indeed, there is a demand effect that leads local and regional administrations, as well as industrial lobbies, to request the inclusion of their territories in the high-speed rail network. The greater these influences, the less efficient the transportation system.

This brings us to the aspects not related to mobility. We emphasize the role played by political models. Politically centralized countries (such as France) have tended to design networks that link the capital to its peripheral cities. This process seems natural in the case of France because of the preponderance of Paris and its area of influence in the country's economic activity and population. By contrast, decentralized countries like Germany or Italy have tended to build more territorially balanced networks. In these cases, the process of selecting routes can be considered as a natural step, in the sense that there is a higher economic dispersion. However, Spain, a country with a relatively decentralized economy has built an HSR network concentrated around the political capital, Madrid. This singularity reflects the will of the Spanish government to build a centralized network for political and administrative reasons.

The response to these issues conditions the design, structure, and functions of the HSR network. In our case-by-case review we cover all these aspects.

ECONOMIC COSTS

There is no doubt that HSR services offer a punctual, comfortable, and rapid mode of transport and are highly competitive over medium distances (between 100 and 500 miles), since by connecting city centers they avoid the need to commute from the airport and the inconveniences of traffic congestion. The maximum distance threshold for which it is competitive may depend on average speed, which in turn depends on the cruising speed and the number of stops.

This said, HSR links involve huge investment costs, which vary with network decisions and their functions. And we cannot ignore the fact that costs do not end with the operation of HSR services; on the contrary, maintenance and operation costs are also very high compared to other modes (de Rus and Nash, 2007). Because of these costs—which are designed to create a very high-capacity service—high-speed rail generates greater net economic benefits as the volume of traffic increases. Construction costs, together with the associated operating costs, condition the social suitability of undertaking HSR projects (Campos and de Rus, 2009); therefore, cost-benefit analyses are essential.

Some of the analyses published show interesting results. For example, de Rus and Nombela (2007, p. 21) estimated that investment in high-speed projects is difficult to justify when in the first year of operation the demand does not exceed eight million passengers for a standard line of 500 km, a distance at which high-speed rail is competitive. Similarly, the European Commission (2008, p 84) stated that "only exceptional circumstances (i.e., a combination based on low construction costs and time savings) may justify a new high speed line with a passenger minimum volume of six million users in the initial year. With normal construction costs and standard time savings a demand of nine million is probably necessary."

For this reason our review of international experiences must pay special attention to the way in which network and design decisions affect investment, as well as the circumstances under which this huge fiscal effort is socially profitable. In short, we seek to determine what can be expected from each dollar spent on the project and how decisions taken—like the ones described above—affect financial results from both private and public perspectives. This economic analysis is of particular interest when public resources are scarce worldwide, a situation that raises the opportunity cost of this social initiative.

MOBILITY AND REGIONAL IMPACTS

As an HSR service enters a given corridor, either as a new or as an upgraded transport mode, its performance can attract new passengers as well as those who had previously used air, road, or conventional rail services. Thus, upgrading rail transportation is expected to affect the airline industry and road usage over medium distances due to both demand shifts and the generation of new journeys. This means that the introduction of an alternative mode of transportation affects choice inside the range for which HSR is competitive, because it can offer time savings and a higher quality of service. These advantages are relevant for medium distances (between 100 and 500 miles), particularly vis-à-vis road transport. However, it is worth mentioning that, for a fair analysis, time comparisons across modes must consider door-to-door trips. This means that point-to-point services like air transportation and HSR must include multimodal steps from the origin to the destination.

But the analysis of HSR impacts must also include the study of what happens to the cities and local and regional economies when they are connected to the HSR network. What can cities and regions expect from HSR? Should we expect gains in productivity, more jobs and firm location enhancement around high-speed rail stations? These are some of the questions that our review of international experiences will examine.

Mobility: Modal Choice

The evaluation of HSR must also consider its impact on mobility and choice of mode because its value added is significant if it increases the number of journeys. The higher quality of the service of HSR may act in favor of this. Unfortunately, if HSR only shifts traffic from one mode to another, then its economic and regional impacts will be limited. Bearing in mind how expensive this transportation alternative is, it is necessary to evaluate whether HSR actually offers something different and covers mobility needs not served by any other efficient transportation mode.

The European Commission (1996) provides data on changes in modal shares following the introduction of HSR on the Paris–Lyon (France) and Madrid–Seville (Spain) lines. On the Paris–Lyon line, between 1981 and 1984, the share of air traffic fell from 31 percent to 7 percent, and the share of car and bus traffic fell from 29 percent to 21 percent, whereas rail traffic rose from 40 percent to 72 precent. In the case of the Madrid–Seville line, between 1991 and 1994, the share of air traffic fell from 40 percent to 13 percent and that of car and bus traffic from 44 percent to 36 percent, while rail traffic increased from 16 percent to 51 percent. Hence, as modal shares are subject to dramatic changes, this review highlights the ways in which the introduction of an HSR line can alter the modal split between two cities.

As this evidence shows, HSR harms air transportation industries. This effect should be considered as an additional social cost of this investment. If there are few new journeys generated, this means that no bottlenecks are alleviated, and so it is difficult to expect any economic impact from the huge investment required for HSR projects.

Moreover, the funding policy will have an important effect on modal choice and market structure. If the service is publicly funded, public resources will be used to affect market competition, favoring rail services over air and bus transportation services. Where private operators are serving the corridor by air or road, the significant public level of interference in market outcomes damages private interests. If HSR cannot guarantee sufficient revenue to cover operation costs (which is basically influenced by the amount of passengers), price settings are controversial; subsidies affect competition, and the absence of subsidies leads to price increases that reduce the demand for HSR even further.

Expected Impacts

Beyond mobility impacts, does high-speed rail generate economic impacts? Does it promote regional economic activity? Which sectors benefit most? Does it increase high-speed network territorial cohesion and productivity? Does it affect the network connection to the business location? These issues will be addressed in the experiences described in the next chapters.

In spite of the hype that usually accompanies HSR projects regarding their economic and regional impact, the literature consistently shows that passengers-only high-speed rail aimed at generating new economic activity does not attract productive investment and has no effect on business location. However, it seems to strengthen and promote existing processes and facilitates intra-organizational mobility for companies and institutions for which mobility is essential.

The use of high-speed freight transport seems to have a greater impact on the efficiency and accessibility of end markets and, therefore, makes a greater contribution to economic development. Nonetheless, there is one necessary condition: there must be an industrial and export base strong enough to build on. Only the services and tourism sectors seem to be substantially affected by high-speed services, although not all the impacts can be counted as benefits. In the case of tourism, it generates a greater number of movements and spending on eating and drinking, but nevertheless it decreases the number of overnight stays. Therefore, the economic balance is indeterminate and depends on the economic structure and context of each experience.

The effects on population growth and the housing market, though expected, are usually marginal. In fact, for regions and cities that are less affluent than their neighbors, network connection speed usually causes them to lose activities—particularly retail and leisure—to larger, more dynamic cities, generating a net negative effect (Givoni, 2006; van den Berg and Pol, 1998; Thompon, 1994).

The French and Japanese experiences illustrate these impacts well, as we see in their respective chapters. Studies of HSR in France show that the most important nodes are those that benefit most (Arduin, 1991). The Paris–Rhône/Alps line is a good example: following the entry into service of the TGV, train travel to Paris increased by 144 percent, while traveling in the opposite direction (where Paris is the source of round-trip travel) grew by only 54 percent. As in Japan, the TGV promoted the centralization of economic activity in service activities in major travel nodes and encouraged intra-organizational contacts. High-speed travel originating in Paris increased by 21 percent, while high-speed travel with Paris as the destination increased by 156 percent (Bonnafous, 1987). In contrast, the impact on industrial activities was irrelevant (Mannone, 1995). Finally, surveys of the effect on the number of overnight stays and reasons for the trip show that train passengers who stayed at the destination fell from 74 percent to 46 percent between 1981 and 1985 with the introduction of the TGV, and the main reasons for travel were intra-company contacts and sale activities (Bonnafous, 1987).

So the size of cities matters. Small and medium-size cities can be, precisely, the main victims of high-speed connection, as their activities may be absorbed by larger, more dynamic nodes. This result is consistently identified in the international experience, particularly in the services sector: the growth generated materializes at the expense of other centers of concentration (Haynes, 1997).

Furthermore, even when the cities served by high speed benefit from improved accessibility, there is usually a negative effect on traditional alternatives. Some reports note that connections are broken down by rail and by air. As we noted above, the existence of the high-speed network creates losers, even in alternative transport modes. In this regard it is not unusual to find what is denoted as tunnel effect: an improvement in access to major cities but at the expense of breaking up the space between them. The increase in dynamism in large nodes, then, is compensated by a decrease in the activity of areas between the connection points.

Arguably the most interesting effects of HSR networks are the economic and regional impacts. Does HSR generate new economic activities and promote job creation? Which sectors benefit most from HSR systems? Does HSR increase regional productivity and cohesion? Does HSR lead to activity dispersion across the territory? Does HSR affect firm location decisions? On these issues, cities served by HSR benefit from improved accessibility, but at the same time there is a downgrading of conventional train services and air services on the lines where an HSR alternative exists. HSR does not appear to attract advanced services companies, which show no greater propensity to locate in areas neighboring HSR railway stations. And while business tourism and conferences benefit from HSR services, a reduction in the number of overnight stays cuts tourist expenditure and the consumption of hotel services. And due to the *tunnel effect* mentioned above, HSR lines do not seem to increase interterritorial cohesion, but rather they promote territorial polarization.

ENVIRONMENTAL ADVANTAGES

Much of the justification and support that HSR technology receives comes from environmental quarters. In fact, the US government has sponsored and promoted HSR as one of the mainstays of their sustainable transportation policy, labeling it as the clean, energy-efficient option (DOT, 2009).

There is no doubt that HSR is more environmentally efficient than its natural competitor, the airline industry. Making medium-distance transportation more environmentally friendly is an obvious justification for building HSR networks. However, the building and operation of HSR systems also causes environmental damage, in terms of land take, noise, visual disruption, air pollution, and the increase in the global warming effect because of the high consumption of electric energy—all this without considering the enormous cost of any environmental gain resulting from the modal shift achieved from planes to HSR.

These costs are unlikely to be recovered through the operation of HSR services, even assuming large-scale time and energy savings. In this respect, Kageson (2009, p. 25) presents comparative evidence of the economic impact of different transport modes, concluding that the CO_2 reduction is small and can take decades to offset the emissions caused by construction. In fact, Kageson considers that recovery would take too long for the traffic to offset the initial generation of emissions, calling into question the environmental advantages of high-speed rail.

Table 3.1. Summary of Elements Considered for the Analysis of HSR Projects

Objectives and Motivation of HSR Projects	Structure and Functions	Economic Costs	Mobility and Regional Impacts	Environmental Advantage
Efficiency: HSR designed to alleviate congestion or solve bottlenecks. Route selection according to demand volume.	*Functions:* Passengers-only or Passengers-Freight complementarities.	*Investments:* Huge investment efforts that require a sufficient level of demand.	*Modal Choice:* Affect modal split, damaging air and road transport industries for services in the range of 100–500 miles.	*Mode Comparison:* HSR is more environmentally efficient than its natural competitor—airline industry—but by seat-mile its superiority disappears against other modes of transportation such as upgraded conventional rail.
Logistics: Improve access of national products to global markets and to intermediate industries.	*Railways:* New railways for HSR or upgraded conventional railways.	*Maintenance and Operation:* High costs with respect to other modes.	*New Journeys:* How many new journeys does it generate? HSR must do something new, or significantly better, to compensate its high cost.	*Building Stage:* Construction involves the emission of large quantities of gases, as well as the use of huge volumes of energy. This must be taken into account. It can take decades to recover.

Equity and Regional Cohesion: Equity to access to HSR network as equity of opportunities and regional economic prosperity.

Network: Influenced by objective. If efficiency, railways on dense corridors. Other objectives provide more random designs.

Structure and Functions: Decisions on network attributes are crucial for cost determination.

Regional Impacts: Depend on railway functions and structure. For passengers-only HSR shows no effects on productivity, labor market, or firm localization. Other services sectors (tourism) are benefited.

Source of Traffic: The final energy and environmental balance is highly dependent on the source of the traffic generated. Attracting traffic from airlines improves the balance, but at high cost.

Mode Substitution: Where distances between large cities do not allow efficient transport by air and road.

Political Context and Private Interests: Centralized countries tend to have centralized networks. Lobbies and political representatives in the territory call for the inclusion of their territories.

Opportunity Costs: Huge investments can have large opportunity costs. Cost benefit analyses are essential.

Expected Benefits: Do not generate new activity, but consolidate current activities. However, there is a drainage of activities from medium cities to large cities and the existence of tunnel effects and disarticulation of traditional regional transport services.

This evidence and the huge economic investment needed have led some authors to advocate improvements in conventional networks to allow higher commercial speeds together with a more restrictive approach to road usage, rather than the implementation of high-speed rail systems. This alternative seems preferable to the creation of a new infrastructure for high speed, because it minimizes the emissions associated with construction (Whitelegg, 1993; Vickerman, 1997).

In addition to the question of the construction period this approach is also supported by an analysis of energy consumption in operation. The data on energy consumption only clearly favors HSR in comparison with air transportation. Some available estimates confirm that the energy consumption per MJ/seat-km is 240 percent higher in air transportation than in rail services. However, HSR services consume 12.8 percent more than cars on the motorway—55.9 percent more if the vehicle uses diesel technology—and 140.9 percent more than conventional trains (van Essen et al., 2003). Estimated in terms of KWh/seat-km, other estimates point to a difference of 32 percent between HSR and conventional rail, to the detriment of HSR (Lukaszewicz and Andersson, 2006). And these differences not only apply to energy consumption: similar results are obtained in the case of pollution (van Wee, van den Brink, and Nijland, 2003).

As a result, the energy and environmental balance of high speed is highly dependent on the source of the traffic generated. Attracting regular passenger air transport will increase energy efficiency, but attracting users coming from the road and heavy rail will have the opposite result—without even considering the environmental costs generated by the construction activity of the HSR infrastructure (see table 3.1).

II

CASE STUDIES WORLDWIDE

4

Japan

Shinkansen

BACKGROUND

Japan's experience with high-speed rail is the world's best known and old-est. The *Shinkansen* ("New Branch Line" in Japanese) or bullet train, as it's been commonly known since its creation, began operating as the world's first high-speed rail service in 1964, connecting the cities of Tokyo and Osaka. In fact, for twenty years, high-speed rail was synonymous with the *Shinkansen*, given that until such services appeared in Europe—in the 1980s—it was the world's only functioning high-speed train.

Today, the *Shinkansen* network basically crosses Honshu Island—the nation's largest island—and enters the southern Kyushu Island. It serves more than 300 million passengers each year, making it by far the world's leading high-speed rail service in terms of number of annual users. For this reason, the Japanese experience is a world reference in high-speed rail and probably constitutes the best example of a successful application because of its adaptation to the needs and conditions of Japanese mobility. Even so, it is possible to find drawbacks in the implementation of high-speed rail in some regions of Japan, where an insufficient demand because of lower population density make the high costs of its development hard to justify.

For all these reasons, an analysis of the impact of high-speed rail in Japan provides a broad, long-term view of what can be expected from investing in and operating high-speed rail in areas where it becomes the dominant mode of transportation over intermediate distances.

In addition to the initial and most commonly used line between Tokyo and Osaka, known as Tokaido, eight distinct lines have also been built that are today managed by various private, regional license-holding companies of the Japan Railways group. Japan Railways is made up of the group of private companies that have operated the interurban passenger and freight railway services in Japan since the privatization of the national railway company in 1987. Japan Railways consists of seven companies, six of which territorially divide passenger services, while a single company is responsible for freight services throughout the entire network.

On Honshu Island alone, there are three passenger companies and one freight company. These companies are the JR East, JR Central, JR West, and the Japan Freight Railway Company for cargo. Thus, the market structure corresponds to a cartel in which different regional monopolies exist—integrated vertically—and which are regulated by the Japanese government. However, most of these companies operate long-distance routes across different Japanese regions, and thus their impact is interregional.

The total length of the network has reached to about 1,300 miles, with speeds above 155 mph and up to 186 mph. Given its enormous volume of passengers per mile and year, the Japanese *Shinkansen* is without a doubt the most used high-speed rail service in the world. In fact, per mile of built line, the Japanese example is an unparalleled model of efficiency in the use of infrastructure. We shall describe in greater detail below the specific characteristics of the world reference in high-speed passenger rail.

OBJECTIVES AND MOTIVATION

The first studies and work carried out on the construction of a high-speed railway line began as far back as 1938, with the goal of connecting the capital (Tokyo) with Shimonoseki, a city located on the southwest coast of the island of Honshu. The planned speed for this train didn't surpass 125 mph, a speed slightly inferior to what the *Shinkansen* eventually reached in 1964 and approximately double the normal commercial speed of the conventional Japanese services at the time.

World War II, however, put the project on hold, although some work was carried out on the construction and design of what was planned to be an electric train. The project was not taken up again until 1957, when a research committee for the *Shinkansen* was created, which guided it to its definitive implementation in the mid-1960s. It was inaugurated shortly before the opening of the Olympic Games in Tokyo in 1964.

The objective pursued by these early planners was to improve services by solving capacity restraints and reducing the travel time between Tokyo and Osaka—located almost 322 miles apart—to four hours thanks to the *Shinkansen*'s speed of 130 mph. Today, the trip takes barely two and a half hours. The importance of commuting ever-greater distances acquired a significant role in Japan's transportation policy due to the elevated costs of housing and the scarcity of inhabitable zones in Japanese territory. The *Shinkansen* was a transportation response fully adapted to these needs.

For this, the primary motivation underlying the railway policy was to promote mobility demand and offer capacity enlargements in overcrowded corridors with favorable characteristics for railway transportation due to the rapid economic growth experienced after World War II. Indeed, 80 percent of Japan's workforce and 85 percent of the value of the country's manufacturing developed in the coastal sprawl northeast and southwest of Tokyo in the postwar period. Between 1945 and 1955, the country's population rose by over seventeen million (24 percent), with another nine million added in the following decade, imposing great pressure on existing rail services.[1] It seems reasonable because of all this to highlight the role of efficiency as the primary motivation for the construction of high-speed rail in Japan, as well as the prioritization of the Tokyo–Osaka corridor. Nevertheless, other motivations, such as regional development and territorial equity, can also be found in the development of some lines in relatively less dense areas.

Along with the clear collapse of the conventional lines and their lack of adaptation to the new reality of Japanese mobility with its increasingly distant commutes, safety must also be considered as one of the primary concerns behind the desire to improve railway services. In fact, the significant congestion of the network and the difficulty of coordinating so many services within the existing network produced some notable accidents that made an impact on the collective mind-set of the Japanese. Some of these accidents occurred in the two years prior to the opening of the first *Shinkansen*. One of the most important tragedies occurred in the Tsurumi accident in 1963, when two passenger trains collided with a derailed freight train (Aoki et al., 2000). The accident in Mikawashima in 1962 was a very similar case of collision and derailment. In the latter case, the number of fatalities rose to 160.

Finally, we mustn't overlook the fact that the political strategies of Japan's political parties and their leaders have played a significant role in the extension of the *Shinkansen* in Japanese territory. According to Christopher Hood (2010), this influence didn't originate with the *Shinkansen* but rather that the conventional lines were traditionally designed according to political and territorial interests. In fact, Hosokawa (1997) argues that "some lines zigzagged from one town to another or looped in a huge half-circle through several towns," and this could only have corresponded to the political motivations that conditioned the Railway Construction Law of 1922.

The Japanese political system favors the tendency of politicians and representatives to attract spending on infrastructure for their districts (Ericson, 1996; Kasai, 2003; Aoki et al., 2000). And this is exactly what happened after the success of the first *Shinkansen* lines. As we shall show farther on, the extension of the network to less dense and more rural zones resulted in an enormously expensive investment that the relatively reduced demand would find difficult to justify.

STRUCTURE, DESIGN, AND FUNCTIONS

Geographic characteristics and a narrow track gauge limited the possibilities of improving conventional lines and achieving greater speeds. For this reason, it was necessary to broaden the width of the track to 4.7 feet (the earlier narrow track measured 3.5 feet) to guarantee a more efficient service capable of absorbing a growing demand for interurban mobility. Because of this, the network was given a new, purpose-built infrastructure—with a different track gauge—and specific vehicles designed to offer commercial speeds of 131 mph. The current top speed is 188 mph. Although the service was designed to serve freight and passengers, the huge passenger demand and maintenance needs—carried out mainly at night—favored a passenger orientation. In addition, its separation from the conventional rail service allowed it to avoid problems derived from these conventional services and its aging infrastructure. Only the Akita and Yamagata lines—branches of the principal Tohoku line—used lines not exclusively for high speed.

Unquestionably, Japan's geographic characteristics, and particularly those of Honshu Island, have favored high-speed rail's suitability as the primary mode of transportation for interurban passenger mobility. Honshu Island, which represents 60 percent of the total surface area of the country, measures 810 miles in length and between 31 and 140 miles in width, with a total area of 88,016 square miles. Honshu Island is thus a narrow island where the comparative advantage of air transportation is only apparent in connecting one end of the island with the other. Furthermore, the principal cities with the greatest population densities are aligned on the plains of the coast, creating a perfect situation for railway transportation.

In such circumstances, an efficient high-speed rail service can enjoy a large share of the market for all those connections between cities located within a range of 300 to 430 miles. This is especially so because the population density of Honshu Island is one of the highest in the world, with a population of 1,170 people per mile^2 and twelve cities with more than a million inhabitants. This density becomes extremely high when considering the fact that the eight most densely populated cities have an average density above twenty thousand inhabitants per km^2, double the population density of Chicago. Such high density favors the accessibility of high-speed rail stations, which are furthermore aided by an efficient system of local conventional services that act as feeders to the high-speed rail service. For this reason, coordination has become one of the most complex but necessary aspects, as well as the best resolved, of Japan's railway system.

Each standard high-speed rail service can transport more than 1,300 passengers—more than other experiences, such as France's or Germany's—and the frequency at rush hour reaches an operating service of one train every three minutes. Some 340 vehicles are daily dispatched on the Tokaido line with a capacity of thirteen trains per hour.

In 1999, many old bullet trains were phased out to make room for the new 700 series Nozomi trains which travel at 186 mph compared to 130 mph for the old bullet trains. At present, there are three types of service: the Nozomi, the fastest (186 mph), makes the least intermediate stops, serving only the most important nodes of the network with nine daily trains; the Hikari, which stops at some intermediary cities; and the Kodama, the least rapid, which serves all of the intermediary stations.

In the case of the Tokaido line between Tokyo and Osaka, the Kodama provides service to fifteen stations. The daily number of passengers is approximately 378,000, which translates annually to almost 140 million, making it the high-speed rail line with the most passengers in the world. Nevertheless, the distance between stations (between eighteen and twenty-five miles) is relatively short in comparison to European parameters.

While geographic characteristics have helped high-speed rail to be adopted as a means of transportation for passengers, the story is quite different in the case of freight. While the railway's market share is very significant for passenger mobility, only 4.5 percent of the tons-mile are transported by rail in Japan. The primary reason for this low participation is due to the high population density of the coast and the ease of access to seaports as the principal routes of entry and exit of goods. In fact, half of the tons transported within Japanese territory use maritime transportation services.[2] On land, road transportation clearly surpasses transportation by railroad.

In terms of the centralization of the network, the "percent of centralization" is a very illustrative indicator, which is calculated as the ratio between the number of origin–destination trajectories that pass through a station and the total number of origin–destination trajectories of the network. The *Shinkansen* has an average centrality of its stations of 36 percent, a low value for an archipelago of Japan's geographic characteristics and the location of its population. Less surprising is that the stations with greater degrees of centrality (see figure 4.1) are Omiya, Tokyo, and Nagoya, all of which are located in the central part of Honshu Island. Cities without positive values in the centrality index are located at the network's extremes.

In addition, the *Shinkansen* has proven to be a highly safe transportation system. Despite its high speed, not a single fatality has occurred since its creation in 1964, which speaks for itself of the great safety in mobility offered by the *Shinkansen*. This figure gains greater importance in light of the accidents described earlier. Even in the face of the frequent earthquakes that occur in Japan, high-speed rail has proven to be invulnerable thanks to its

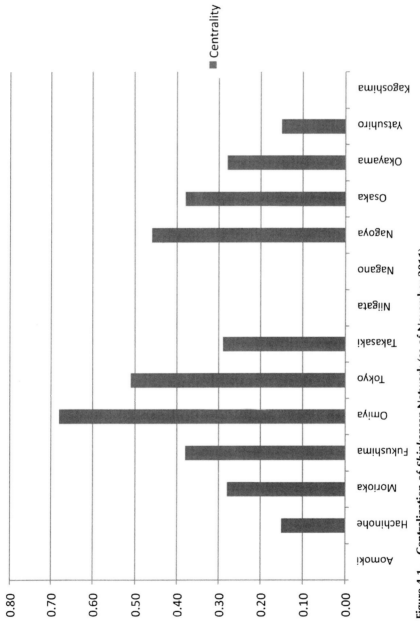

Figure 4.1. Centralization of *Shinkansen* Network (as of November 2011)

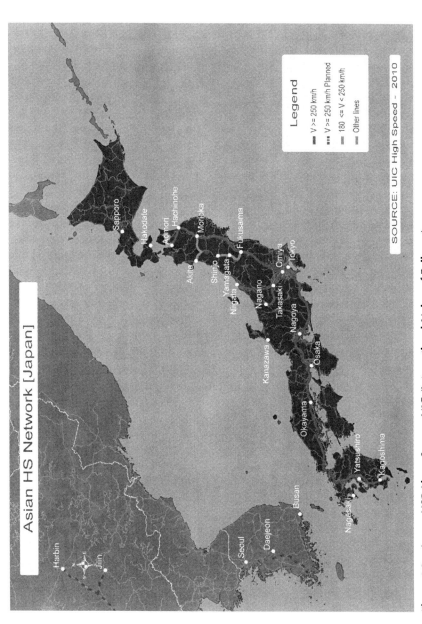

Figure 4.2. Japan: HSR Lines. Source: UIC (International Union of Railways)

advanced design. Similarly, the punctuality of the *Shinkansen* is astonishing, with an average delay of thirty seconds. Earthquakes, snowstorms, and heavy rains cause the most important delays, which are greatly superior to the average. In 2004, when the average delay increased to forty-two seconds as a result of typhoons, earthquakes, and some other problems, it was considered a disgrace (Hays, 2009).

On the other hand, the technology chosen was intrinsically Japanese, with public-private participation between the government, technology research institutions, and private companies such as Kawasaki Heavy Industry, Nippon Sharyo, Hitachi, Tokyu Car, and Kinki Sharyo. Its success has made it possible to export technology to different countries, such as China, Taiwan, and the United Kingdom, although at lower levels of internationalization and volume of business than those achieved by French and German technologies.

Lastly, mention should be made of the technological development that can provide high-speed services at velocities approaching 373 mph. We refer here to the superconductivity magnetic levitated superexpress technology, known as "Maglev." This technology dates back to the early 1960s and in fact, in 1974, 4.3 miles of testing track were built in Miyazaki. The most recent tests made in 2003 in Yamanashi resulted in speeds of 361 mph, which encouraged JR Central to commit to introducing this technology between Tokyo and Nagoya (Chuo Shinkansen) by the year 2025. If successfully installed, the time savings for each vehicle would be approximately one hour, making the journey between origin and destination forty minutes. The same technology applied on the Tokyo–Osaka route (344 miles) would save one hundred minutes per vehicle between origin and destination, making it eight minutes faster than air transportation.

INVESTMENTS AND PROFITABILITY

Work on the world's first high-speed line (see figure 4.2) was begun in 1959 and was financed by a loan of eighty million dollars from the World Bank, funds from the Japanese government, and the issuing of bonds. The total nominal cost of the Tokaido line was around one billion of 1964, around eighteen billion dollars in 2011 terms to facilitate comparisons with present projects, some fifty-two million dollars per mile (table 4.1). The debt accrued had to be paid back through the income obtained from service fees.

By its third year, the Takaido *Shinkansen* generated sufficient income to cover and surpass the costs of its operation, and within a few years (1971) it even managed to cover the costs of the spending made on its development. Nonetheless, not all of the Japanese lines generate such satisfactory profitability. Table 4.1 provides information on the total cost and the rela-

Table 4.1. Selected *Shinkansen* Lines. Construction Costs

Line	Year Beginning Operation	Miles	Total Cost (US $ Billion of 2011)	Cost per Mile (US $ Million of 2011)
Tokaido	1964	347	17.96	51.7
Sanyo	1975	389	20.6	52.9
Tohoku	1985	335	40.3	120.4
Joetsu	1985	209	24.7	118.2
Kyushu*	2010	78.7	9.6	122.4

Source: Authors' own, adapted from Taniguchi (1992) and from * UCL project plan for Kyushu line. Exchange rate applied 1 USD = 78.5389 JPY (January 2012).

tive cost per mile. Such high costs need sufficient demand to justify an effort of such magnitude. In fact, in 1985, only the Tokaido and Sanyo routes managed to cover operating costs. The Thoku and Joetsu routes presented significant operating deficits with incomes that only managed to cover approximately half of the expenditures (Taniguchi, 2009). As various authors and testimonies have indicated, the construction of these loss-making routes through relatively less populated territories was due strictly to political motivations derived from pressure from territories that desired a high-speed rail service similar to the Sanyo and Tokaido routes (Peterman et al., 2009; Clever and Hansen, 2008).

One of the most notable examples of political pressure as a determining factor in the design of the routes is found in the Joetsu line and the leadership assumed by Tanaka Kakuei, the most influential politician of the Liberal Democratic party in the government, who promoted the connection between Tokyo and his native prefecture of Nigata. This loss-making line, which cost US $24.7 billion of 2011—118 million per mile—was never expected to be profitable. Nor was the Tohoku line. As indicated by the reports of the JNR, these projects served to establish closer ties with Tokyo and promote regional development. Consequently, these two *Shinkansen* stand in stark contrast to the Tokaido and Sanyo lines, which were built to serve areas of high economic activity (Takashima, 2001).

The country's infrastructure policy, however, has not been determined solely by political or territorial interests, and indeed we cannot overlook the role special interest groups have played. In this context, Haruo Kondoh (2008) empirically evaluates the distribution of spending and public capital on a local level, finding that the policy of local spending has been profoundly affected by the interests of the construction industry. One mustn't forget that this industry in Japan is highly dependent on public works.

The Japan National Railway was suffering from huge financial deficit accumulated year by year. Investment, maintenance and operation costs were basically self managed by the JNR. Rapid motorization in urban and regional transport led the JNR to severe financial distress. In particular, the expansion of the railway network in rural areas amplified the problem. Accumulated loss of the JNR skyrocketed from 83 billion Yen in 1965 to 678 billion Yen in 1975 at which point it was still growing fast. The government and the JNR took steps to restore financial distress by increasing fares. [. . .] Railway fares continued to be increased until the JNR was privatized in 1987. (Yamaguchi and Yamasaki, 2009, 7)

This financial distress and accumulated debt led to the privatization of JNR as extreme policy. In face of this difference between profitable routes and loss-making ones, it seemed inevitable that the surpluses earned by the profitable lines would serve to cross subsidize the rest of the high-speed lines, as well as other local and regional lines. In fact, in 2002, the Tokaido route on its own was still capable of carrying more than half of the passenger-miles of the entire high-speed network. Although this line represents approximately 25 percent of the total miles of the JR Central, it generates 85 percent of the total turnover. In terms of the total *Shinkansen* network, the Tokaido line was 25 percent in 2005, while its percentage of total passengers and passenger-miles was 44 percent and 56 percent, respectively.

Given this form of financing, the fees in the profitable services are necessarily higher than the inherent cost of the service with the goal of permitting cross subsidization. Thus, the passengers of the profitable routes, particularly the Tokaido route, bear the weight of the loss-making routes. And whatever the case, the price of the high-speed service increases with the distance traveled and the quality of the reservation.

Nonetheless, a series of requirements have existed since 1988 concerning the prioritization of spending that act as counterweights to what we have just described. Among these criteria, we find the following:

- Long-term profitability in the railway business
- The effects of spending on the national economy
- Future business outlooks and policies for the construction of *Shinkansen* railways
- Consensus reached by residents in affected areas

Since 1997, the financing model of recent high-speed lines in Japan has been based on a cofinancing between the national government and those local governments served by the new high-speed lines. Even so, participation in the spending is unequal, with the central administration assuming a two-thirds part and the remaining third corresponding to the local authorities. Thus, the infrastructure used by the high-speed services is public property, and an independent state agency charges Japan Railways, the company responsible for the services, for the use of the infrastructure.

In terms of the structure of the spending, we find that in the case of the Sanyo line between Shinosaka and Okayama (103 miles), 58 percent was dedicated to infrastructure, while the second-most important sum was the price of the land, a great deal higher than the electrical equipment (11 percent) and the tracks (5 percent). In fact, anecdotes exist in cities, such as what occurred on the section between Ueno and Omiya, where local opposition to the project seems to have followed a collective strategy to increase the compensations for expropriation (Groth, 1986, 1996; Hood, 2006).

Compared to other experiences, the cost per seat of the *Shinkansen* is relatively lower, as is the maintenance cost of the vehicles. In contrast, the cost of the investment was very high due to the significant use of tunnels and viaducts, amounting to 49 percent and 35 percent of the total miles of the route, respectively. On the Osaka–Tokyo line alone, three thousand bridges and sixty-seven tunnels were built, which gives an idea of their elevated impact on the total spending. Some of the more recent lines of the *Shinkansen* have mostly been built with viaducts and bridges, which explains their greater relative cost in respect to older lines. For example, 70 percent of the initial section of the Kyusku *Shinkansen* is in tunnels.

Some cost-benefit analyses reveal interesting results. The cost-benefit analysis for one of the more recent lines, the Kyushu, shows a net positive benefit and cost/benefit ratio of 1.1. The not very high benefit rate is around 4.6 percent. The primary benefit of introducing this line is the time savings of some ninety minutes and a 225 percent increase in demand in the first year of its functioning. This is a considerable increase and can be explained above all because the travel time between Hakata and Kagoshima—the two important cities located at the ends of the Kyushu line—is now ten minutes less than the same journey by air. Nevertheless, the price of the journey increased around 55 percent with the entry into service of the *Shinkansen* between Fukuoka and Kagoshima and 75 percent between Kumamoto and Kagoshima. Even so, the price is still decidedly lower than the price of traveling by air for the same routes.

DEMAND AND MODAL COMPETITION

Demand forecasts for the first *Shinkansen* services proved to be underestimated. From the beginning, the *Shinkansen* was a success. While the number of passenger-miles was 17.6 billion in 1965, with the opening of the Expo '70 held in Osaka, this figure rose to forty-three billion passenger-miles, and just ten years after the inauguration of the *Shinkansen* this figure reached to more than eighty billion. In terms of passengers, the increase was from thirty-nine million daily passengers in the first year, to 157 million in 1975

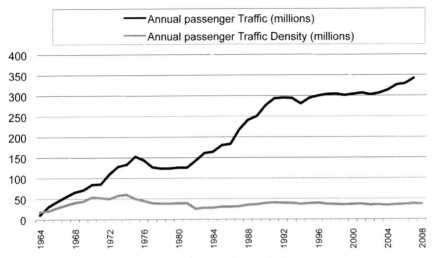

Figure 4.3. *Shinkansen* **Passenger Traffic Trend 1964–2008**

(Taniguchi, 1992). The story of the *Shinkansen* is, therefore, a success story that has seen its total volume of annual passengers in the network constantly increase, rising from the eleven million in its first year of service to the present 330 million (see figure 4.3).

The economic crisis and intermodal competition, encouraged by the liberalization of the air transportation sector and the expansion of Tokyo's airport, were the primary factors behind the stagnation of demand that began in the late 1990s and which lasted until the mid-2000s at 300 million annual passengers. Since 2004, there has been a clear upturn in demand that has situated it at around 330 million, although the figures for the last years of the decade seem to indicate an end to the rise.

A comparison of the numbers of annual passengers for the different lines reveals the great weight of the Tokaido lines (149 million in 2008) and Tohoku (128 million in 2009) in the totality of the network, even with the entry into service of additional lines (see figure 4.4). The disparity between the demand of the two principal lines and that of the rest helps us to understand the reason for the doubtful social benefits of the spending made on some recent routes, such as the Hokuriku and Kyushu lines, with a volume of passengers in 2009 of 10 and 4.2 million passengers, respectively (see figure 4.5).

On the other hand, the *Shinkansen*'s largest rise in traffic density, measured as passenger-mile per mile of system length, occurred in the mid-1970s during a moment of significant expansion and before other lines with lower traffic demand had been incorporated (see figure 4.6). This indicator of use of the infrastructure shows us that the Tokaido route is

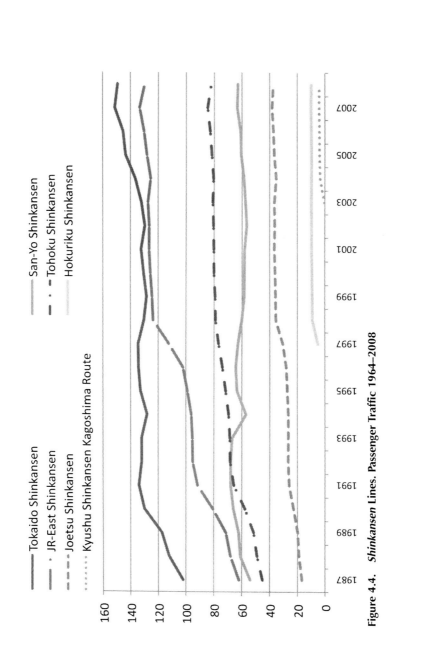

Figure 4.4. *Shinkansen* Lines. Passenger Traffic 1964–2008

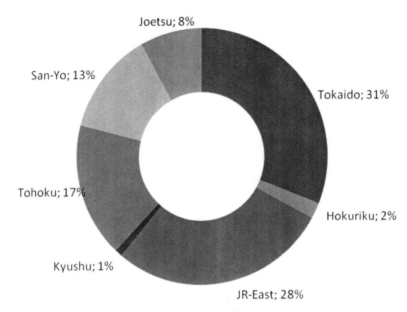

Figure 4.5. *Shinkansen* **Lines. Passenger Traffic 1964–2008**

unquestionably the densest, with more than 129 million passenger-miles per mile of track, while other lines such as the Sanyo and the Tohoku have densities lower than forty-eight million, which even so is still a density greatly superior to those presented by the Hokuriku and Kyushu lines with 7 and 5.5 million passenger-km per mile of track in 2009, respectively.

This vigorous demand can be explained by the dense population located along the lines, which is the geographic setting and advantage of the *Shinkansen* and which in turn promotes its popularity. The Tokaido and Sanyo routes alone serve two-thirds of the Japanese population and three-fourths of its economy. Most existing *Shinkansen* lines run through densely populated areas in Japan and at distances that favor the competitiveness of rail travel over other means of transportation. An example that reveals the ferocious impact of the *Shinkansen*'s introduction on competing means of transportation was the closing by airlines in 1964 of the air route between Tokyo and Nagoya, comparable in distance to the route between New York and Washington, DC (Clever and Hansen, 2008). Other routes abandoned by air transportation after the introduction of high-speed rail services are those that connected Tokyo with Sendai, Niigata, Aichi, and Iwate. All of these routes are less than 350 miles long, a distance at which air transportation has a difficult time competing with high-speed rail.

In fact, estimates show that for routes between 313 and 460 miles, 66 percent of the Japanese choose high-speed rail as their means of transportation,

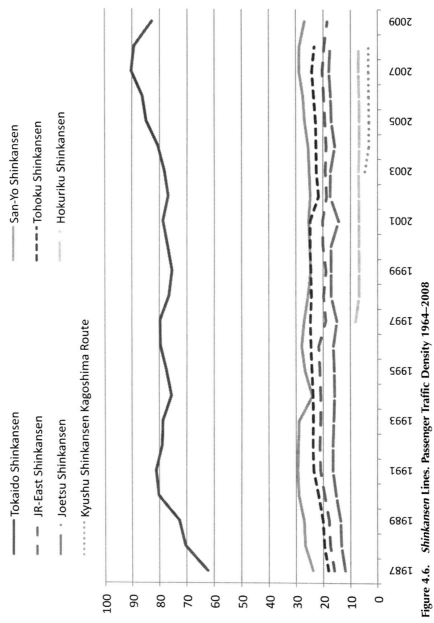

Tokaido Shinkansen
San-Yo Shinkansen
JR-East Shinkansen
Tohoku Shinkansen
Joetsu Shinkansen
Hokuriku Shinkansen
Kyushu Shinkansen Kagoshima Route

Figure 4.6. *Shinkansen* Lines. Passenger Traffic Density 1964–2008

Chapter 4

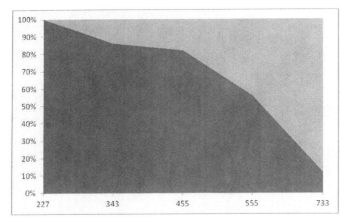

Figure 4.7. Market Share (%) of *Shinkansen* per Route Distance (Miles)

as opposed to the 21 percent and 11 percent who choose air and road transportation, respectively (Matsumoto, 2007). In terms of distance, the market share of the *Shinkansen* is always greater than that of air transportation for routes of less than 600 miles (see figure 4.7). In Japan's case, this is significant because up to fourteen important cities—including Osaka, Nagoya, Kobe, and Kyoto—are located at distances of less than 400 miles, which offers a very attractive potential market for the *Shinkansen*.

The shorter travel time achieved by air transportation on the Tokyo–Osaka route is negligible when taking into account the time necessary to travel between the centers of the cities of origin and destination and their respective airports, as well as the time spent on check-ins and arriving at the embarking gates. All of this eliminates the theoretical advantage of air transportation, which, within the vehicle, is estimated to save an hour and forty minutes. Furthermore, one of the factors that most contributes to the preference for high-speed rail on this route is the fact that air travel costs its passengers approximately 50 percent more than what users of high-speed rail have to pay for their journey. For all of these reasons, rail's market share continues to be above 80 percent, despite competitive efforts introduced by the air industry through a greater presence of low-cost companies.

In effect, the characteristics of Japanese mobility and geography don't permit a hub and spoke strategy for airlines, and because of this they must focus on exploiting point-to-point routes in which low-cost companies can take advantage of the economies of density and be competitive both with the rest of the airlines and high-speed rail. Nevertheless, the fact that most of the population is concentrated in city centers or has efficient access to these centers gives high-speed rail an advantage that is difficult for air transportation to overcome on routes of medium distance.

Furthermore, the high reliability of the *Shinkansen*, which offers an extremely punctual service, gives it a significant competitive edge over the quality of the service offered by the air industry. Indeed, the airlines that provide service between cities served by direct high-speed rail lines operate 97 percent of their services with a maximum delay of fifteen minutes.

Needless to say, the advantages of the *Shinkansen* in respect to road travel are much clearer on routes of this distance, given that by bus the route between Osaka and Tokyo takes eight hours and by private vehicle, an average of seven hours. Apart from the travel time, it has been necessary to finance the high cost of the expressways—given the geography and the conditions imposed by the regularity of earthquakes—by tolls. As a result, users of these large-capacity roadways must pay high tolls, which facilitates the competitiveness of the HSR on routes of shorter distances where the natural rival is the road.

Among the effects produced by the *Shinkansen* is the dismantling of some conventional services. Although in Japan some of these services have been oriented to feed the stations of the *Shinkansen*, others have been suppressed, reduced, or substituted by bus services. As a result, following the start of service of the *Shinkansen*, travel on these regional routes now takes longer.

ECONOMIC AND REGIONAL IMPACTS

Time savings are estimated at 400 million hours per annum. This savings in travel time forms the basis for the primary economic impact of the *Shinkansen* (Kamel and Mattewman, 2008). Population growth offers interesting results as well. Cities with HSR railway stations achieved average rates of 1.6 percent, while those by-passed by the service only increased at a 1 percent rate (Hirota, 1985). It was found that HSR stations resulted in marginal population impacts and that these were more marked in cities with an information exchange industry, access to higher education, and expressway access (Nakamura and Ueda, 1989). However, as Haynes (1997) and Huang and Sussman (2011) have pointed out, the route selected paid particular attention and chose its stations based on expectations of population growth, thus casting doubt on the direction of the cause-and-effect relationship. At any rate, the real impact of the *Shinkansen* on the population is still difficult to determine.

According to the study made by Koösoku Tetsudö Kenyükai *Shinkansen— Koösoku Tetsudö no Gijutsu no Subete* (Everything About the Technology of High-Speed Railways) edited in 2003 by Sankaido (Tokyo) (quoted in Hood, 2010), the figures are positive between the mid-1970s and the mid-1990s. Between 1975 and 1995 those cities with a *Shinkansen* station experienced an average population increase of about 32 percent as compared to the 12 percent increase of the national average. In terms of business location, it is notable that cities with high-speed rail stations experienced an increase in the number of businesses listed there by 46 percent between 1975 and 1991, doubling the national average, which was 21 percent.

Similarly, municipal finances improved by 155 percent between 1980 and 1993 in cities served by the *Shinkansen*, while the average Japanese increase was 110 percent. In fact, finances improved at a rate even greater than those of population and businesses.

What seems clear is that having a *Shinkansen* station favored population and business concentration at a time when all of Japan was growing economically and demographically. This growth favored the enormous migration from rural zones to the country's three main economic areas (Tokyo, Osaka, and Nagoya) until 1975, fueled by the huge disparity in income and work opportunities. After that year, only Tokyo continued to absorb rural workers in a significant way. However, during the recent decades of economic and demographic stagnation, no correlation seems to exist in respect to the existence of a high-speed rail station.

Nonetheless, expectations regarding the economic gains of HSR led to political pressure and demands for high-speed rail stations, a fact that affected the economic viability of the system through debt increases and annual losses (Imashiro, 1997). In fact, debt surpassed US $200 billion by 1987, leading to a financial crisis ending with the privatization of the railway (O'Toole, 2008). As reported in ADB (2006), it was decided to transfer ownership of the *Shinkansen* facilities to the operating Japanese Railways companies at a price determined by the national government. The purchase price (in Japanese Yen) of the *Shinkansen* lines was as follows: JR East–JYen 6,527 million per mile; JR West–JYen 2,830 million per mile; and JR Central–JYen 15,911 million per mile. The average price of the three *Shinkansen* lines was JYen 8,047 million per mile.

In terms of the impact on the economic structure, according to Hirota (1985) employment growth in retail, industrial, construction, and wholesaling was 16–34 percent higher in cities with a high-speed rail station, and land value increased by 67 percent. Also of particular interest has been the dynamic generated in those cities with a greater weight in the sectors of information exchange (business services, banking services, real estate) and higher education. In contrast, cities with an important industrial base, such as Nagoya, have had much more difficulty in making use of the *Shinkansen*.

Studies of the economic impact of HSR show that services were the most favored economic sector in Japan. Service industries became highly concentrated in the cities of Tokyo and Osaka, resulting in the centralization of this sector in the country's major nodes. Indicative of this trend is the fall in employment in Nagoya, a city located between Osaka and Tokyo, following the inauguration of the high-speed line. According to Alain Plaud (1977), this fall was estimated at around 30 percent from 1955 to 1970. For the same period, the increase in employment in Osaka, Kyoto, and Kobe was 35 percent. Tourism also showed significant growth—rising from 15 to 25 percent between 1964 and 1975. In the case of the retail industry, Tokyo became the dominant force following the opening of the high-speed rail service. Similarly, since intra-organizational journeys have become easier, business travel has increased, albeit with a reduction in the number of business overnight stays in hotels in Tokyo and Osaka. Indeed, the reduction in travel time is the main impact of the *Shinkansen,* and its mean delay time of just two minutes provides extremely high standards of reliability (Daluwatte and Ando, 1995).

In conclusion, despite efforts by various researchers to determine the impact of the *Shinkansen* on Japanese cities, it is difficult to establish any clear cause-and-effect relationship. Several reasons exist for this. The first problem is the numerous fusions between cities. The second, the diversity in the business and demographic dynamics of the cities that has nothing to do with the *Shinkansen.* Third, the simultaneous expansion of other transportation infrastructures such as expressways that have connected most of the cities with access to the high-speed rail network.

The regional impact of the *Shinkansen* has also been evaluated. On the one hand, according to the study by Komei Sasaki, Tadahiro Ohashi, and Asao Ando (1997), its expansion led to regional dispersion from developed regions to some extent, although the magnitude of the effect doesn't seem overly significant. In fact, although one might think that the construction of infrastructure favors less developed regions, the truth is that this infrastructure likewise favors accessibility to the more developed center and thus acts in a contrary direction because of the relative attractiveness of the different areas. In this respect, Christopher Hood (2010) points out the huge economic variations between prefectures across Japan that the *Shinkansen* would actually have contributed to further exaggerating. In effect, the *Shinkansen*'s success doesn't seem to have been distributed uniformly.

Another aspect that casts doubt on the net impact of high-speed rail, and concerning which there is a significant lack of information, is whether the investment generates new activity or simply displaces activity from dispersed zones to the more dynamic center, near high-speed rail stations.

ENVIRONMENT AND OTHER EXTERNALITIES

The *Shinkansen*'s energy consumption per passenger-mile is a fourth of that of air transportation (Matsumoto, 2007). Taking into account the fact that electricity is also generated by nuclear power, CO_2 emission from the *Shinkansen* is significantly lower than that of other modes of transportation. Its emissions are only one-fifth of that from aircraft and one-eighth of that from automobiles. The specific comparison of the 700 Series Nozomi to the 747 Boeing is even more remarkable, the CO_2 emissions of the first being one-tenth of the latter. Its energy consumption is one-sixth (Kasai, 2003).

According to declarations made by the president of Japan Railways, Yoshi-yuki Kasai, the substitution of all of the flights from the airport of Haneda, 110 of which connect to the cities of Osaka, Okayama, and Hiroshima, with high-speed rail services, would reduce 200,000 tons of CO_2 a year. However, the *Shinkansen* consumes an enormous amount of electricity.

In the case of the Kyushu line, there has been an increase in tons of CO_2 emitted by the railway due to the significant increase in traffic caused by the *Shinkansen*. The tons emitted by air transport, meanwhile, have decreased because of air's reduced market share as a result of competition with the *Shinkansen*. On average, it is estimated that the total emitted tons of CO_2 has fallen 20 percent (sixteen tons a day).

Although the *Shinkansen* presents an environmental advantage in the operation of its service—leaving aside the emissions produced in its construction—the introduction of Maglev technology, which we previously presented as a technology capable of reducing travel time by approximately 40 percent—will also mean an increase in CO_2 emissions per passenger-mile. The estimates show that Maglev technology would multiply the *Shinkansen*'s emissions by three. In the specific case of the route proposed between Tokyo and Nagano, the volume of pounds of CO_2 emitted per passenger-mile would change from eighteen pounds to fifty-three pounds. Despite the increase, this amount continues to be quantitatively much lower than the amount emitted by air transportation, although not on this route given that it has no air service. In a similar vein, the intensity of CO_2 grams per passenger-mile is some four times the intensity of the *Shinkansen*.

Additionally, one of the *Shinkansen*'s most important environmental problems, requiring the most regulation, has been and continues to be noise. The primary cause of this noise is the friction between the front structure of the vehicle and the air, particularly in the moments before and after the numerous tunnels found on its routes. Technical refinements have focused on improving the design of the noise of the *Shinkansen* after stricter laws against noise were passed in the 1970s. The success of these efforts has made the train's sides (some 400 meters, or 1,312 feet) into the current, still-to-be-resolved noise problem. Standard measures to resolve the problem of noise have included the use of antinoise walls along the tracks. Despite these efforts, noise has become a true problem of public acceptance in the train's passage through urban zones, as is the case in the city of Nagano.

SUMMARY

The Japanese experience as the world's pioneer in the use of high-speed rail technology astonished the international community and, with its spectacular increase of traffic on the Tokyo–Osaka line, established the first major success for this mode of transportation. Still today, this line, the world's most transited, is the global reference. The geographic and demographic characteristics of Honshu Island—Japan's main island—favors the conditions in which high-speed rail can compete and contribute to mobility. In a country where most freight is moved by road and maritime services, HSR's orientation toward passenger service offered an efficient and reliable alternative that quickly won a large market share on the country's most densely populated corridor. In the face of Japan's strong economic growth after World War II, railway modernization emerged as a goal of efficiency for an economy that had serious problems of congestion and saturation on its primary corridors of mobility.

The successful results of the first lines and a political system favoring the attraction of investment to rural districts promoted an extension of high-speed lines to increasingly less densely populated areas. This extension, which raised construction costs for a lower demand, caused economic and financial problems for the state railway company. High debt and operating deficits led to a financial crisis that partially explained the railway's restructuring and privatization. In Japan, the high traffic demand on major routes offsets the enormous construction costs arising from the difficulties of expropriating land and the intensive use of viaducts and tunnels to overcome the obstacles imposed by the country's rugged topography.

The impact of high-speed rail has been extensively evaluated in Japan, although not without significant methodological problems. The *Shinkansen*, which seems to have benefited some areas of the services sector, has not had a uniform impact throughout the territory. Instead, it has promoted the concentration of activity in the hubs connected to high-speed rail, particularly benefiting the largest hub of the network. It has also had a severe impact on the air industry for routes of distance less than 500 miles, which includes fourteen of Japan's primary cities, and has lead to the dismantling of conventional rail services. The high accessibility offered by the station located in the center of major cities and design in which conventional and regional services are aimed at feeding the *Shinkansen* hubs, provides a competitive advantage relative to alternative modes that can produce time savings for the "in vehicle" journey.

In all, Japan remains the global benchmark for an efficient and safe network and which furthermore—on its main Tokaido and Tohoku lines—is profitable from the standpoint of economic and social development. Only the expansion to less populated areas limits the results of the *Shinkansen* because of the resulting need to use cross subsidization between profitable lines and loss-making ones.

NOTES

1. Data obtained from Railway-technology.com's article "Japanese bullet trains 40 years at the forefront" (published online on September 3, 2007), www.railway -technology.com/features/feature1216/.

2. G-7 countries: Transportation highlights US Department of Transportation. Bureau of Transportation Statistics, 1999.

5

France

Train à Grande Vitesse (TGV)

The *Société National des Chemins de Fer Français* (SNCF) was created in 1938 through the merger into a single entity of the five private companies and two public ones that had built France's railway network in the nineteenth century. The SNCF was originally a mixed public-private enterprise, 51 percent of its capital being public property and the remaining 49 percent being private. As Dunn and Perl explain (1994, p. 318), the private participation took the form of nontransferable preferred stock that would be repurchased through annual payments made by the government from 1939 until 1982, the year in which the original period of the concession ended. Although the plan was to make the payments by way of SNCF's operating profits, the financial performance of the company didn't allow this on a regular basis and so the French Treasury assumed responsibility for these payments. After 1982, the company became entirely public property.

After recovering from the effects of World War II, the railway's competitiveness in respect to road and air transport deteriorated in a constant way, and the worsening of SNCF's financial results, along with the corresponding fiscal repercussions, led to large and growing deficits, which became a matter of unavoidable concern for the French government. This situation led to the drawing up of the Nora Report, which established a new strategy for the SNCF. On the one hand, public service contracts were to govern those SNCF services considered to be an obligatory public service. On the other hand, the rest of the operations had to take into account the competitive logic of France's transportation market (Dunn and Perl, 1994). In this context, SNCF's services had to successfully compete with road and air transportation, or else abandon those of its services that were not competitive.

Within this framework of greater emphasis on the commercial orientation of SNCF's services, the company used the Paris–Lyon route as the primary opportunity to modernize itself. The level of congestion on the rail link joining Paris and Lyon—the gateway to southeast France—led to the introduction of high-speed rail service in France (*Train à Grande Vitesse*—TGV) with the building of a new, separate network. The line was named "Paris Sud–Est" and was constructed between 1975 and 1983, initially with 264 miles, and now 278 miles. The total number of rail passengers increased following its inauguration, rising from 12.5 million in 1980 to 22.9 million in 1992—18.9 million of whom were high-speed train (HST) passengers according to Vickerman (1997)—and increased to over 25 million by 2008.

The success of the Sud–Est (Paris–Lyon) line led to the promotion of an investment plan that provided the funds to construct connections from Paris to Le Mans (1989), Tours (1990), and Calais (1993). The Rhone–Alpes (1994), the Méditerranée (2001), and the Est-européenne (TGV Est, partly still under construction) were the next corridors to be served. The subsequent expansion of the HST network was carried out chiefly to serve corridors with sufficient traffic, connecting cities of significant size. The policy was to invest only in lines that expected to be socially profitable:[1]

- The TGV Atlantique (Paris–Tours/Le Mans), with 176 miles, was the second line to be constructed. Work began in 1985, and the TGV began service in 1989–1990. This line has two different branches, the Paris southwestern branch (near Tours) measuring 144 miles, and the western branch (near Le Mans), measuring 32 miles.
- The TGV Rhone–Alps (Lyon–Valence) was the third to enter into service, between 1992 and 1994. It is 71 miles long and extends the Paris–Lyon line toward the south. The TGV Rhone–Alps line connects with the TGV Med.
- The TGV Nord (Paris–Calais/Belgian frontier) entered into service in 1993 at the same time as the TGV Rhone–Alps. It is 207 miles long. This line connects Paris with Belgium and with the Canal Tunnel through Lille.
- The TGV Méditerranée (Valence–Marseilles/Nimes) entered into service in 2001 and completed the Paris–Marseille connection and extended it to the region of Languedoc/Roussillon. It is more than 160 miles long.
- The LGV Est européenne (LGV Est) currently connects Paris with Baudrecourt, near Metz and Nancy, and plans to also connect Paris with Vendeheim, near Strasbourg. At present, almost 190 miles have entered into service (in 2007), and 62 miles remain to be opened, for a total of 252 miles.

- The TGV Rhin–Rhône is the first province-to-province HSR line that is not centered on Paris. The 87-mile route from Dijon to Mulhouse began commercial operations on December 11, 2011. Another 31 miles will be constructed in the near future to complete the Eastern branch of TGV Rhin–Rhône. With the western and the southern branches (both connecting Dijon with points of the TGV Sud–Est) the TGV Rhin–Rhône will be used in the future to connect destinations in southern Germany and Switzerland with the French TGV network.

By the end of 2011, France's HST network comprised around 1,250 miles of line. Figure 5.1 displays the French HSR network. Traffic demands, time savings, and construction costs were all considered in the French project. Indeed, France decided only to create a new, separate network along congested links, to use conventional services along less crowded connections, and to access big cities when construction and expropriation costs were likely to be exorbitant. As a result, and in contrast to Japan, France has a mixed HSR infrastructure system. In fact, the current share of specifically HSR lines in the total network is just 37 percent, serving more than 100 million travelers. However, even with this system, commercial speeds fluctuate between 150 and 200 mph but are lower on the conventional network (130 mph). All in all, HST has meant an 80 percent increase in speed on average.

OBJECTIVES AND MOTIVATION

The rationale underpinning the HSR network in France was the modernization of rail services, with the goal of improving their commercial competitiveness in respect to the transportation alternatives of road and air transport. The aim of improving the commercial competitiveness of rail service placed emphasis on passenger transportation, and thus the network has been designed exclusively for travelers without significant effects on freight services.

To improve rail's commercial competitiveness and attractiveness, the implantation of the TGV was begun on the corridor with the most serious congestion problems, both in terms of rail traffic and traffic in general. Priority was thus given to the Sud–Est corridor and Paris–Lyon route in the implantation of the TGV. The objectives planned for the TGV were amply fulfilled. Rail traffic grew rapidly, and the number of train passengers on the corridor almost doubled between 1980 and 1992. Furthermore, the TGV achieved great hegemony as a transportation mode on the journey between Paris and Lyon, almost entirely displacing air transportation. According to

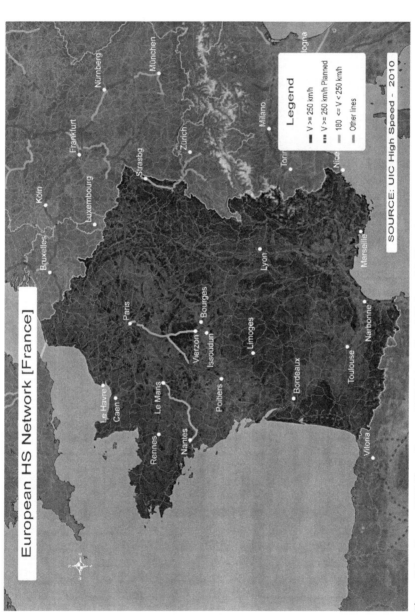

Figure 5.1.   France: HSR Lines. Source: UIC (International Union of Railways)

data provided by the European Commission (1996), between 1981 and 1984, the modal share of air traffic fell from 31 to 7 percent and that of car and bus traffic fell from 29 to 21 percent, whereas rail traffic rose from 40 to 72 percent.

The TGV Sud–Est was a success not only in winning passengers but also financially: the Sud–Est link is estimated to have provided a 15 percent financial rate of return and a 30 percent return in social terms. It was already amortized by 1993 (Vickerman, 1997). These factors were decisive for the extension of the network in France, which continued to be implanted in sections where the demand was strongest.

STRUCTURE, DESIGN, AND FUNCTIONS

The structure of the network was decisive to the commercial goal SNCF pursued to expand the TGV. In order to provide service on corridors where the demand was strongest, the network was extended on corridors connecting to the city of Paris, in keeping with mobility patterns in France. By 2001, the four main metropolitan areas of France, those articulated around Paris, Marseille, Lyon, and Lille, were already linked by TGV through the Sud–Est, Nord, and Méditerranée corridors. Only one French metropolitan area with a population of more than a million, Toulouse, still lacks today a TGV connection. Furthermore, the TGV now has a transborder connection with the United Kingdom and Belgium. To understand the pattern followed in the extension of the network, it is necessary to take into account the demographic and economic weight played by the metropolitan area of Paris-L'Île-de-France in France: Paris-L'Île-de-France has 11.8 million inhabitants, that is, 19 percent of the French population, and a population density of almost one thousand inhabitants per square meter. Its GDP is close to 30 percent of the country's total GDP. Because of this, Paris-L'Île-de-France attracts a large portion of mobility in the country.

With the expansion of the TGV network, conventional and regional services have been designed to complement high-speed rail services. This makes it possible to significantly reduce the travel time between Paris and other cities and metropolitan areas that are not yet connected to the TGV network, or for which no plans exist to connect them to this network in the future. Nonetheless, the modernization strategy of rail infrastructure in France doesn't call in any significant way for intermediate standards, such as high-speed services (in the range of 130 and 140 mph), between high-speed services and conventional ones. Furthermore, the high concentration of railway spending on TGV lines has left very little room for investment in improving regional networks used in a much more regular way by regular passengers. Furthermore, as mentioned above, the implantation of TGV in France has been made with new lines geared exclusively for passenger use without mixed characteristics capable of combining passengers and freight.

In terms of the degree of centralization of the TGV network, we may complete the view gained by the analysis of the network map using the same exercise applied previously in the Japanese experience, where we have identified the degree of centrality of each network hub in respect to the total origin–destination pairs in November 2011. As figure 5.2 shows, the network is highly centralized on the Paris hub, which has 80 percent of the trajectories among the origin–destination pairs of the TGV network. The second-most important hubs of the network are the stations of Lyon and Valence (both on the same route), with centrality values of 46 percent and 36 percent, respectively. The rest of the hubs located at the extremes of the network have much lower values, making them into end hubs of the network. Unquestionably, the design of the French high-speed rail network corresponds to a centralized structure whose primary hub is the political and economic capital of France. This hub acts as the hub and spoke for most of the trajectories in the high-speed rail network.

Lastly, in terms of the technology of the vehicles, SNCF operates a fleet of some four hundred units of seven different types of TGVs or derivatives of the TGV currently in operation in the French rail system: the TGV Sud–Est, TGV Atlantique, TGV Reseau, the Thalys PBA, Eurostar, TGV Duplex, and Thalys PBKA. Another type currently being tested also exists, the TGV POS, which will link France with southern Germany. The maximum velocity of these units is normally between 185 and 200 mph. The most used fleets, consisting of about one hundred units each, are (1) the TGV Sud–Est fleet, built between 1978 and 1988, initially used for the Paris–Lyon line, and

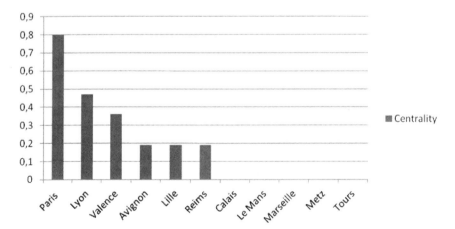

Figure 5.2.   Centralization of TGV Network (as of November 2011)

which were adapted for use on the Méditerranée, to Marseille and Nimes; (2) the TGV Atlantique fleet, built between 1988 and 1992 and used on the corridor of the same name; and (3) the TGV Réseau fleet, developed in the 1990s, used on the TGV Nord corridor and on the TGV Atlantique. Some of these transformed units of the TGV Réseau fleet are used for the connection with Belgium (Thalys PBA). The Eurostar is used for the connection with the United Kingdom. The technology used on the TGV lines is French, produced by the Alstom company, and has successfully implanted itself in some of the neighboring countries with which a connection already exists, and also in Spain, Korea, and the United States (the Acela Express, built jointly with the Canadian company Bombardier).

INVESTMENTS AND PROFITABILITY

As mentioned above, the Nora Report established a new strategy for SNCF that gave this company autonomous management over long-distance trains—rapid and express ones—(Campagne, 2004). For this reason, these operations had to take into account the competitive logic of the transportation market and achieve commercial viability. In practice, the development of HSR in France has always given priority to economic objectives in order to demonstrate that public enterprise can make money from operating the network. Unlike other projects with these same objectives, state officials did not permit any public debate on how to distribute the HSR network and were immune to any social and regional pressures.

The expansion of the network has followed spending criteria only in lines where spending was socially profitable; the lines have been financed according to their expected profitability, with required rates of financial and socioeconomic return, which have been flexibly applied (Vickerman, 1997). For example, the Paris to Bretagne project envisioned a financial return of 7.4 percent and a socioeconomic one of 13.6 percent; or the Côte d'Azur project, with a financial profitability of 8.4 percent and a socioeconomic one of 11 percent.

For this reason, those in charge of railways in France—who haven't mixed politics with spending—have always been reluctant to satisfy demands of a territorial type that go against the principle of social profitability. Priority has been given to service on corridors with sufficient traffic, connecting cities of a significant size. Because of this, it has almost always been necessary to connect cities with Paris to justify the investment. The first three lines built connected the French capital with the country's other main metropolitan areas: Lyon, Marseille, and Lille. This has generated a star-shaped network, centered on Paris. It is interesting to note that the use of conventional services for connections with lower traffic density, as well as for the access of the TGV to the large cities, has been maintained given that the costs of expropriation and construction would have been exorbitant.

The initial expectations concerning financial and social profitability were exceeded on several lines (Vickerman, 1997). For instance, the TGV Paris–Lyon was completely financed by SNCF with the expectation of obtaining a financial rate of return of 12 percent. In fact, the Sud–Est link is estimated to have provided a 15 percent financial rate of return and a 30 percent return in social terms. It had already been amortized by 1993, just twelve years after entering into service. However, the other lines have provided lower rates of return, which have been decreasing in parallel to the increase of the length of the network and the lower number of users relative to the first line. Increase in construction costs over time has played a role as well in the reduction of profitability (see table 5.1).

Table 5.1. *Train à Grande Vitesse* Construction Costs in Some TGV Lines

TGV Line	Year Beginning Operation	Miles	Total Cost (2011 US $ Billion)	Cost per Mile (2011 US $ Million)
Paris–Lyon	1981	264	3.0	11
Méditerranée	2001	155	6.5	42
Est–partial	2007	190	5.1	27
Rhin Rhone–partial	2011	67	3.5	52

Note: The total cost of the TGV Méditerranée estimated by the Cour des Comptes of France was 5.8 million euros in 2004 terms (including rolling stock). This amount greatly increases data previously provided by SNCF of 3.8 million euros in 1994 terms (Cour des Comptes, 2004, p. 232). However, we take into account the amount provided by SNCF, because the figure provided by the Cour includes rolling stock as well.

In September 2009, an agreement was reached to launch the tender for the second phase of TGV Est, of 66 additional miles, for a total amount of 2.01 billion euros.

The construction costs estimate for the TGV Rhin–Rhône is preliminary (as in the funding agreement of 2007) and includes TGV stations. Hence, that figure might underestimate the actual construction costs.

We used the average exchange rate by the end of 2011 to get nominal US dollars (1 euro = 1.30 US dollars).

Source: Adapted from information in Arduin and Ni (2005) for Paris–Lyon, Cour des Comptes (2004) for TGV Méditerranée, Réseau Ferré de France for LGV Est (www.lgv-est.com/medias/pdf/medias1359.pdf), and French Ministry of Ecology, Sustainable Development, Transport, and Housing for TGV Rhin–Rhône.

Because of this, public funding has been made available for the most recently constructed lines or those under construction. For instance, the French government contributed to the TGV Atlantique with a subsidy covering 30 percent of the costs. In this sense, the need for public subsidies has grown as the network has expanded. The TGV Est line (Paris–Strasbourg), which initially was expected to generate a financial rate of return of 4 percent but for which estimations were later lowered, has received subsidies from the central government and the regions involved. Thus, 61 percent of the construction of the network has been financed (Arduin and Ni, 2005) with public funds, contributed by the central government, seventeen local governments, the European Union, and Luxembourg. Another 17 percent has been financed by Réseau Ferré de France (French Rail Network, the company created in 1997 to own and maintain the French railway network) and the remaining 22 percent (which includes rolling stock for 800 million euros) by the operator of the service, SNCF. After the entry into service of this line, it reached a volume of traffic of thirteen million passengers in 2010 (and by June of 2011 had accumulated fifty million journeys), but its financial evolution has not been as stimulating, leading the commercial director of the TGV Est line to declare in September 2011 that "the TGV Est is an important commercial success, but it isn't profitable."[2]

In December 2011, the sixty-seven-mile long Dijon–Mulhouse trajectory of the eastern branch of the TGV Rhin–Rhône line entered into service. According to the figures supplied by the French Ministry of Ecology, Sustainable Development, Transport, and Housing, the investment cost of building the line is estimated at US $3 billion in 2007 terms (1 euro = US $1.30), of which approximately 75 percent has been subsidized with public funds from the central government, some regional governments, the European Union, and a marginal participation (3 percent) from the Swiss government. These estimations are provisional (from the financial agreement signed in 2007), and the definitive figures will probably reveal that the cost has been higher. On the other hand, SNCF has invested nearly €1.56 billion in rolling stock and stations in the TGV Rhin–Rhône line, of which US $0.25 billion in 2007 terms was in stations. Recently, an agreement has been reached to invest US $1.3 billion in the thirty-one miles remaining to complete the Eastern branch. The expected demand for this line is twelve million annual journeys.

The trend toward progressively worse results as the network expands is the principal reason for the moderation in plans to create new lines in the future. Indeed, France's plans are more modest that those of other countries, such as Spain, which has surpassed France in the expansion of its network in terms of service and even more so in terms of its network under construction; this is due to the considerable negligence in Spain over the budgetary implications of the costs of extending the HSR. Later we shall return to the Spanish experience and analyze these matters in much greater detail.

DEMAND AND MODAL COMPETITION

After thirty years of service in France, the TGV's commercial success as a means of transport is undeniable. In 2010, the TGV network transported 114.5 million passengers, a figure that amounts to almost 100,000 passengers per mile of network, making it the world's second-most traveled network after that of the *Shinkansen* in Japan, the world's pioneer. The long French experience with the TGV combined with the important tradition of geographic studies and territorial planning in France has allowed this country to produce a growing number of valuable studies on the effects produced by high-speed rail on a varied range of topics. These include HSR's effects on aggregate mobility and its competition with other modes of transportation offering an alternative service.

Bonnafous's work (1987) has had one of the broadest and most significant impacts internationally. This work analyzed the results of two studies realized in 1980 and 1985 concerning train and airplane users traveling for business reasons between Paris and the Rhone–Alps region. A survey was also made among 453 businesses of the Rhone–Alps region before the TGV line entered into service in 1981. One of the first notable results in Bonnafous's study is the fact that between 1980 and 1985 journeys between Paris and Rhone–Alps increased by 56 percent, within a context of economic expansion. This change in traffic, however, was marked by very varied characteristics: train journeys increased by 151 percent, while airplane journeys fell by 46 percent. On the other hand, the journeys originating in Paris (return trips originating in Paris) increased by 20 percent, much less than the journeys originating in Rhone–Alps, 86 percent. In terms of the modal distribution of the journey between Paris and Lyon, the airplane fell by 48 percent to 17 percent, while the train rose from 52 percent to 83 percent (note that journeys by road are not considered). The duration of the stay at the journey's destination underwent significant changes: stays of less than a day went from 26 percent to 54 percent, while overnight stays fell from 74 percent to 46 percent.

Vickerman's work (1997) provides information on the change in mobility on this corridor within a somewhat broader time frame. This study reports that the number of train passengers on the Paris–Lyon corridor rose from 12.5 million in 1980 to 22.9 million in 1992,[3] of which, 18.9 million were TGV passengers. It is important to note that the increase took place almost entirely during the first years of operation, with twenty million passengers (15 of them in TGV) in 1985, and then became much more moderate beginning in 1989. Although the increase in traffic received a new boost with the successive extensions of the TGV Sud–Est line (Mannone and Telemme, 1997), the growth in traffic has remained much more modest in recent years, and at present the number of trips is around twenty-five million. The cause of the increase in TGV traffic was the airplane, which fell by almost half between Paris and Lyon. Road traffic was also captured, as indicated by the fact that the growth in traffic on the A6 expressway, an alternative to the Paris–Lyon train, was only a third of the growth rates on other expressways, such as the A4 (Paris–Strasbourg) and the A13 (Paris–Caen) (Vickerman, 1997).

The evolution of traffic on the second corridor to enter into service, the TGV Atlantique, was not as successful as that of the Paris–Lyon line. Global traffic on the TVG Atlantique corridor increased only between 2 percent and 4 percent in the first four years of the TGV's service, from 1989 to 1993 (Klein, 1997; Klein and Claisse, 1997). The effect of the economic crisis in that period caused traffic to stagnate, creating quite a different context from the economic growth of the first half of the 1980s when the TGV Sud–Est began operating. On the other hand, the evolution of traffic by modes on the TGV Atlantique showed significant segmentation according to distances and travel times (Klein, 1997). For the shortest distances, less than one hour and thirty minutes travel time by TGV, the train lost passengers in a precipitous way, while road travel gained them. This negative evolution in short-distance journeys can be explained by the lower importance of the time saved traveling by HSR, the increase in the price of the journey,[4] and the degradation of conventional rail service. For intermediate distances, from between one hour and thirty minutes and three hours of TGV travel time, an important increase occurs for train travel, a more limited increase for road travel, and sharp reduction for air travel. It is in this interval of time that the TGV enjoys its greatest comparative advantage, gaining both volume of traffic and modal share. Lastly, for distances of over three hours' travel time by TGV, the train loses passengers, while the airplane is the winner.

In sum, distances of between one hour and thirty minutes and three hours are the most favorable to the TGV, whose attraction also depends on the difference in price in respect to conventional rail services. Furthermore, the business traveler, who for work reasons is more sensitive to time costs and less sensitive to monetary costs than the leisure traveler, is more likely to travel by TGV. Among business travelers, those with the highest ranking, such as executives, use the TGV the most; HSR attracts them away from the airplane for distances of less than three hours' travel time.

ECONOMIC AND REGIONAL IMPACTS

As in the case of HSR's effects on demand and the modal distribution of traffic, the French experience has also generated a particularly abundant literature on the economic and regional effects of high-speed rail. Such effects have been most scrutinized in relation to the experience of the TGV Sud–Est line. One of the first things to stand out, and which constitutes one of high-speed rail's most significant impacts, is that the most important hub benefits the most from HSR (Arduin, 1991). The Paris–Rhône–Alps route illustrates this point, as flight and train journeys to Paris for the purpose of buying or selling a service increased by 144 percent, while journeys in the inverse direction only experienced a 52 percent increase due to the HSR connection (Bonnafous, 1987). This means that round-trips originating in Paris increased much less than round-trips originating at the other end of the city-to-city connection. Although a compatible network allowed the HSR network to be extended, the region surrounding Paris (L'Île-de-France) has enjoyed the largest increase in its HSR supply mainly due to the spatial concentration of the population. As in Japan, HSR has promoted the centralization of economic service activities in big hubs and favored intra-organizational business trips. Such trips originating in Paris are up 21 percent, while those with Paris as their destination are up 156 percent (Bonnafous, 1987).

By contrast, the impact on industrial activities has been largely irrelevant. And the impact of HSR on business location decisions within the service sector also seems negligible. Mannone (1995, 1997) designed a survey to analyze how HSR was viewed by firms established in Dijon, the capital of the French region of Bourgogne, between 1981 and 1994. One-third declared that HSR was a factor they considered in their decision, but only four firms out of a total of 663 claimed it was a key determinant in their choice of location. Similar results were obtained in Valence and Avignon. These findings are consistent with those obtained from preliminary examination in Bonnafous (1987).[5] Consequently, it is consistently found that HSR has neither accelerated industrial concentration nor promoted administrative or economic decentralization from Paris. On the contrary, it is more likely that economic activity is attracted to the principal hub, as pointed out earlier. Thus, for example, as Manone (1995) notes, the arrival of HSR on the TGV Sud–Est line to Dijon (some 200 miles from Paris) meant an extension of the market of specialized services (such as computer assistance or marketing) for Parisian companies, increasing Dijon's dependence on Paris for these activities.

The surveys carried out on business trips provide additional information on the number of overnight stays and the reason for the journey. Train passengers staying at least one night at their destination fell from 74 to 46 percent with the introduction of HSR (1981–1985), and the main purposes were stated as being internal contacts and buying/selling services (Bonnafous, 1987). On the contrary, stays of less than a day went from 26 percent to 54 percent. These facts about the TGV Sud–Est suggested that the increase in volume of traffic didn't necessarily bring with it an increase in the demand of hotel services, given that the final effect on the total number of overnight stays is uncertain even though there is a large increase of mobility on the corridor.

Lastly, still in terms of the Paris–Sud–Est corridor, it is appropriate to highlight the analysis by Mannone (1997) concerning the effects of policies of station improvement as a consequence of the development of the TGV network and resulting urban transformations. This analysis of the functional and social transformations of cities with TGV stations reveals that high-speed rail generally has small influence on urban dynamics. Its primary effect is to shift centrality toward the neighborhood where the station is located, although this is not enough of a factor to modify its functions. On the other hand, the potential increase in economic activities, above all in respect to commerce and real estate, in the zone where the station is located occurs mainly because of the restructuring of activities within the city itself, and not through any significant creation of new activity or attraction of activities previously located outside of the zone.

Very detailed analysis has also been made of the effects of TGV service on the TGV Atlantique corridor in studies by Klein (1997) and Klein and Claisse (1997). These studies show that the implantation of the TGV worsened conventional train services, negatively affecting short-distance rail services through loss of quality and the increase in price of the new TGV service. Likewise, the origin–destination analysis of TGV mobility on the corridor showed that journeys made to sell advanced services (business consulting, advertising) increased much more for trips originating in Paris and much less for those originating in Le Mans, Tour, or Vendôme. This fact, which reflects the much greater imbalance of economic potential between these cities and Paris in contrast to what occurred between Paris and Lyon, resulted in an expansion of the market for Paris-based companies in these sectors, these having a competitive edge over companies from the small provincial cities.

In terms of the duration of the journeys by train, Klein and Claisse (1997) observe that between 1989 and 1993, very strong growth occurred, with half-day journeys doubling, while there was a decrease in the number of daylong journeys and above all those that lasted more than a day and required overnight stays: in this last case, those of two or three days fell by 11 percent, and those that required four or more days dropped by 32 percent. Given that other modes of transportation experienced an increase in these types of journeys, the drop in the number of journeys by train with overnight stays at their destination corroborates the idea that the effect of the change in mobility on hotel demand can be negative.

The study by Bazin et al. (2006) has examined in great detail the effects on the corridor, and furthermore the period examined (1990–1999) is longer than in the previous cases, making it possible to observe more consolidated changes. The most important results of this study can be systematized as follows:

Effects on the real estate sector: In general, there is a trend toward increasing real estate prices, which occurs in the two years prior to and the two years following the entry into service of HSR, with a later stabilization of prices. In the well-known case of Vendôme, located just over 100 miles from Paris, property prices rose sharply in the moments prior to the entry into service of the high-speed train. The rise increased to about 20 percent and was especially intense in the neighborhood where the HSR station was located. Nevertheless, prices later returned to more moderate levels, and the local market followed an evolution similar to the property market on a national level. Overall, the change seems to have led to an increase in the attractiveness of the neighborhood where the HSR station is located, within a radius of less than fifteen minutes from the station. Similar trends have been observed in the city of Le Mans, some 130 miles from Paris. The increase in prices was much more acute in the city of Tours (some 150 miles from Paris) in the city center, although these also later stabilized. Furthermore, in the cases of Le Mans and Vendôme, local authorities set in motion real estate projects and urban planning geared to take advantage of the potential effects of welcoming businesses. Nonetheless, it's necessary to point out that the real effects have been much less important than the expectations created by local authorities and economic agents in relation to attracting companies.

Global effects on employment: HSR can favor retaining existing companies but doesn't always prevent the relocation of companies. The existence of HSR service is not systematically associated with the creation of employment or with acting as an important attraction for outside companies. For the TGV Atlantique line, Bazin et al. (2006, p. 92) have statistically contrasted the hypothesis of a link between the presence of HSR service and an employment growth rate higher than the rest of France, and they have found that the phenomena are independent and unrelated. In practice, the creation of employment in cities with HSR service reflect the greater or lesser creation of employment in the territorial areas in which these cities are located: TGV cities with greater employment creation are found in regions with greater employment creation, and the TGV cities with less creation of employment are located in less dynamic regions. On the other hand, the study of the cities of Tours, Le Mans, and Vendôme show a relocation of companies to the vicinity of the TGV station in the heart of the agglomeration that receives the TGV service or will receive it shortly, which is consistent with Mannone's results (1997) for the cities of the TGV Sud–Est line.

Effects on sectors of employment: HSR service is not significantly associated with strong employment growth in any of the types of employment examined. The arrival of the TGV reinforces previously prevalent specializations. In particular, the total creation of urban higher employment and in the sub-sector of "business services" is independent of the availability of HSR service. As an exceptional case, a measure of urban employment in "research" work is created in large urban units associated with the availability of HSR service. In terms of companies in the "consulting services" sector, it is particularly notable that for companies operating in a national market located in the province to which HSR has arrived, the arrival of HSR helps reinforce the opening of the local market and thus the arrival of Parisian companies in tertiary activities of high specialization. This observation is consistent with the one made by Klein and Claisse (1997 for this same line) and by Mannone (1995) for small cities of the TGV Sud–Est line.

Effects on tourism: In and of itself, the TGV doesn't excite curiosity, except for sporadic initial demand to become familiar with the service. Analysis of the available experiences shows that the availability of HSR gives value to already known and popular tourist destinations but is not sufficient on its own to promote the development of barely known or little-valued tourist spots, even when the arrival of HSR brings with it important accompanying policies. Clearly, it can favor a measure of development of business tourism, if there is an increase in the number of events that spark such forms of travel, as occurred in Le Mans after the entry into service of the TGV Atlantique. On the other hand, there is a decrease in the length of overnight stays, which can accelerate the restructuring of the hotel and catering industry. Thus, in the city of Le Mans, small hotels with limited attractions disappeared, while large national chains increased their offer, providing better quality more in keeping with the characteristics of the demand of business tourism.

The effect on purely leisure tourism is much more limited. Many projects promoting tourism based on the arrival of HSR to little-known destinations with limited attraction have failed. Bazin et al. (2006) explain that the project to create a golf course in Vendôme was abandoned. The same occurred with the tourist circuits organized for visits to the castles of the Loire region, with return to the Tours station. This type of result has also been observed in the TGV Sud–Est, in respect to the circuits organized for visiting Dijon and the vineyards of the region. This last case is very illustrative, given that the proposals were for foreign tourists, with a significant presence of Americans, who sharply increased the number of visits to the region of the Côte d'Or, where Dijon is located. From the late 1970s to the mid-1980s, the number of tourists tripled, reaching 85,000 in 1985. That number, however, later rapidly fell to 31,470 in 1994 (Mannone, 1995, p. 173).

Effect on cultural activities: A somewhat surprising and unexpected result, which reflects the evaluation of the effects of the TGV Atlantique, is the low level of vitalization of recreational, cultural, and sporting activities in cities served by the TGV, except Le Mans. A plausible explanation for these results is that the improved accessibility to Paris's cultural and recreational offer, as well as that of the principal cities of the region, weakens the cultural and recreational offer of small and medium-size cities, which are incapable of attracting outside visitors to compensate for the exit of local residents to activities in Paris or the principal cities of each region.

Effects on commercial activity: The availability of HSR services increases the attraction of products of a regional type in the new locations served by high-speed rail. Furthermore, in respect to this type of product, there is an increase in activity in locations near the station, although analogous activity is reduced in zones of the city located farther away from the station. In contrast, the commercial activity of high added value and luxury products suffers in the new destinations, given that shopping trips to Paris and the primary regional hubs, which have much greater commercial attraction, hurt activity in this subsector in small and medium-size cities. This evolution was anticipated by the results of a study made of the city of Le Mans shortly before the arrival of the TGV to evaluate the risk of commercial flight for commerce in luxury products, as noted by Bazin et al. (2006, p. 178). Among those interviewed within a radius of 1,000 meters from the train station, 78 percent responded that they weren't going to change their shopping behavior because of the TGV, while the remaining 22 percent responded that they would. In respect to the latter, 80 percent thought that their change of behavior would favor Paris, and only 20 percent thought it would favor Le Mans. As for the merchants interviewed, most thought that the effect of HSR would be commercial flight to Paris, and this percentage was much higher in the case of luxury products (88 percent) than in the rest of the subsectors (43 percent).

Policies of support: Furthermore, in general, policies of support are necessary to strengthen the effects of high-speed rail, but are not enough in any mode. Table 5.2 presents a summary of the way territorial authorities carried out (or not) policies of support related to the arrival of the TGV to Mans, Tours, Saint-Pierre-des-Corps, and Vendôme.

In fact, the effects of the TGV were perceptible in Le Mans, which had carried out policies of support, but less perceptible in Vendôme and Saint-Pierre-des-Corps, which had also applied support policies. Likewise, general effects were not notable in Tours, which had chosen not to apply any policies of support.

A general reflection that comes to light from the study of the TGV Atlantique is that good accessibility for conventional rail is as important as HSR service, especially for cities closer to Paris, where the competitive advantage

Table 5.2. A Critical Synthesis of the Support Policies Carried Out in Le Mans, Tours, Saint-Pierre-des-Corps, and Vendôme upon the Arrival of the TGV

	In the Economic Field	In the Tourist Field	Others
Le Mans	• Creation of Novaxis (office spaces near the TGV station) for outside (nonlocal) companies, although in the end it was primarily local in effect. • Communication from Novaxis with projects indirectly linked to the TGV. • Emphasis on attracting investors. • Strong cooperation of local actors (city, department . . .) to set up the projects.	• No high-level products exist in Le Mans (exception 24hh) • Proposed products: Train + golf; Train +24h of Le Mans; Train + visit to the historic city center. • Tourist development policies were applied in relation to the TGV in the department and region. Effects were limited, above all, because of the modal discontinuity after the arrival to Le Mans.	• Negotiation to maintain *corail*-type trains. • Negotiation of prices for season tickets for the SNCF.
Tours	• No project related to the TGV in Tours because of the cul-de-sac of the service and the weakness of the expected demand. • The conference center was opened ten years after the arrival of the TGV. • View that it wasn't necessary to stimulate activity in the center given its natural attractiveness. Rents and rates were already high, and the city center was often congested.	• Implementation of the "formula plus" with SNCF (train + overnight stay + gourmet menu) • Low interest in tourist sector, also because of the modal discontinuity.	None
Saint-Pierre-des-Corps	• Urban planning operation with the aim of creating a new station, an office building of 10,000m², a parking garage with 460 spaces on 7 levels, a hotel with 100 rooms, and a complete restructuring of the track network. • Reorganization of an industrial zone. • Creation of a 900m² municipality facility. • Creation of a zone for activities.		None
Vendôme	• No supporting project prepared in 1990, although a service park of 140 hectares was in the project since 1986. • Implementation of a 111-hectare activities park with the goal of it being commercialized and a tourist terminal. • Project to study the fitting out of the station. • Realization of a mixed real estate operation (offices / residences) after the arrival of the TGV.	• Evaluation of heritage. • Project to create a Tourism Office and Information Center near the station. • Proposal for circuits to the castles of the Loire, the Loire Valley, and the Sarthe.	• Renegotiation of the timetables of the SNCF.

Source: Adaptation of Bazin et al. (2006), 235–38.

of the HSR in respect to the road and conventional railway is more limited. On the other hand, the availability of HSR is a supplementary attraction to the availability of good road service.

ENVIRONMENT AND OTHER EXTERNALITIES

The first environmental protest against the construction of a TGV line in France occurred in May of 1990, during the planning stage of the TGV Méditerranée. The protestors, who blocked a train viaduct, called for the existing line between Lyon and Marseilles to be used instead of a new line being built, given the environmental impact the latter option would cause. However, environmental aspects of the TGV have not been a fundamental issue in France, either in the public debate or in the analysis and evaluation of experiences. Two factors can help explain why environmental questions have not been central issues. First, the fact that the substitution of the airplane was very intense (in modal share) and extensive (in quantity of use) in the initial experiences at medium-range distances may have helped limit protests; indeed, substituting the airplane is high-speed rail's most favorable environmental impact. Second, nuclear power's hegemony in the production of France's electricity means that CO_2 emissions generated by electricity consumption are very low; for this reason, the environmental outcome of increased use of the train can be even more favorable.

Even so, environmentally motivated opposition has grown in recent years and is being voiced with greater emphasis against projects such as the TGV line between Bordeaux and Toulouse. Environmentalists argue that the TGV is environmentally inefficient if the costs of creating the new line are taken into account, and point out the declining importance on recent lines of substituting air travel, which casts doubt on environmental benefits. Furthermore, criticism is made of the disrupting effect on the rural environment by the so-called tunnel effect: the TGV joins medium-size and larger cities for point-to-point journeys and disrupts the rail offer in the smallest cities and in rural areas, through both the reduction in conventional service and the progressive degradation of the conventional infrastructure. Lastly, the growing financial problems created by the extension of the TGV network have also been used to justify opposition to the TGV by environmental groups, who question the high cost of achieving environmental improvements that, in the best of cases, are very limited.

SUMMARY

The French experience offers very interesting lessons on the effects of high-speed rail in many areas: demand and impact on other modes of transport, economic effects, and regional effects.

High-speed rail is primarily competitive at intermediate distances and for in-vehicle TGV travel times of between one and a half and three hours. For shorter distances, the modest time gained in the overall journey by HSR combined with the higher price of the service make it less attractive. For in-vehicle journeys longer than four hours the advantage of the plane is clear, even though the price of the TGV may be more attractive, as occurs in the experiences analyzed in the French case, which has a relatively low TGV price and experiences prior to the development of the low-cost model of air transport.

The financial performance of the TGV and its socioeconomic profitability were high in the initial moments of its development, led by the Paris–Lyon line, which, along with Tokyo–Osaka line, is the only line in the world to have entirely repaid its costs. However, after the development of the second line, the TGV Atlantique, public subsidies for construction began to be necessary and have subsequently risen. For example, the development of the TGV Est Européenne line has required subsidies of more than 75 percent of the cost of construction. Thus, after the network's good start, there has been ever-greater pressure applied to the taxpayer, and this despite the fact that with 114.5 million journeys in 2010, France's TGV network is the world's second in terms of volume of use, after the Japanese system.

The economic effect of HSR is extremely limited, when they are positive. The positive effects are very far from being systematic. Employment growth has not been stronger in cities served by high-speed rail, given that it plays a very secondary role in attracting the implantation of companies. Its arrival, which results in the relocation of local companies in the center of the agglomerations, can favor the continued presence of some companies but doesn't always stop relocations from occurring. There is no regular evidence of vitalization of the tertiary sector in high-speed rail cities. And on the other hand, it can broaden the business reach of high added value service companies located in the network's primary hubs, which are generally more competitive than those of smaller cities. In fact, this dynamic allows the large hubs to capture new market areas, attracting economic activity away from the smaller points. Furthermore, in terms of commerce, HSR generates an attraction of shopping activity—above all, of luxury products—in favor of the network's primary hubs.

The effects of the TGV on tourism are also quite inferior to the expectations created. The TGV makes possible the revaluation of cities that already enjoy strong tourist appeal and which are already known. In these cases, its potential impact is limited to urban, green, or sports tourism, and for short stays. It can favor business tourism more strongly. But it can, overall, have the effect of reducing the number of overnight stays and, with this, hotel demand. The global balance is not clear. In the case of cities without previous tourist potential, the tourist effect is irrelevant, given that people don't travel to places that lack a reason to be visited. In all, it can produce an increase in the demand for restaurant services given the increase in short journeys, and a reduction of hotel demand as a result of the shorter duration of the visits. In this sense, as mentioned earlier, the strongest employment growth in the tourist sector occurs in places that already have a strong appeal, but the results are much more mediocre for the rest of the locations. This combination of factors has caused concern in the South of France over the expulsion effect of tourism toward Barcelona (Masson and Petiot, 2009), when this city becomes totally linked to the cities of the French Midi.

Another interesting result is that small and medium-size cities with TGV located relatively near the large hubs of the network can find their offer in recreational, cultural, and sporting activities harmed, given the increased accessibility for their residents to the offer of these activities in the nearby large cities.

Property and residential real estate markets seem to be vitalized by the prospects of the arrival of high-speed rail, which causes a notable rise in prices, of variable proportions. Nevertheless, over the long term, this rise doesn't usually lead to sustained higher prices. The entry into service of an HSR line doesn't lead to the transformation of the cities near Paris into dormitory-cities. Indeed, the work-residence migrations continue to be limited, although they rise with the first HSR services. There is a slight rise in the number of home buyers outside of the city.

In sum, the positive effects of high-speed rail are not evident except in the presence of strong local potential. The number of stops, ticket prices, and timetables are crucial to realizing the potential effects. The articulation between HSR and the network of local stations is also decisive in respect to the potential effects.

NOTES

1. Social profitability is defined as the net social return, in terms of economic welfare of the society, of an investment project. It results from the comparison between social costs and social returns instead of comparing private costs and private revenues, which is the traditional financial analysis of a private project evaluation. The social rate of return is the rate of return achieved by society—this is considering all externalities generated—with an investment project.

2. "TGV Est : un succès pas rentable," *Républicain Lorrain*, September 22, 2011, www.republicain-lorrain.fr/actualite/2011/09/22/tgv-est-un-succes-pas-rentable.

3. Note that the variation in train journeys is less in this case than in that of Bonnafous (1987), probably because in the case the latter study business trips were analyzed, on which the TGV has a much greater impact. The evolution of trips by plane between Paris and Lyon is much more similar in both studies, as seen below, probably because business trips by air had significant hegemony over leisure trips.

4. The combination of the lower impact of the time savings in vehicle on the total time (door to door) of the journey and the increase in the price of train tickets make the gained hour of time in the early 1990s a higher monetary cost on the shortest journeys, up to 80 francs per hour—12.2 euros—(Klein, 1997). The monetary cost of the hour saved by the TGV fell continually with the distance traveled, until reaching some 52 francs per hour (7.93 euros) on the longest journeys (Klein and Claisse, 1997).

5. Similarly, in a survey realized for the regions of Bretagne and Pays de la Loire, Ollivro (1997) found that while the existence of swift forms of transport was a criterion for locating strategic functions for 13.3 percent of the businesses surveyed, the existence of an HSR station was an important criterion for only 4.7 percent of these.

6

Germany

Neubaustrecken

BACKGROUND

After overcoming the difficulties imposed by the destruction of its infrastructure in World War II and the division of the country for four decades, the next necessary step in the modernization of Germany's railway services was to overcome the forced north–south orientation of West Germany in order to incorporate and integrate the territories of East Germany. The German unification of the 1990s meant rethinking transportation infrastructure and services and the necessary realization of new planning in which high-speed rail came to have a decisive role.

The *InterCity Express*, as high-speed rail is called in Germany, began functioning in June of 1991, a decade after the introduction of high-speed rail in the Old Continent. There were several reasons for this delay. Besides the obvious problems of constructing an HSR system in the country's mountainous terrain, it proved considerably more complicated to obtain the necessary legal and political approval to begin construction (Dunn and Perl, 1994). At any rate, the high-speed rail plan for the 1990s designed in 1984 used the experience of the recent French HSR as its model. After the development of the plan, it had to be brought up to date in 1991 in the midst of the country's reunification so that its objectives and priorities could take into account the new political and economic context.

The first routes chosen in Germany were the line between Hanover and Wurzburg and the route between Mannheim and Stuttgart. Both were conceived as mixed lines combining passenger and freight traffic, which is one of the features distinguishing the German experience from others that centered on providing services exclusively for passenger mobility.

The network quickly grew with the addition of a route between Wolfs-burg and Berlin in 1998—known as the east–west route—which broke the traditional north–south orientation. This route displaced as a priority the rest of the planned lines following the political unification between the Democratic Republic of Germany and the Federal Republic of Germany. The need to connect the new political capital, Berlin, with the primary cities in the country's west was the reason behind this decision.

Later, the line between Cologne and Frankfurt entered into service in 2002, and the one between Nuremberg and Munich in 2006. Both lines were geared exclusively for passenger traffic, which is why their cruising speeds reach 186 mph in contrast to the rest of the routes that opted for mixed passenger and freight traffic in exchange for slower speeds. In fact, on the same Nuremberg–Munich line, numerous sections exist, particularly on the southern section of the route, in which the train's speed doesn't surpass 124 mph; new upgrades are expected to increase this speed to bring it on par with the rest of the sections on the route.

OBJECTIVES AND MOTIVATION

The rationale underpinning the HST network was somewhat different in Germany. Given the west–east orientation of the rail network constructed before World War II and the current north–south patterns of industrial co-operation, Germany sought to reform the network so as to facilitate freight transportation from the northern ports to the southern industrial territo-ries. For this reason, the first two *neubaustrecken*—new lines—were those linking Hanover and Wurzburg and Mannheim and Stuttgart, respectively. The main goal was to solve congestion problems in certain corridors and to improve north–south freight traffic. Furthermore, following the country's political reunification, the need to connect east and west became an ad-ditional priority.

One example demonstrating the interest in achieving efficiency and relieving congestion is the route between Cologne and Frankfurt. This route since 1994 has formed part of the European Union's priority axis of Paris–Brussels–Cologne–Amsterdam–London because of its very high use—among the highest on the continent—and because it provides service to Germany's large economic conglomerations: Rhine–Ruhr and Rhine-Main. Because of the complex process of planning and approval of infra-structure projects in Germany, the bottleneck that had existed on this route since the 1970s wasn't resolved until the 1990s. The solution was found in a high-speed rail service that, in contrast to regional services—which fol-low the Rhine River—directly connected the two capitals of the two regions following the route of the A3 expressway to minimize environmental and economic costs, while also minimizing the time of the route. This design, however, left out some important cities, such as Koblenz and the capitals of the states of Hesse and Rhineland Palatinate, Wiesbaden and Mainz, respectively. Construction began in 1995 and wasn't finished until 2002, achieving a reduction of twenty-eight miles (from 138 to 110) and an extraordinary time savings that reduced travel time from two hours and thirteen minutes to fifty-nine minutes (Brux, 2002).

STRUCTURE, DESIGN, AND FUNCTIONS

Regarding the determining factors behind the network's design, no better source can be found than Eberhard Jaensch (2005), who was responsible for designing the network system at DB Netz AG in 2005. Jaensch sustains that geography and the location of industry were the forces that determined the functions and form of the railway networks in Germany. In particular, the initial design took into account as a starting point the InterCity (IC) long-distance system that had functioned throughout the territory of West Germany (before political unification). For this reason, the *InterCity Express* had to adapt to the existing system and substitute conventional services in a gradual way. As a consequence, Germany opted to improve technology and upgrade infrastructure and service instead of building separate new lines dedicated exclusively to high-speed rail services, as is the case in most HSR routes in Japan and Spain. In fact, high-speed rail services also use the same tracks that regional conventional services use in areas where no new infrastructure has been built.

Germany has also opted for a mixed strategy in the construction of new infrastructure (*neubaustrecke*) and improving existing tracks to accommodate them to high speeds (*ausbaustrecke*).

As in France, conventional and regional services are designed to complement high-speed services, thereby broadening territory accessibility in a country where the population is quite dispersed. However, high-speed rail in Germany has also been designed to complement mobility by air transportation, with HSR stations located in the air terminals themselves.

In contrast to France, Germany's population of eighty million is dispersed throughout the territory, and thus the high-speed rail network has tended to reproduce this decentralized (polycentric) design without a center or dominant hub. Nevertheless, its population density (593 inhabitants per square mile) is significant and in fact higher than the densities of France, Italy, and Spain, which makes it possible to justify using the services of a high-speed rail network.

Among the largest hubs of the network, only four cities have populations of more than one million (Berlin, Hamburg, Munich, and Cologne).

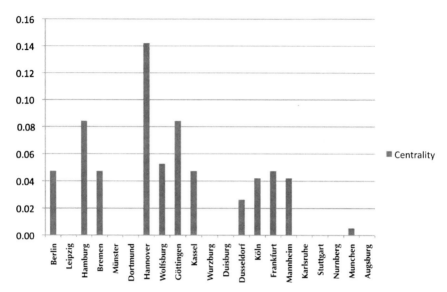

Figure 6.1.   Centralization of *InterCity Express* Network (as of November 2011)

Analysis according to metropolitan area, in contrast, shows how this, in combination with the dispersed population and the decentralization of the network, impedes wide-scale use of direct high-speed rail and makes necessary a service with efficient connections.

Analysis of the centrality of the different HSR network hubs (see figure 6.1) shows the decentralization of the network with very few hubs having a significant value of centrality in the network. In fact, in contrast to other experiences, such as those of the Japanese or French, we find that the primary hub in terms of centrality has a value of only 14 percent. This means that of all the origin–destination pairs of the German high-speed rail network, 14 percent pass through its station. This hub is Hanover, which plays an important role in the connections between the east and west of the country. The rest of the hubs all have values lower than 10 percent. It should be remembered that in the case of Japan the primary hub has a value of 70 percent, and in the case of France Paris enjoys a centrality value of 54 percent. There is no question that the design of the network reproduces the existing decentralization found in the system of German cities.

As in other experiences, the design of the network and very particularly the number and selection of intermediary stops between large cities has been controversial and characterized by enormous pressures from regional governments (the German *länder*), municipal governments, and different local pressure groups. This complex negotiation has primarily occurred in peripheral areas, not only because of problems of economic viability but also because of the significant impediment to the efficiency of high-speed rail services that are forced to constantly stop, thereby reducing their competitive potential with other forms of transportation.

The route between Cologne and Frankfurt was considered the best given the restrictions imposed by the objectives of the *Deutsche Bahn* (the service operator) in view of economic, environmental, and network costs along with those related to the efficiency of service on the one hand, and the pressures applied by the federal states to maximize the number of stations within their respective territories on the other (Ashlfeld and Feddersen, 2010).

Such results are not out of the ordinary if one takes into account the enormous weight of regional governments (*länder*) in the German political system, and quite particularly in terms of infrastructure projects. The project of the Cologne–Frankfurt route involved three of these states: North Rhine Westphalia, Rhineland-Palatine, and Hesse. Nonetheless, the initial design didn't envision any stations in the intermediary state of Rhineland-Palatine, leaving the intermediary cities of this state isolated even while the infrastructure passed through their territory. Negotiations with the state of Rhineland-Palatine dragged on as this regional government threatened to block construction, definitively affecting the political decision-making process. As a result of this arduous conflict—the last legal challenge to the project wasn't resolved until September of 1998—Rhineland-Palatine obtained one high-speed rail station in its territory, but in exchange the other two states each added another intermediary station in their own territory. A curious thing about these intermediary stations in different states is the fact that the distance between Montabaur and Limburg is only 20 km—some twenty-two minutes by road and greatly below the average distance between stations in Germany, which is approximately 95 km. Furthermore, the municipalities have very low populations, totaling 12,400 and 33,400 inhabitants, respectively. Only political motivation explains the insertion of both of these stations. The weight of regional governments and that of the political economy of infrastructure spending appear in a reoccurring way in all high-speed rail experiences. The German case, furthermore, is particularly intense given that HSR projects must be approved by the territorial parliaments, where the federal states have a new opportunity to establish their positions and apply new pressures on the network's design (see figure 6.2).

If there is a feature that distinguishes the German experience from others it is precisely the network's capacity to function for two forms of mobility: passengers and freight. Passenger services primarily use the network during the day, while freight is transported at night. However, on some routes with more than one line of conventional service with trajectories close to the Rhine or which were introduced in densely populated urban zones, it was decided to build a new infrastructure dedicated exclusively to passengers, as is the case on the route between Cologne and Frankfurt. The maximum

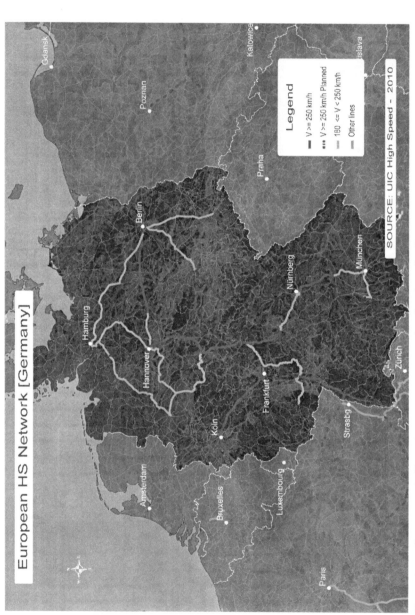

Figure 6.2. Germany: HSR lines. Source: UIC (International Union of Railways)

mass carried by freight trains of the new mixed traffic lines is restricted to 2,500 tons.

Apart from its effect on spending, the choice of a mixed model of passengers and freight meant renouncing greater commercial speeds (with a maximum of >150–160 mph) in order to gain the stability and safety required for adapting the infrastructure to the restrictive characteristics of high-speed freight transportation. This decision was controversial and was extensively debated in Germany, according to Klaus Ebeling (2005). On the one hand, the Ministry of Transportation and the promoter of the infrastructure debated over whether to build tracks exclusively for passenger traffic, following the French and Japanese models, or else to construct infrastructures capable of combining passenger traffic with that of freight. Their position in favor of the mixed model was greatly influenced by the significant volume of income freight traffic generated for the state railway company. In this sense, it was believed that the enormous necessary investment could be compensated for by the high use of the railway for transporting freight and by its thus elevated capacity to generate income for the public railway company.

On the other hand, some experts favored specialization and the separation between passengers and freight, as the pioneering countries in HSR had done with experiences that could be considered successful. An example of the importance of this debate can be seen in the delay in construction of the Cologne–Frankfurt line. Although originally it was planned to be the first high-speed rail line to open in Germany, the intense debate over the functionality of the infrastructure made it the third line after the opening of the Hanover–Wurzburg and Mannheim–Stuttgart lines, and in the end it was relegated to the fourth position after the previously mentioned connection Wolfsburg–Berlin was given priority. In fact, the first design had double functionality in mind, but the experience with the rest of the lines already in operation showed that freight traffic could only function in very restrictive conditions:

- *Timetable*: It was difficult to coordinate the daytime schedule and design a reasonable and reliable timetable for passenger and freight services because of their different average velocities.
- *Slots*: Slots couldn't be distributed at night because of the extensive maintenance requirements of high-speed rail lines, which can only be realized at night.
- *Weight*: The restrictions imposed by the weight of the freight train on the alignment of the infrastructure also favor the separation of passengers and freight services. Freight service requires greater alignment and thus more tunnels, which increases cost.

Another trade-off that required making a choice of model was the incompatibility of short-distance services in conurbations and high-speed rail. In fact, the prioritizing of short-distance passenger services is one of the main causes behind freight train delays.

Finally, it is necessary to keep in mind that high-speed rail services in Germany are not restricted to the national territory and also provide services beyond the country's borders to Austria, France, Switzerland, Belgium, and Holland despite the technical problems derived from the different technology, infrastructure, and signaling. Some of these services are operated by Thalys, the international operator present in many trans-European lines and in which Deutsche Bahn holds a 10 percent stake. In Germany, Deutsche Bahn is responsible for services, while its branch Deutsche Netze has been in charge of infrastructure since 2008, resulting in an accounting division between services and infrastructure.

In terms of the vehicles and their technology, different versions and generations exist. Up until the present, five different vehicles have been produced, from the ICE 1 (used in 1991) to the ICE TD (2001). The technology used is primarily German, although the ICE 3 version was developed jointly between Siemens and the Canadian Bombardier. The development of this technology has made it possible to export it to other countries, such as China, Russia, and Spain that use the ICE 3 version (Siemens Velaro). The development of Maglev technology described in the Japanese experience has also been tested in Germany. In fact, such testing began there two years earlier than it did in Japan, and German planners expect it to provide greater speed with less negative externalities, although at a higher cost.

SPENDING AND PROFITABILITY

The first thing to draw attention to is the fact that Germany is among the group of countries with high construction costs. This is due to the unevenness of the terrain and its geological characteristics, as well as to complex construction procedures that must be complied with, in contrast to other countries.

Choosing a mixed traffic service for passengers and freight has resulted in much higher upgrading costs and, arguably, operating costs, although the industrial centers served have enjoyed greater benefits (Haynes, 1997). The German multipurpose HSR system was conceived, therefore, to spread benefits rather than concentrating them. In fact, as Heinisch (1992) claims, the main consideration when designing the new lines was not faster passenger traffic but rather the highly profitable overnight traffic between the North Sea ports and the industrial areas and consumer markets in southern Germany. Goods transport was deemed more important, because it contributes considerably more to the turnover than is the case of passenger traffic. A further difference with the HST in France is that the HSTs in Germany are heavier, wider, and more expensive to run but offer greater flexibility (Dunn and Perl, 1994).

The choice of a mixed model has obvious consequences for investment costs. First of all, and given the unevenness of the terrain, the number of necessary tunnels increased significantly. The restrictions imposed by freight services on the alignment of the infrastructure impeded the flexibility necessary to avoid passing through tunnels. As an example, the percent of miles of tunnels on the mixed line between Hanover and Würzburg is 37 percent, whereas the proportion of tunnels over the whole length of the high-speed line between Cologne and Frankfurt is only 21 percent, and the average tunnel length is one mile. It is estimated that the decision to build a line exclusively for passenger service reduced construction costs by 15 percent on that line.

Building delays and Germany's topography resulted in higher-than-expected construction cost overruns, as well as operating deficits and increasing debt burdens, which increased the financial pressures to reform the system. The source of some of these overruns according to Dunn and Perl (1994) was the need to satisfy the multiple, and at times conflicting, criteria of a wide range of policy participants. As a consequence, the German lines have been much more expensive than the French lines, a situation that can be attributed to the more challenging nature of the terrain, its urban structure, and various political and legal obstacles.

Furthermore the network only serves around sixty-seven million passengers a year. For this reason, the utility of continuing investment in HSR is being questioned, since it is seen as an expensive solution that might not provide the environmental gains that could be achieved with a more restrictive approach to road transport (Whitelegg, 1993; Vickerman, 1997).

Although the average net revenue per train-mile of the *InterCity Express* service was 1.7 times higher than the average for its other long-distance services (Ellwanger and Wilckens, 1993), operational deficits are due in large part to the dispersed nature of the German population and the small average size of German cities. The urban structure of Germany lacks France's mono-centric focus, and so for many years the country's intercity rail system had been based on a complex, interlinking network of services with interchanges that provided regular hourly or two-hourly connections between most major German towns and cities, and more frequent services on certain key lines (Vickerman, 1997, p. 28). This means there are few corridors providing sufficient demand. Compared to the nine million annual passengers using the HST link between Cologne and Frankfurt, the Paris–Lyon link can boast twenty-five million passengers and the Tokyo–Osaka link 130 million; i.e., more than ten times the Cologne–Frankfurt figure. Likewise, low population densities lead to higher accessibility needs, which

Table 6.1. *Neubaustrecken* Construction Costs

Lines	Year Beginning Operation	Miles	Total Cost (US $ Billion of 2011)	Cost per Mile (US $ Million of 2011)
Hanover–Würzburg	1988 and 1994	203	12.8	63
Mannheim–Stuttgart	1991	61.5	3.0	49
Cologne–Frankfurt	2002	110	8.3	71
Nuremberg–Ingolstadt	2006	55	4.7	86

Source: Adapted on info from European Commission (1996), from Deutsche Bahn web page, and from the International Union of Railways High Speed Department.
Note: We updated according to inflation rates, and conversion was made applying the average exchange rate by the end of 2011 to get nominal US dollars (1 euro = 1.3 US dollars).

usually result in high regional transportation costs and shorter distances between stations, which—in turn—negatively affect commercial speed.

In short, the dual function and compatibility of German HSR with conventional services, together with the country's mountainous terrain— freight traffic requires low gradients—have resulted in higher construction costs (Gutierrez-Puebla, 2004). For a comparison between lines, a summary of the total and corrected costs per mile is given in table 6.1, where we offer information in 2011 terms.

In terms of their operation, the vehicles of the *InterCity Express* are up to three times more expensive than the French technology of the TGV due to the greater complexity of their electronics, monitoring, and diagnostic systems.

DEMAND AND MODAL COMPETITION

The time reduction achieved by the *InterCity Express* for a route of a standard distance of approximately 217 miles was an average of an hour and a half. In percentage terms, this reduction is between 35 percent and 50 percent (Jaensch, 2005). For the Cologne–Frankfurt route of 112 miles, the *Inter-City Express* shortened the travel time of two and a half hours to only one hour and a quarter. In the case of the Nuremberg–Ingolstadt line, the travel time was reduced from one hour and forty-one minutes to approximately one hour.

Even with renouncing the fastest possible speeds to provide mixed passenger and freight services, the average time reduction contributed by the *InterCity Express* high-speed rail is around 60 percent.

The business of high-speed rail passenger service has grown, as was the case with its predecessors in Japan and France. In the year 2004, the volume of traffic was already 19.6 billion passengers per mile, which meant 60 percent of the total passenger railway traffic. The total traffic per year is

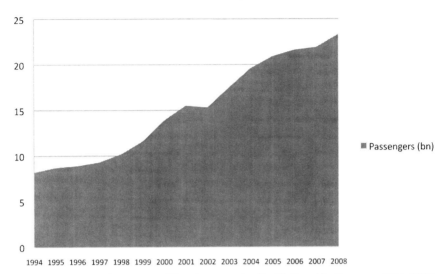

25

20

15

■ Passengers (bn)

10

5

0

1994 1995 1996 1997 1998 1999 2000 2001 2002 2003 2004 2005 2006 2007 2008

Figure 6.3. *InterCity Express* **Billion Passenger-km Traffic Trend in Germany 1994–2008**

115 million passengers, with an average journey length of 174 miles within the long-distance passenger transport system in Germany. The train-miles amount to 95.8 million. Average train occupation is 130 passengers (pass-mile/train-mile).[1] The evolution of passenger traffic up to 2008 is shown in figure 6.3.

The average increase in market share achieved by the introduction of the HST was 11 percent (Ellwanger and Wilckens, 1993). Its impact on air transportation has been much greater than on road transportation. Furthermore, transportation policy in Germany has made an effort to include the principal airports (for example, Frankfurt and Cologne, among others) within the high-speed rail network in order to promote substitutability in short and medium-range journeys.

Nevertheless, on the Cologne–Munich route, the travel time by train is approximately four hours and thirty minutes, given that part of the route cannot be made at high speed, and there are several stops due to the elevated density of the urban network in the west of the country. Given such a lengthy travel time, air transportation has maintained its services between these cities. In fact, air services have even increased in recent years thanks to the implantation of low-cost airlines that seem better able to compete with high-speed rail services than the flag carrier airline Lufthansa. This company, which increased its services after the entry into service of the Cologne–Frankfurt line by complementing its services, was later forced to reduce the frequencies of its flights with the entry into service of the high-speed rail line between Cologne and Munich (Dobruszkes, 2011).

On routes that have high-speed service over their entire length, much higher time savings are achieved. For example, the Hanover–Berlin route takes only an hour and a half, while the travel time on conventional trains takes up to five hours, or three hours by car.

The elevated cost of high-speed rail also has another negative externality on conventional medium-range services. According to Klaus Ebeling (2005), medium-distance services enjoy a decreasing flow of public funds, which doesn't occur in relation to short-distance services given their characteristic of being an obligatory public service. In this sense, medium-distance services suffer more from the displacement of public resources toward high-speed rail. This has caused criticism of the spending being made on high-speed rail, given that many people in Germany feel that this form of transportation will end up carrying a lower volume and more elite (businessmen) group of passengers, in detriment to the quality of the trains carrying ordinary passengers.

ECONOMIC AND REGIONAL IMPACTS

The double functionality of the German network was especially conceived to provide service to the industrial system, reducing the travel time for freight, and not solely for passengers. For this reason, the entry into service of these services has had greater economic impact than in other experiences. Nonetheless, few scientific analyses have been made contrasting these expected effects.

One of the most recent studies is that by Gabriel Ashlfeld and Arne Feddersen (2010), who have produced favorable results concerning the impact of high-speed rail on the economy and regional development in the case of one of the most traveled and previously most congested routes, the line between Cologne and Frankfurt. Their results show how the entry into service of this line significantly increased economic activity as measured by GDP and improved market access thanks to the improvement achieved in the accessibility of peripheral and remote zones. These effects were anticipated even before the inauguration of the line. For example, according to their estimates, the authors found that in the surroundings closest to the high-speed rail stations of Limburg and Montabaur, an increase of 2.7 percent of GDP occurred in contrast to the rest of the regions analyzed, all of which were peripheral and similar to these two. This effect can be attributed, according to the authors, entirely to the arrival of high-speed rail, in the same way several French cities showed before. Even if this effect continued in following years, there has been a return to the local growth trend existing prior to the shock caused by the new infrastructure.

ENVIRONMENT AND OTHER EXTERNALITIES

The environmental impact of the *InterCity Express* has been carefully considered in the network's design, particularly in terms of conserving the landscape. This is one of the most complex challenges in the planning and construction process and usually generates problems related to cost overruns. With the goal of reducing to a maximum the environmental impact, many of the high-speed rail routes run in parallel and as close as possible to expressways.

Another problematic aspect of high-speed rail in Germany as elsewhere is its elevated energy consumption, along with the noise it produces and its barrier effect (Ebeling, 2005). According to studies made by Christian Van Rozycky, Heinz Koeser, and Henning Schwarz (2003) on the Hanover–Wurzburg route, the CO_2 emissions per 100 ICE passenger-miles are calculated as being 24.6 pounds. This quantity is dominated by the energy consumption processes. The total energy consumed per 100 ICE passenger-km is estimated in 117 MJ. Rail infrastructure provides only less than 15 percent of the total cumulative energy demand per 100 passenger-miles. For most rail infrastructure components, the construction phase dominates the life cycle of these components. For the rail tracks as a whole, the cumulative energy demand of the construction phase is fifteen times larger than that of the operation phase. Furthermore, train capacity utilization, traction energy, train load, and the share of tunnels have a strong influence on the ecological impact of the transport system.

Compared to other experiences, the energy consumption of German high-speed rail is approximately 5 percent more than the French (Campos and de Rus, 2009). This difference is apparently explained by the existence in France of a less expensive source of energy (nuclear) and because in this country it is the operator itself that directly acquires energy instead of energy being included in the infrastructure canon as occurs in Germany. In fact, when the operator itself negotiates its own energy contracts, the incentives for greater energy efficiency and cost reduction are stronger.

In terms of safety, high-speed rail in Germany has also proven to be safe. Nonetheless, in 1998 a very serious accident occurred that has been considered the "but" in the German railway system since 1947. The unfortunate accident, a derailment in Eschede, caused the death of 101 passengers and injured 88. The cause of the accident was attributed to the poor condition and breakage of one of the wheels and a flange connection. Other lesser accidents occurred in 2008 and 2010. The first, from the collision between a train of the Hanover–Wurzburg line and a herd of sheep near Fulda, which caused the derailment of the vehicle, slightly injuring nineteen passengers. The second occurred when a train collided with a garbage truck in Lindenberg, injuring nine passengers with no mortalities.

SUMMARY

The German *InterCity Express* is characterized by some special features that distinguish it from the rest of the earlier experiences. On the one hand, it is a network with a double functionality for passengers and freight in which maximum speed is sacrificed in order to be able to also serve the industrial sector. On the other hand, it is a markedly decentralized network with no hub, having a marked centrality within the network and which faithfully reproduces the polycentric system of cities in Germany.

The objectives of the planners of the *InterCity Express* can be divided into two large groups. On the one hand were the goals of efficiency that led to the design of the routes with bottlenecks and significant congestion problems, and a north–south orientation that made it possible to connect the industrial zones in the south with the large international ports in the north. On the other hand, political goals decisively affected not only the design of the network but also the prioritizing of the lines. Political unification required the inclusion of the east, quite particularly the new political capital, Berlin, in the high-speed railway network in order to link the east and west of the country by way of a large and modern infrastructure.

In Germany, as in other experiences, the investment cost has been high, but in contrast to other experiences, the great care taken with environmental aspects and the topological and geological characteristics have significantly increased these costs. Furthermore, costs have been higher because of the decision to combine passengers and freight, given that the technical requirements for freight services impose a notable cost overrun on the infrastructure. The process of approving projects in which the various regional and local governments have a significant say has likewise imposed numerous limitations and conditions on the development of the network.

Despite all of these problems, the *InterCity Express* is a growing business which slowly but constantly increases the number of passenger-miles served annually even though the service operates at a deficit because of the marked dispersion of the population. The complementariness of high-speed rail with conventional regional services and air transport unquestionably acts in favor of its intermodal use. Despite this complementariness, in Germany as elsewhere the inauguration of high-speed rail has affected some regional services that have been forced to shut down, as well as affecting the air transport industry. Nevertheless, low-cost airlines seem to compete better with these services than do the regular and flag carrier airlines, such as Lufthansa. The impact on territory seems positive—above all, for the most remote zones that have gained greater accessibility—although few studies have been carried out to rigorously examine the question.

NOTE

1. This information is obtained from "High speed and network extension additional information," *Railway Technical Review: The International Journal for Rail Engineers, Operators and Scientists* 02/05, 12–18.

7

Spain

Alta Velocidad Española (AVE)

Beginning in the 1920s and growing more acute in the 1950s, the railway in Spain underwent a sustained loss of competitiveness and attractiveness as first road and later air transportation was developed. The great drive to extend high-capacity roads in Spain occurred in two stages (first, from the mid-1960s to the 1970s, and later beginning in the mid-1980s), which strongly reduced travel time by road and further diminished rail's competitiveness (Bel, 1994). In this context, the Spanish government decided in the late 1980s to modernize the railway. The corridor chosen to begin the modernization was the one connecting the political capital, Madrid, with Andalusia. While the original objective was to modernize the existing infrastructure to improve services, in late 1989, in a somewhat improvised way and in a swift process void of any public or technical debate, it was decided to modernize the Madrid–Seville route with a new track of international width (UIC) and high-speed capacity. These were the origins of high-speed rail in Spain.

In Spain, high-speed rail has been termed *Alta Velocidad Española* ("Spanish High-Speed," or AVE, its Spanish acronym). Such nomenclature of an identifying nature is unique among developed countries, where the name given to this form of railway lacks national connotations (with the exception of Korea, *Korea Train Express*). The first AVE railway was installed on the Madrid–Seville route, where it entered into service in 1992. When implanting the new route, the decision was also made to apply the international track gauge for the new lines. This decision, whether correct or not (a question outside the scope of our discussion), was independent of the requisites necessary for implanting high-speed rail. The entry into service of the Madrid–Seville AVE, with intermediary stations at Ciudad Real,

95

Puertollano, and Cordoba, occurred shortly before the inauguration of the Universal Exposition of Seville in 1992.

There was a paradoxical element to the choice of the Madrid–Seville line as the first line of the implantation of the AVE in Spain: although the international track gauge was chosen with the goal of integrating the Spanish network into the European one, rather than beginning the modernization along one of the connecting routes with France (still incomplete as of late 2011), an island of high-speed rail was instead created on the Peninsula.

By the end of 2011, the *Alta Velocidad Española* (AVE) had almost 1,300 miles of service (at speeds greater than 155 mph). It is the most extensive network in the OECD and the second in the world, surpassed only by that of China. Measured in AVE miles per million of population, or in miles of line per thousands of square miles, Spain also clearly surpasses China in terms of high-speed rail infrastructure. Spain's leadership has grown even more with the entry into service of the 93 miles (using Iberian Peninsula track width) of the Ourense–Santiago–Coruña line, which forms part of the Madrid–Galicia corridor, on December 10, 2011, at a cost of more than 3.3 billion euros (well over US $4 billion).

The Spanish network surpasses those of the two pioneering HSR countries: Japan and France. And this despite the fact that the passengers transported by high-speed rail in Spain number only slightly more than 6 percent of those transported by the *Shinkansen* in Japan. The fact that the AVE network is the most extensive of the OECD despite transporting a volume of traffic greatly inferior to countries such as Japan and France, as well as Germany and Italy, makes the development of high-speed rail in Spain a unique phenomenon and, when viewed comparatively, a system with some truly precarious ratios of passengers per miles of network.

Even so, the extension of the high-speed rail network is the centerpiece of infrastructure planning in Spain for the next decade. The *Plan Estratégico de Infrastructuras y Transportes* (The Strategic Plan for Infrastructures and Transportation) (PEIT) foresees 43.7 percent of spending made in the period 2005–2020 to be dedicated to interurban rail. Within the railway mode, high-speed rail is planned to receive three-quarters of the interurban railway spending, amounting to 33.5 percent of the total investment (Bel, 2007). The driving idea behind AVE planning is to connect all of Spain's provincial capitals with Madrid by 2020, as figure 7.1 shows.

The sum of sections in service or under construction of the AVE in Spain amounts to almost 2,800 miles, as shown in table 7.1, and constitutes nearly 50 percent of the total high-speed rail in the European Union. In fact, Spain currently leads the world in high-speed rail construction projects, given that 80 percent of the miles under construction in the EU correspond to AVE projects. In global terms, one out of every five miles of HSR under construction in the world corresponds to a mile of the AVE in Spain.

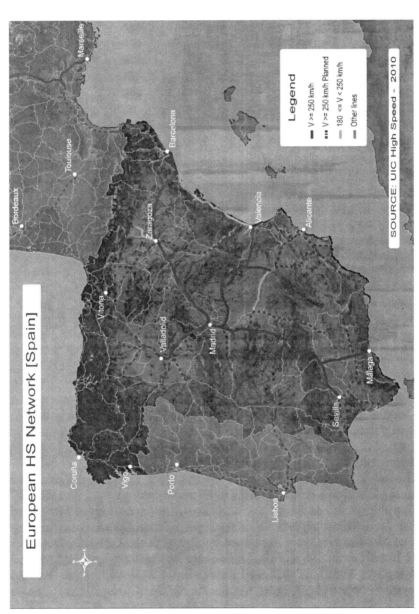

European HS Network [Spain]

Legend
— V >= 250 km/h
▪▪▪ V >= 250 km/h Planned
— 180 <= V < 250 km/h
— Other lines

SOURCE: UIC High Speed - 2010

Figure 7.1.   Spain: HSR Lines. Source: UIC (International Union of Railways)

Table 7.1.   Lines in Service and under Construction of the AVE in Spain in 2011

In Service	Length (km)	Length (miles)
Madrid–Seville	477	296
Madrid–Barcelona Sants	667	414
Córdoba–Málaga	155	96
Zaragoza–Huesca	79	49
Madrid–Valladolid	201	125
Madrid–Toledo	21	13
Madrid–València/Albacete	438	272
Connection Los Gavilanes	6	4

Under Construction	Length (km)	Length (miles)
Barcelona–French Border	131	81
Madrid–Badajoz–Portuguese Border	258	160
Transversal axe of Andalusia: Antequera–Granada	126	78
Mediterranean axe: Castelló–València–Xàtiva– Murcia–Almería	701	436
Bilbao–Vitoria–San Sebastián	177	110
Madrid–Galicia	459	285
Valladolid–Burgos–Vitoria	235	146
Venta de Baños–Palencia–León–Asturias	279	173
Other	85	53

Source: ADIF (2011, p. 34)

And if we exclude China, more than half of the miles under construction are located in Spain. The goal of implanting HSR is being sought with such intensity that, in practice, the development of AVE projects has been one of the areas of spending to be least affected by the spending cuts begun in 2010 in order to reduce the public deficit.

The public policy decisions in relation to railway spending in Spain have been made within a context lacking open and rigorous debate—in terms of both public policy and academic analysis—about the effects of high-speed rail in its different aspects. Of course, specific analyses on concrete projects of AVE lines in Spain have been published in the economic literature. Cost-benefit evaluations of the Madrid–Seville line have appeared (de Rus and Inglada, 1993), as well as of the Madrid–Barcelona line (de Rus and Román, 2006). In both cases, the results obtained from the cost-benefit analysis offered very poor prospects for the AVE's economic profitability and its contribution to social welfare.

Nevertheless, economic analysis of the spending on high-speed rail has lacked persuasive power and has played a marginal role in the formation of infrastructure policy in Spain (Albalate and Bel, 2011). Excessive emphasis on financial analysis of the spending and on aspects intrinsic to the journey has sidestepped a great many of the multiple aspects and various arguments that have fueled the public debate and served the government design of high-speed rail.

OBJECTIVES AND MOTIVATION

The central government's enormous spending on high-speed rail projects is based on a goal that is unique—for being exceptional—among comparable cases: to connect the country's political and economic capital, Madrid,[1] with all of the provincial capitals by high-speed rail, just as it was expressly established by the president of the government, José María Aznar, in the investiture debate for the 2000–2004 legislation (*Diario de Sesiones del Congreso*, 2000, n° 2 [April 25], p. 29) and in the *Plan Estratégico de Infrastructuras y Transporte* 2005–2020, drawn up by the socialist POSE government at the end of 2004. This goal arises from an understanding that at times is defended openly and other times implied: high-speed rail and its connection with the political and economic capital favor territorial cohesion and regional development.

This explains why, in contrast to all of the significant high-speed rail experiences, such as those of France, Japan, Germany, or Italy, the corridors served by high-speed rail are not chosen with the social benefits of the spending in mind. In other words, the potential of passenger volumes and the mitigation of congestion are not considered as determining factors in the selection of routes. This explains why Spain doesn't conform to the minimum potential demands recommended by the European Commission. Let us recall that the European Commission (2008) established that projects with less than six million passengers in the first year of service were only justifiable if construction costs were very low and time savings were significant. For medium costs and time savings, the minimum should be at least nine million passengers. The Barcelona–Madrid corridor had barely more than five million passengers in its first year, while currently the annual traffic is around six million. The prospects for the additional sections and projects incorporated into the high-speed rail network are even worse, given that the projected demand for the Madrid–Valencia AVE in its first year of service (2011) was lower than three million passengers in the point-to-point relation, and close to four million with its extensions to lesser capitals. Provisional figures indicate that traffic will be almost a million passengers lower than the initial previsions.

If we compare the volume of annual passengers per mile of track in the initial project in Spain for the year 2008 with those transported in the initial

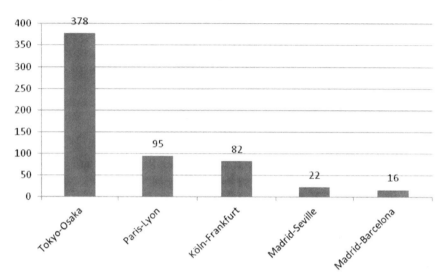

Figure 7.2.   Annual Passenger Ratio (Thousands Passengers) per Mile of Length of High-Speed Rail Tracks on the First Routes (Speed > 155 mph) in Japan, France, Germany, and Spain

project in Japan, France, or Germany, we can quickly see that high-speed rail in Spain doesn't correspond to specifically transport-related goals (see figure 7.2). While on the Tokyo–Osaka line the number of annual passengers per mile of network is almost 380,000, on the Paris–Lyon 95,000, and in the Köln–Frankfurt 82,000, the Madrid–Seville line—even including the Puertollano and Malaga branches, as well as all services realized by units on international track gauge—is barely more than 22,000 passengers a year per mile. Therefore, even including a calculation of maximums, it is not possible to reach a level of use for the first AVE comparable to that of the initial projects of other national experiences even two decades after the Spanish line's entry into service.[2] We find a similar result in the case of the Madrid–Barcelona AVE. The first complete year of service for the AVE between Madrid and Barcelona was 2009, during which period its annual traffic per mile was close to 16,000 passengers per mile.

What factors lie behind Spain having such a different goal from those of other nations? Japan and France aimed for efficiency in transportation; Germany pursued an industrial policy goal of connecting ports and industrial zones by high-speed rail; Italy observed the competitive advantage of high-speed rail in respect to air transportation, given its structure of cities and geography. Spain, in contrast, pursued a goal of territorial policy—to connect all provincial capitals with the capital city—under the rhetorical claim of regional development and cohesion.

The political motivation and territorial structuring of Spanish high-speed rail would logically condition its design, its development, and its economic viability. These aspects are evaluated below.

STRUCTURE, DESIGN, AND FUNCTIONS

Faced with the different possible combinations of infrastructure characteristics, Spain chose the most costly, the least productive, and the least generative of spillover effects for the Spanish economy. First, Spain decided to build a totally separate network from the conventional one, which meant greater spending on construction and particularly in the expropriation of land in urban settings. Second, it oriented its infrastructure exclusively to passengers, leaving only a marginal role for freight, even though freight transportation is much more likely to generate an economic impact on the territory. And third, in contrast to Germany, France, and Japan, it has used foreign technology, generating jobs and innovative technology in France and Germany, where the primary producers of the technology used for the Spanish high-speed rail are located (Vickerman, 1997).

Another characteristic element of Spanish high-speed rail is its centralization around the political capital following a unique and exclusively radial design, as much in the development stage as in the planned, final goal. In this respect, the case of Spain resembles that of politically centralized states with urban systems of satellite cities around a large hub, as is the French case with Paris, which has reproduced this layout in the design of their high-speed networks. In contrast, the territorially decentralized states with structures of dispersed cities in the territory, such as Germany and Italy, have reproduced a dispersed and decentralized design, without a hub that systematically enjoys greater accessibility and connectivity in the network. Proof of this centralization is figure 7.3, which shows a centrality degree for Madrid of 75 percent. This value is close to the centrality of Paris for the French network using this methodology.

INVESTMENTS AND PROFITABILITY

The investment for the extension of the AVE has been very high (see table 7.2). The gross cost of the first line, Madrid–Seville, was $3.5 billion in 1992 (de Rus and Inglada, 1993, p. 37), amounting to more than $6 billion in 2010 terms. In respect to spending on the lines that entered into service beginning in 2007 and ones currently under construction, the *Memoria Económica de 2010* for the Administrador de Infraestructuras Ferroviarias (ADIF) reports that at the end of 2010 AVE activity had been contracted

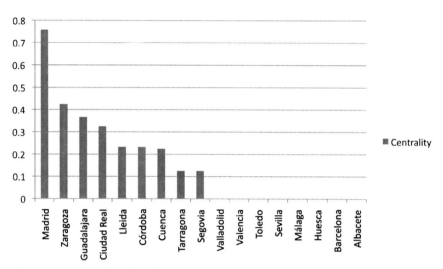

Figure 7.3.   Centralization of AVE Network (as of November 2011)

for $52 billion and spending of $44 billion had been made (ADIF, 2011, p. 58), part of which was cofinanced by the EU. Table 7.2 presents figures for the primary lines in service at the end of 2010. Note that these figures don't include the spending on the Madrid–Seville line, the branch on this line to Toledo, and the Zaragoza–Huesca line. Taking into account these three lines, the volume of spending made on AVE activities up until the end of 2010 is well over $55 billion (contracted) and close to $50 billion (executed), including lines in service and lines under construction.

These high-speed rail projects have enjoyed cofinancing from the European Union, thanks to regional development subsidies (ADIF, 2011, p. 68). The European contribution to financing high-speed lines in service in Spain up to the end of 2010 is around $10 billion.

The volume of spending made on the extension of the AVE is impressive. However, the total traffic of the Spanish high-speed rail network is low in comparison to other experiences: slightly over 6 percent of the passengers of those of Japan's network, less than 20 percent of those of France's, and around 25 percent of those of Germany's. This suggests that rates of return for the high-speed rail projects in Spain are, at the least, very poor. The principal reason is clear: the volume of population served is relatively reduced, and furthermore competition with the airplane is much greater than in the domestic traffic of other countries such as France, Germany, or Italy. In fact, time savings are slight in respect to the airplane, and construction costs are high.

The development of high-speed rail in Spain has been made without the aid of a cost-benefit analysis, properly speaking, of the different projects.

Table 7.2. Spending Contracted and Realized on the AVE by the End of 2010 (Lines Not Yet Totally Finished by 2010)

Lines	Contracted (Million €)	Executed (Million €)	Executed (%)	Contracted (US $ Million)	Executed (US $ Million)
Madrid–French Border	12,569.9	11,426.7	90.9	16,341	14,855
Madrid–Levante	9,129.4	7,736.0	84.7	11,868	10,057
Madrid–Valladolid	4,489.1	4,442.0	98.9	5,836	5,775
Córdoba–Málaga	2,711.3	2,644.4	97.5	3,525	3,438
Variante Pajares	2,632.6	2,517.4	95.6	3,422	3,273
Ourense–Santiago	2,113.8	1,698.8	80.4	2,655	2,208
Vitoria–Bilbao–San Sebastián	1,029.5	503.4	48.9	1,338	654
Valladolid–Burgos–Vitoria	737.5	266.7	36.2	959	347
Bobadilla–Granada	737.3	406.8	55.2	958	529
Venta Baños–Palencia– León–Asturias	623.6	325.9	52.3	811	424
Connection Atocha–Chamartín	591.6	182.5	30.8	769	237
Almería–Región de Murcia	494.0	194.6	39.4	642	253
High-Speed Stations	851.7	806.3	94.7	1,107	1,048
Other Investments	1,551.8	696.5	44.9	2,017	905
Total	40,263.1	33,848.0	84.1	52,248	44,003

Source: Based on information from ADIF (2011, p. 58) on contracted spending figures to December 31, 2010. De Rus and Inglada (1993) for the cost of the Madrid–Seville line.

Note: The conversion of euros to US dollars has been made with an exchange rate of 1 euro = $1.30, the average rate at the end of 2011. The table does not include the cost of the lines totally finished by the end of 2010: Madrid–Seville (2,704 million euros of 1992, or 1992 US $3,515 million); Zaragoza–Huesca (221.5 million euros of 2005, or 2005 US $288 million), and the line La Sagra–Toledo, of 21 km, for which cost has not been possible to establish.

The limited existing analysis of this type has been carried out by academics. For example, de Rus and Inglada (1993, 1997) have shown how no economic justification existed for the Madrid–Seville project, in that it generated a clearly negative social result. In particular, de Rus and Inglada (1993, p. 44) obtained an internal rate of return of 0.52 percent for the Madrid–Seville line, which they qualify as very low, and these authors add, "even if the IRR had been high, alternative projects should have been evaluated." Some more recent analysis (de Rus and Román, 2006) continue to show that the demand on the Madrid–Barcelona route—the connection with the highest volume of passengers—doesn't compensate for the high cost of the spending, while the time savings are insignificant.

In keeping with the information facilitated by de Rus (2010), the distribution between variable and fixed costs on the marginal cost associated with the high-speed rail projects depends on the volume of traffic. For a demand of five million annual passengers, for example, 65 percent of the marginal cost refers to the fixed cost, while the remaining 35 percent to variable costs. For lines with 2.5 million passengers, the distribution changes to 79 percent for fixed costs and 21 percent for variable ones. The fact that it is difficult for fees to recover even the variable costs of Spanish high-speed rail sheds light on the importance of the public subsidies granted to the high-speed train in Spain.[3] Even assuming a fee rate that would make it possible to recover the variable costs, and for projects with a demand twice that of the Madrid–Barcelona line, subsidies would be necessary for the value of half of the marginal cost.

Public aid for high-speed rail has sparked significant criticism, as well as an important sanction for Spain from the European Union for illegal competition. It is very worrying that exploitation of the AVE is loss-making, as demonstrated by the fact that the European Commission declared illegal the aid to cover the losses of exploitation of its long-distance services, which include high-speed rail. Such aid reached a sum of more than $300 million in 2007, and may have risen to more than $500 million in later years.[4] Future prospects are even dimmer, given that new lines entering into service will have progressively lower traffic densities and ones lower than those currently in service.

Lastly, it is appropriate to observe the very high opportunity cost assumed by the excessive (in fact, exclusive) emphasis placed in Spain on high-speed rail, particularly passenger high-speed rail. In fact, the significant spending on the railway made and planned in Spain (the largest in the EU in terms of percentage of GDP) has been disengaged from the forms and services that make a greater contribution to productivity and social welfare, such as local passenger trains and freight trains. Freight rail, furthermore, cuts road congestion, reduces environmental impacts, and has a direct repercussion on the productivity of the country's industrial fabric. Nevertheless, the market share of transportation by freight train has done nothing but decline over the last decade: as table 7.3 shows, between 2000 and 2007 it fell more than 40 percent, a much higher percentage than the 10 percent for Europe as whole. In fact, passenger transportation by train likewise shows no large benefits from such a large investment: its share in Spain has declined, while in the EU it has remained stable. The figures for 2008, with the latest lines of the AVE already in service, suggest that the passenger train's market share grew between three- and four-tenths (at great economic cost); the freight train's share, however, lost between two- and three-tenths, placing it below 4 percent.

DEMAND AND MODAL COMPETITION

The AVE undeniably offers high levels of comfort and satisfaction to its users, who furthermore avoid paying a large part of the cost thanks to the subsidy that covers practically the entire cost of the infrastructure (something much less common for medium/long-distance journeys in other modes of transportation). Having noted the AVE's contribution to the comfort of its users, we shall next examine its overall impact. In this sense, the results cannot be favorable.

In terms of its efficiency as a transportation infrastructure, the first thing to be noted is that it has been quite effective in acquiring a dominant, if not hegemonic, share of passengers in the primary connections served by the AVE at distances in which it is competitive. Thus, according to the operating company, in 2009, the AVE had an 85 percent share of the Madrid–Seville line, more than 70 percent of the Madrid–Malaga line, and very close to 50 percent of the Madrid–Barcelona line, in detriment, above all, to the airplane. Observe how the share falls as the distance increases, from the 293 miles of the Madrid–Seville to the 386 miles of the Madrid–Barcelona.

The AVE's results for journeys of more than 400 miles are much more modest. In Spain's case, there are routes between Barcelona and Seville and Malaga, which can now be made nonstop after the entry into service of the Madrid bypass in early 2009 (the radial character of the Spanish network makes it necessary to pass through the capital when traveling between the north and the south of the peninsula, even though this means traveling greater distances). The bypass reduces the trip between Barcelona and the Andalusian capitals by some fifty minutes; table 7.3 shows the results of this improvement almost a year after its implementation.

In effect, the AVE's market share at these distances is much more discreet. Specifically, the AVE only enjoys around 30 percent of the share of seats—not necessarily of passengers—on the route. In fact, high-speed rail's point-to-point (origin–destination) share is necessarily lower, given that

Table 7.3. Service by AVE and Airplane between Barcelona and Seville/Malaga. Daily Seats (Total in Each Direction) for October 7, 2010, and Prices (for a One-Way Trip)

Relation	AVE Seats	Airplane Seats (Direct)	AVE Price € [1] (minimum/medium/ maximum)	Airplane Price € (minimum/medium/ maximum)	Units in Circulation [2]
Barcelona–Malaga	1,264	From 3,000–3,600	101 / 117 / 140	5 / 31 / 65	AVE: 4 (2 in each direction) Airplane: 20 (10 in each direction)
Barcelona–Seville	1,264	From 3,300–3,960	56 / 98 / 129	5 / 48 / 119	AVE: 4 (2 in each direction) Airplane: 22 (11 in each direction)

Source: The authors, from information from the web pages of the operating companies. Information obtained on September 23, 2010.
[1] The minimum and maximum prices (for adults) have been taken as offered on the RENFE reservations web page, independently of the class of reservation.
[2] For flights on the Barcelona–Seville and Barcelona–Malaga routes (and vice versa), only the direct routes (without stopovers) have been considered. In contrast, high-speed trains make six intermediary stops between the stations of origin and destination.

it makes six intermediary stops, and thus a significant number of its users don't travel the entire route between Barcelona and the Andalusian capitals.

The AVE's low participation on these routes can be explained by the fact that the time in vehicle on the high-speed train is five hours and thirty minutes, while by plane it's one hour and thirty-five minutes. The total time of the journey (door to door) by AVE is almost twice as long as by plane. Furthermore, the fact that the AVE's frequency is only two units in each direction (except at specific points) means it offers much less convenience than the plane with its ten and eleven flights in each direction on the Barcelona–Malaga and Barcelona–Seville routes, respectively. In contrast, and despite the subsidy for the infrastructure and the longer travel time, the price of the AVE ticket is even more expensive than that of the plane on the Barcelona–Malaga route. Even on the Barcelona–Seville route, most of the flights provided by air transportation offer tickets at lower prices than the AVE, as indicated by the average airplane ticket price shown in Table 7.3. In fact, we find a single flight with a price higher than the average price of the AVE.

Upon analyzing the AVE's impact on mobility it is necessary to remember that the convenience of a mode of transportation depends crucially not only on the distance/time of the journey but also the frequency of nonstop services. The latter is generally a more significant limitation for the passenger AVE than for the airplane.

ECONOMIC AND REGIONAL IMPACTS

In terms of territorial impact, no case studies exist for Spain that evaluate the specific impact of the AVE's arrival at and service for a particular city. For this reason, allusions to the AVE's effect on a territory are often of a strictly anecdotal nature. A clear example of this is found in the recent work *Alta velocidad en el ferrocaril* (High-Speed in the Railway), which states that "It is reasonable to think that the AVE has played a relevant role in the demographics and university life of Ciudad Real. Note, in effect, how during the period from 1992 to 2007 the population increased by 25 percent, and how the city has a university of a significant size" (López Pita, 2010, p. 250). The fact is, however, all of the capitals of Castilla–La Mancha except Guadalajara have experienced a similar growth of the corresponding campus of the UCLM in the provincial capital. And, more importantly, the comparative figures of population growth don't show an especially notable growth for Ciudad Real since the entry into service of the AVE until 2007 (+ 25 percent). According to figures from the INE, population growth was higher in other capitals of La Mancha, such as Toledo (31 percent) and Albacete (27 percent), and similar in Cuenca (24 percent) and Guadalajara

(22 percent). In contrast, the city of Puertollano, which also received the AVE in the early 1990s, lost a few dozen of inhabitants.

Of course, there is no analytical substance to this comparison. Many things could have occurred in the various capitals of Castilla-La Mancha during those fifteen years that the infrastructure was on the ground: the arrival of the AVE to Toledo in 2005, shortly after having arrived at Guadalajara. . . . Nonetheless, another assessment—without pretending to be causal analysis—may shed light on the AVE's territorial effect (or its absence). Clearly, the population of Ciudad Real has grown significantly since 1992; however, is the AVE the factor behind that growth? We can attempt to answer this question by comparing the growth in population and housing stock in Ciudad Real and the other city of Castilla-La Manch that has had AVE service since 1992, Puertollano, with the rest of the capitals of Castilla-La Mancha.

Highly useful information is obtained by analyzing the evolution of the population and housing stock between 1991 (a year prior to the entry into service of the AVE) and 2001, the last year for which we have an official census. Furthermore, this interval of time is very appropriate because no relevant improvement of infrastructures occurs in the various cities of Castilla-La Mancha other than Ciudad Real and Puertollano (none of the other cities had AVE service in 2001). The case of Puertollano is even more spectacular given that it is the only city that lost population during the period analyzed.[5]

We find a very similar result for the housing stock (see table 7.4). Despite being one of the cities to grow the most, Ciudad Real is surpassed by Toledo and equaled by Albacete. The case of Puertollano is even clearer: its housing stock only grows more than Cartagena. In terms of Ciudad Real, good reasons exist for thinking that a significant part of its increase in housing stock is due to the creation of a new university campus, much more so than

Table 7.4.   Growth of Population and Housing Stock in Ciudad Real, Puertollano, and Comparable Cities of Castilla-La Mancha

	Inhabitants 1991	Inhabitants 2001	Δ 1991– 2001 (%)	Housing 1991	Housing 2001	Δ 1991– 2001 (%)
Ciudad Real	57,030	63,251	10.9	21,664	28,799	**32.9**
Puertollano	50,910	48,086	−0.6	19,118	22,669	18.6
Albacete	130,023	148,934	**14.5**	51,892	67,448	30.0
Guadalajara	63,649	68,248	7.2	23,958	29,825	24.5
Cuenca	42,817	46,341	8.2	18,647	23,902	28.2
Toledo	59,802	68,382	**14.3**	22,164	30,167	**36.1**

Source: Census 1991 and 2001. Instituto Nacional de Estadística.

the service offered by the AVE, as a result of what is shown by the analysis of the population.

It does seem more likely that the AVE can have a significant impact (still difficult to measure, given its recent entry into service) in the cases of Toledo (2005) and Segovia (2007). For both these cities, the AVE serves for the daily commute to Madrid; its travel time and monetary cost make this possible. In this sense, the AVE functions as a "luxury local train." Obviously, it is yet to be determined whether the effect will be to vitalize the smaller hubs of the network, or in contrast, to attract more activity to the larger hub, Madrid. Comparable experiences (Bonnafous, 1987; Givoni, 2006; Van den Berg and Pol, 1998; Thompson, 1994) indicate that the second scenario occurs much more often than the first.

ENVIRONMENT AND OTHER EXTERNALITIES

Although very little information is available on the real environmental impacts of high-speed rail, we can nonetheless evaluate the CO_2 emissions of high-speed rail compared to the conventional railway, thanks to figures contributed by the work of García-Alvarez ([2007] 2008). The information on average distances, emissions, and capacity make it possible to compare the emissions per passenger-mile on three high-speed rail lines and their corresponding conventional services. On two routes (Madrid–Seville and Madrid–Barcelona), no significant differences exist in emissions per passenger-mile.[6] Nonetheless, the emissions per passenger-mile in the case of the Madrid–Toledo line are almost 50 percent higher for high-speed rail. While the first two routes are routes of medium distance, the Madrid–Toledo route is clearly one of short distance (> 100 miles). Thus, greater distance can favor the environmental impact of high-speed rail, but in no case does it appear to contribute to a lower amount of CO_2 emissions per passenger-mile.

High-speed rail compares much more favorably to the plane or car. For example, García-Alvarez ([2007] 2008) finds that while high-speed rail emits 9.2 kg of CO_2 per passenger on a fully loaded train on the Madrid–Barcelona routes, a fully loaded plane or car emits 50.13 kg and 18.9 kg of CO_2 on this same route. Under the same conditions described above, the bus, for its part, emits slightly less than 9 kg of CO_2 per passenger, a figure very similar to that of high-speed rail, although its speed is much less.

It goes without saying that none of these comparisons includes the CO_2 emissions produced during the period of construction of high-speed rail nor the fact that, as Kageson (2009) points out, during the first thirty years of operating service it will be difficult for HSR's emissions savings—in relation to air transportation—to recoup the emissions generated during its construction.

SUMMARY

The most salient characteristic of infrastructure policy in Spain in the 2000s has been the accelerated expansion of the high-speed rail network using international track width, which began in the early 1990s. The emphasis on this sub-mode of transportation has led to Spain becoming by late 2010 the world's second leading country, behind China, in miles of high-speed rail. In relative terms, Spain is the world leader in miles of track per inhabitant and square miles of area.

Since 2000, the reason given for accelerating the expansion of the high-speed rail network has been the desire to reinforce Spain's articulation and territorial cohesion. The rhetoric emphasis on either articulation or cohesion has depended on the political party in power. The result has been the same: the explicit physical goal of the network's extension has been to join all provincial capitals with the political capital. The primacy of meta-policy-type goals over ones appropriate to transportation policy has resulted in the permanent ignoring of criteria of economic efficiency in the AVE's development. This has led to spending with very poor financial and social benefits, the very low results of which contrast the data from the rest of the international experiences. This situation will tend to worsen as new lines with ever-lower transportation demand enter into service.

The facts have proved eminent analysts of the history of the railway system in Spain to be right. Such is the case of Uriol Salcedo (1992, p. 448), who questioned, "What will the demand for high-speed rail lines be in Spain? We're afraid the subject hasn't been studied in depth and that its results won't be good in terms of traffic or in terms of incomes and expenses." Or Gómez Mendoza (2005, p. 48), who more recently concluded his very expressively titled article "From the Railway to the AVE. The Same Historical Mistakes?" by saying that "In contrast to what occurred with the train in the second half of the nineteenth century, the benefits of high-speed rail are quite limited . . . the decision to assign enormous amounts of public resources to provide high-quality resources to a minority of Spanish society is a matter of dubious equity."

On the other hand, the offer of high-speed rail doesn't promote—as the Japanese and French experiences have shown—the development of cities and regions equipped with high-speed rail, with the exception of the central hubs of the network. Furthermore, the environmental balance can be negative when the CO_2 emissions from the construction process are taken into account, and HSR's lower efficiency compared to the improved conventional train and the bus. In the most favorable case for HSR, when it manages to attract a large volume of traffic away from the airplane, it turns out to be an extremely expensive way of achieving only modest reductions of emissions.

The concerns raised by these results of the AVE in their various dimensions are multiplied if we take into account the fact that the enormous use of public resources to finance high-speed rail projects comes with a very high opportunity cost. As did the use of European Cohesion and Regional Development Funds to finance these projects instead of others that would have greater impact on the economic and industrial fabric—such as the freight train or technological infrastructures. Very good reasons exist, therefore, for ceasing all further extension of the high-speed rail network in Spain, except for those sections whose entry into service is imminent.

Lastly, the Spanish experience offers another lesson of great importance: it is essential to increase the transparency and sharing of data by the government and the public agencies and companies involved. Finding data for the demand of the AVE according to corridor or route is extremely difficult, and finding detailed cost data on the final cost of the different lines is a true work of investigative journalism. Such a lack of transparency explains why there is so little existing information in Spain on the matter, which makes any public debate about the policy difficult. And indeed, to encourage social debate on public policies is a good way to improve the decision-making process and thus to improve the quality of the policy itself.

NOTES

1. The centralizing policy of transportation infrastructures financed by funds from the national budget has been a standard model in Spain over the past three centuries, as shown in Bel (2011, 2012).

2. The figures presented correspond to 2008, although it should be noted that the figures for 2009 are even lower than those of 2008.

3. According to declarations by the former Minister of *Fomento* (Public Works), José Blanco, to the *El País* newspaper in April 2010 (April 10, 2010), the cost of maintaining a mile of the AVE would be more than $200,000 and more than $400,000 in the case of a mile of tunnel. www.elpais.com/articulo/economia/posible/autovias/AVE/lleguen/puerta/casa/elpepieco/20100410elpepieco_7/Tes el día 10/04/2010. Interview downloaded on September 23, 2010.

4. *Expansion*, January 22, 2010, offers details on the communication of the European Commision.

5. In respect to the rest of the cities reached by the AVE in 1992, during the period from 1991 to 2001, Cordoba experienced a population growth of less than 2 percent; in Seville's case, its population growth was even lower: 0.2 percent.

6. García-Alvarez (2007) details some of the physical and technical reasons for why the high-speed train's consumption is not very different from the consumption of the conventional train.

8

China

'Zhōngguó gāosù tiělù

BACKGROUND

The economic miracle of the People's Republic of China, with its spectacular economic growth that took off after political reforms were initiated in
1978, has astonished the world, particularly Western countries, which view
the Asian giant as an emerging power capable of questioning the status quo
and the world's power relations. Some of the determining factors that have
laid the foundations for this incomparable growth have been economic
openness—still very limited—to the market economy; the corporatization
of some activities of the public sector; decisive involvement in international
commerce; and a policy of intensive capital investment. These factors have
allowed the country's GDP to expand by an average annual rate of between
10 percent and 11 percent over the past three decades, which has made the
Asian giant into the world's second largest economy—third if we consider
the European Union as a whole—after the United States, and the most important emerging actor in global politics and the world economy.

In the realm of transportation, and particularly in respect to infrastructures, China has likewise experienced outstanding development. Chinese
interest in the modernization of ground transportation has its roots in
the desire to improve the country's economic productivity. This interest
involved improving road and railway networks in order to free up capacity
for freight mobility. In this respect, productivity gains in freight transportation and logistical improvements have been the centerpiece of Chinese
transportation policy at the end of the twentieth century and early twenty-
first century.

With this framework, railway transportation has played a decisive role for China's economy. Proof of this can be seen in the fact that half of the ton-miles of the country's economy are transported by railway, as well as a third of its passenger-miles (Rong and Bouf, 2005). Vigorous economic growth and the resulting increase in traffic have imposed strong pressure on current infrastructure capacity. Between 1978 and 2010, the ton-miles transported by the Chinese railway network went from 535 billion to 2,764 billion, with an annual increase of 5 percent. Similarly, the volume of passenger-miles increased from 109 billion passenger-miles to 876 billion passenger-miles, an average annual increase of 6.73 percent (Wang et al., 2012). According to the World Bank (2009, p.1) China Rail is the second biggest carrier of rail freight and the biggest carrier of passenger transport in the world. It has the largest combined rail traffic task of any national railway system in the world, carrying about a quarter of the world's railway traffic on about 7 percent of the world's route-mile of public railway.

For this reason, decisive commitment was made to high-speed rail technology in order to modernize the railway network through the approval in 2003 of the plan to invest in high-speed rail over the middle and long term; this plan established the goals for the HSR network up until 2020. The plan addressed the chronic capacity problem in the context of both the expected national growth and development and the expected evolution of other transport modes with the novel strategy of separating passenger traffic through the construction of lines exclusively for passenger transport (World Bank, 2009).

Spending recommenced in 2005 and since 2008 has been developed within the framework of the Chinese government's economic stimulus plan.[1] According to this plan, 8,100 miles of high-speed rail network are expected by 2012, and 12,400 by 2020. Of these, some 5,000 miles are expected to support maximum speeds of 217 mph, while the remaining 310 will be tracks for services with maximum speeds of 155 mph (Amos, Bullock, and Sondhi, 2010).

Despite this recent interest and commitment, China's entry into the world of HSR has been vertiginous thanks to its impressive investing power; indeed, in little over six years the country has created the world's largest high-speed rail network. At present, the portion of its HSR network capable of speeds of more than 186 mph has reached an extension of 2,184 miles. If we include speeds equal to or greater than 155 mph up to the previously mentioned 186 mph, China's HSR network extends for nearly 4,000 miles (at the end of 2011), making it the world's most extensive HSR network, above pioneers Japan and France and even surpassing Spain's expansion of the AVE.

The impressive nature of the Chinese experience is not limited to the vigorous expansion of its network, which began commercial operations in April of 2007,[2] but is also evident in the network's exuberant activity in construction and planning. In October of 2010, there were twenty-seven lines or line extensions under construction in Chinese territory, designed for high-speed services greater than 155 mph (Takagi, 2011). With these, the network will reach an extension greater than the sum of all of the world's high-speed rail networks already built and planned.

These prospects are possible thanks to financing provided by the Chinese government—and by provincial governments—in the economic stimulus plan of 2008 in response to the 2008 global financial crisis, in which HSR and expressways were the centerpiece of the country's countercyclical policy of investment in infrastructures. In fact, the packet more than doubled the investment funds available for railways for the years 2008 to 2010, which made it possible to accelerate and advance the execution of high-speed rail projects (Amos, Bullock, and Sondhi, 2010).

Nevertheless, recent developments in Chinese high-speed rail, which will be highlighted over the course of this chapter and which are related to problems of quality and safety, financing and indebtedness, as well as corruption, have forced the Chinese government to rethink the design and planning of high-speed rail, postponing 80 percent of the projects in the fall of 2011.

OBJECTIVES AND MOTIVATION

For most of the period since 1990, the development of China's rail system has been a response to the imperatives of growth in traffic, rather than any wider national transportation strategy (World Bank, 2009). The main challenge facing China was the need to bolster its rail capacity for economic development given that the primary objective was to transport freight and passengers over long distances (Takagi, 2011).

To increase the capacity of freight transport, the 2003 spending plan for the middle and long term proposed a novel strategy based on the construction of lines exclusively for passenger use that would liberate capacity on conventional lines equipped to transport freight. The aim was to unblock bottlenecks, alleviate road backups, and boost both productivity and regional development.

In addition to increasing capacity, the Chinese goal of improving productivity and logistics led to the need to increase the speed of the services, even in the existing conventional network. For this reason, the Ministry of Railways designed six rounds of acceleration of services between 1997 and 2007 to increase average service speed on existing tracks just before the incorporation of the high-speed rail networks.

Along with the goals of efficiency and productivity, other objectives relating to spending on railway infrastructures were included in the government's

2008 stimulus plan. These included lowering dependence on expressways and reducing oil imports (Wang et al., 2012).

Above and beyond these objectives, the Chinese government has a concept of a network, rather than individualized corridors. In this respect, and in a similar way to the Spanish case, the goal set by the Chinese government has been to connect all provincial capitals by high-speed rail by the year 2020. In contrast to the network designed in Spain, however, China imposed a less demanding objective. Only those provincial capitals with populations of a minimum of 500,000 inhabitants will be connected to the network (Wang, et al., 2012).[3] In such a network, it is estimated that 90 percent of the population will be served by high-speed rail in 2020 (Amos, Bullock, and Sondhi, 2010), as long as the envisioned plans are carried out.

STRUCTURE, DESIGN, AND FUNCTIONS

The Chinese high-speed rail network is located in areas where most of the population is concentrated, that is to say, in the east and south of the country, as figure 8.1 shows. Nonetheless, the network's design doesn't appear radial, as in France or Spain, and in fact has greater similarities to the decentralized design existing in Germany and Italy, where the large cities tend to be connected with one another and where no one hub has a significantly higher degree of centrality than the others.

These coastal provinces are home to China's largest cities in terms of area and which furthermore have the highest population densities. Among these is the political capital, Beijing, with its more than nineteen million inhabitants, located in the northeast of the country. This city is connected by high-speed rail to the city of Tianjin, which has thirteen million inhabitants and is located on the east coast. Then there are other cities, such as Shanghai, further south, with twenty-three million inhabitants, which has high-speed rail connections with Beijing, as well as with the cities of Ningbo and Nanjing, with seven and eight million inhabitants, respectively. Thus, high-speed rail in China has been designed, on the one hand, to connect the principal hubs of population density in the country. On the other, it is designed to facilitate connection between rural zones and more remote areas in the west of the country with the areas of greater prosperity in the east and south. All of this makes it possible to free up capacity for freight transport, which, as we've noted, makes massive use of the railway.

China suffers from a considerable geographical imbalance that creates huge transport demand originating at the major raw material production centers, which are located at considerable distance from the rapidly developing coastal regions (Rong and Bouf, 2005). This imbalance makes it necessary to connect large distances by rail. On the other hand, migration

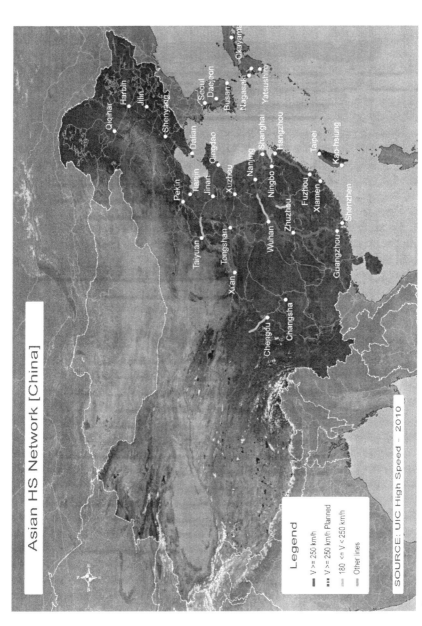

Figure 8.1.   China: HSR lines. Source: UIC (International Union of Railways)

from the country's most depressed zones to the prosperous coastal regions also generates significant long-distance transport demand. Thus, the design of the Chinese high-speed rail network complements the connection of the large cities with the long-distance links to less developed zones of the country.

The Chinese experience is based as much on upgrading conventional tracks as on building new tracks specifically for high-speed rail geared for passenger use. As much in the construction of new infrastructure as in the work of upgrading, the resulting design in terms of speed of service and functionality—mixed or solely passenger—varies from project to project. This diversity depends on the characteristics of the corridors served. The high-speed lines with mixed freight traffic tend to operate at lesser speeds, while the exclusively passenger lines operate at speeds of up to 217 mph.

High speed—at a minimum of 186 mph—can be reached both on newly built lines and on upgraded ones realized on already existing tracks. In fact, the sixth and final round of the campaign to increase speed on conventional lines (1997–2007) included the adaptation of 525 miles to high speed. New construction, therefore, primarily obeys the need to liberate capacity on the tracks most used for freight.

Lastly, since 2004, China has the world's first regular service using Maglev technology. The train line is designed to connect Shanghai Pudong International Airport and the metro system of Shanghai in just seven minutes thanks to top speeds of 268 mph.

The high-speed rail lines currently operating in China are detailed below, with their inauguration date, the distance between the primary hubs, the top speed, and the orientation type for passengers and freight (see table 8.1).

In respect to stations, many city governments are planning massive new development zones around the newly built stations in the hope of better connecting them to their urban centers. Some of these stations are located forty minutes from the center of some cities that have expectations of benefiting from economic prosperity associated with HSR. The participation of local and provincial governments in high-speed rail projects is evident, above all, through the contribution of land. For this reason, these governments have tended to contribute terrain outside of the city centers, which means a trajectory cost between these stations and the final origin and destination. In addition to assuming a lower cost of the value of the contributed land, this location aimed to develop remote and less attractive zones with the influx of economic, commercial, and tourist activity associated with the arrival of high-speed rail (Wang et al., 2012). With HSR projects, local governments have tended to raise the land value of these areas and thus take advantage of the boom in private and public construction in China.

In this sense, James Wang et al. (2012, p. 5) point out that the eagerness to build HSR lines is largely due to interprovince and intercity competition.

Table 8.1. Chinese Operating HSR Lines

Route	Name Line	Opening	Designed Speed	Distance	Type
Shanghai–Airport	—	2004	268 mph	19 mi	Maglev
Qinhuangdao–Shenyang[a]	Qinshen	2003/2007	124/155 mph	251 mi	Pass-dedicated
Beijing–Tianjin	Jingjin	2008	217 mph	73 mi	Pass-dedicated
Hefei–Nanjing	Hening	2008	155 mph	103 mi	Mixed
Jinan–Qingdao	Jiaoji	2008	155 mph	226 mi	Pass-dedicated
Hefei–Wuhan	Hewu	2009	155 mph	218 mi	Mixed
Wuhan–Guangzhou	Wuguang	2009	217 mph	601 mi	Pass-dedicated
Wenzhou–Fuzhou	Wenfu	2009	155 mph	185 mi	Mixed
Shijiazhuang–Taiyuan	Shitai	2009	155 mph	118 mi	Pass-dedicated
Ningbo–Taizhou–Wenzhou	Yongtaiwen	2009	155 mph	166 mi	Mixed
Haikou–Sanya	Hainan	2010	155 mph	191 mi	Pass-dedicated
Xiamen–Fuzhou	Fuxia	2010	155 mph	185 mi	Mixed
Shanghai–Nanjing	Huning	2010	217 mph	187 mi	Pass-dedicated
Shanghai–Hangzhou	Huhang	2010	217 mph	93 mi	Pass-dedicated
Zhengzhou–Xian	Zhengxi	2010	217 mph	283 mi	Pass-dedicated
Nanchang–Jiujiang	Changjiu	2010	155 mph	81 mi	Pass-dedicated
Beijing–Shanghai	Jinghu	2011	217 mph	819 mi	Pass-dedicated
Changchun–Jilin	Changji	2011	155 mph	69 mi	Pass-dedicated
Guangzhou–Shenzhen	Guangshengang	2011	155 mph	72 mi	Pass-dedicated

Note: Operating lines: January 23, 2011.
[a]The line was opened in 2003; however, maximum speed did not reach 155 mph until 2007 with the last speed-up program of the Railways Ministry.

In China, HSR connection is widely viewed by local governments as a critical means to bring in more economic opportunities for their cities or regions rather than to operate transport services and make profit per se. Thus, the subsidiaries of local governments for railway development don't expect to pay off their loans by HSR operation on its own but by other means such as property development at railway stations and surrounding areas.

INVESTMENTS AND PROFITABILITY

Estimates of investment costs up until the present ascend to $395 billion for high-speed rail alone, a figure greater than 6.5 percent of the annual GDP of the world's second largest economy.[4] An unrivaled investment effort. Investment in fixed assets like factories and the rail network accounted for more than 95 percent of China's 7.7 percent growth in the first three quarters of 2009 and made up 45 percent of gross domestic product, which is higher than any major economy in history, according to declarations by Stephen Roach, chairman of Morgan Stanley Asia, to the *New York Times*.[5] This enormous cost for China's coffers is related not only to the length of the lines built and planned but also to their design. First of all, it must be pointed out that the routes designed to support maximum speeds of 217 mph are much more expensive than routes in other experiences that have lower maximum speeds, given that costs increase with each marginal increase of speed.

Secondly, tunnels and viaducts have been used on a massive scale in China, and these infrastructures vastly increase the cost of the projects. Solely on the Beijing–Tianjin and Beijing–Shanghai routes, 80 percent of their trajectories make use of these infrastructures (*Caixin Weekly*, 2011).

Thirdly and lastly, just as in most other experiences, the construction of HSR has imposed large cost overruns in respect to estimates. The Beijing–Tianjin line is a very illustrative example. While the National Development and Reform Commission, the government's economic planning agency, originally approved a $1.9 billion investment for the Beijing–Tianjin project, by the time the line opened in 2008, the cost had risen to roughly $3.4 billion, this being one of the network's most expensive in terms of miles of distance at a unit cost of $46.6 million. While the original plan was to use a speed of 124 mph, the increase of the maximum speed to 217 mph has only contributed to a time reduction of ten minutes (*Caixin Weekly*, 2011).

Despite all of this, the average cost per mile in China is lower than the cost of the European and Japanese experiences, as table 8.2 shows:

Before 2004, the budget for new railway construction came from a surcharge on freights, based on a special policy implemented in 1992. This was far from sufficient to cover the proposed expenses of the plan. The Ministry

Table 8.2. Total Cost and Cost per Mile in Selected Lines

Line	Designed Speed	Length (miles)	Total Cost (US$ billion)	Cost per Mile (million/mile)
Qinshen	124/155 mph	251 mi	2.5	9.9
Jingjin	217 mph	73 mi	3.4	46.6
Hening	155 mph	103 mi	4.0	38.4
Jiaoji	155 mph	226 mi	1.7	7.7
Hewu	155 mph	218 mi	2.7	12.2
Wuguang	217 mph	601 mi	18.5	30.8
Wenfu	155 mph	185 mi	2.9	15.4
Shitai	155 mph	118 mi	2.7	22.9
Yongtaiwen	155 mph	166 mi	2.6	15.5
Hainan	155 mph	191 mi	3.2	16.7
Fuxia	155 mph	185 mi	2.4	13.0
Huning	217 mph	187 mi	7.9	42.2
Huhang	217 mph	93 mi	4.7	50.9
Zhengxi	217 mph	283 mi	5.6	19.7
Jinghu	217 mph	819 mi	35.0	42.7
Changjiu	155 mph	81 mi	0.9	11.1
Changji	155 mph	69 mi	1.5	21.7

of Railways had to find other sources to raise the necessary funds (Wang et al. 2012). This financing essentially came from loans and debt issuance, as well as collaboration agreements between the Ministry of Railways and local and regional governments.

In 2007, nearly half of rail-accumulated investment was funded from domestic bank loans and bonds, about 16 percent from provincial governments and public enterprises (through use of the joint venture model), and about 15 percent from a construction surcharge on freight (Amos, Bullock, and Sondhi, 2010). Financing has thus been shared by state-owned banks and financial institutions, the Ministry of Railways through dept issuance, and regional and local governments, normally through the ceding of land.[6] The Ministry of Railways alone, through its financing arm, the China Rail Investment Corp., issued an estimated $150 billion in 2010 dollars in debt to finance HSR construction from 2006 to 2010, including $49 billion in the first ten months of 2010. CRIC has also raised some capital through equity offerings of the Beijing–Shanghai line, such as the stock sold to the Bank of China, although it retained 56.2 percent ownership of that line.

Despite impressive figures of passenger use, virtually every completed line has incurred losses in the first years of its operation. For example, in its first two full years of operation, the Beijing–Tianjin Intercity Railway delivered over forty-one million rides. The line cost $3.4 billion to build and $290 million per annum to operate, including interest payments on its $1.6 billion loan obligations. Solely in its first year of operation, with a volume of traffic of 18.7 million passengers, the line lost $111 million.[7] In fact, it is estimated that an annual volume of thirty million passengers is necessary to avoid losses, while this volume must reach forty million to be able to return the principal of the debt and loans.

Such a massive investment made in the short period of time that China has developed its network has had immediate consequences for the finances of the Ministry of Railways. The Ministry was nearly $318 billion in debt and clocking up losses at the rate of about $311 million a quarter by mid-2011. To meet the plan, another $444 billion has to be found in the next three and a half years.[8] These financial problems, in addition to the doubts cast on the quality of the work carried out at low cost but for very high speeds—higher even than 186 mph—and the suspicions of corruption in the awarding of contracts, may have been behind the removal and later expulsion from the Communist Party of the Minister of Railways, Liu Zhijun, in early 2011.

According to the British newspaper *The Telegraph* and the weekly magazine *The Economist*, Liu Zhijun allegedly received between $119 million and $152 million in bribes over various years for contracts linked to high-speed rail.[9,10] Zhang Shuguang, another top official in the railways ministry, was later dismissed for corruption. Just a month after these dismissals, the State Auditor of China said in March of 2011 that construction companies and private individuals had diverted $28 million in funds destined for the connection between Beijing and Shanghai.

Why so much speed and so much investment in such a short time? Liu won fame for being obsessed with high-speed rail. According to declarations mentioned in *Caixin Weekly* (2011), the now ex-Minister Liu had declared:

> Rail currently has a favorable, opportune moment for low-cost development [. . .] With rapid economic and social development, resource shortages will become increasingly prominent, and land acquisition and relocation costs, material prices and labor costs will grow higher [. . .] This is an irreversible trend. So the earlier we carry out large-scale railway construction and the faster we push it forward, the lower our costs will be [. . .] Seize the opportunity, build more railways, and build them fast." (*Caixin Weekly*, 2011)

Despite the enormous opportunities of the moment glimpsed by Liu Zhijun, after his dismissal HSR in China fell on bad times. In view of the financial problems that appeared in the Ministry of Railways, the scandals related to corruption, and the cost cutting made at the cost of safety standards, the only thing needed to even further complicate the development of HSR projects was a serious accident. This accident occurred in Wenzhou in July 2011. Forty passengers died in it. After this unfortunate event, China decided to suspend 80 percent of its new high-speed rail projects to conveniently revise its planning and reduce the speed of its services currently in operation from 217 mph to 186 mph.

Although the decision to stop all HSR projects was made because of popular concern and criticism over safety, there is no question that the revelations concerning the finances of the Ministry of Railways played a decisive role in the decision to rethink the HSR model in China. In fact, one of the consequences of the Wenzhou accident and the doubts it raised about the safety of the system was the significant increase in the costs financing the projects. Chinese banks ceased to loan money for HSR construction as they waited to learn the government's new moves and decisions in respect to high-speed rail, with the resulting difficulty on the part of the Ministry of Railways to refinance itself and pay its suppliers. All of this led to a cash crunch that threatened the continuity of the suspended projects, the employment of more than six million workers, and the recuperation of the investment made by construction companies that have yet to receive payment for the work realized.[11] The two most important construction companies in China—China Railway Construction Corporation Limited and China Railways Group Limited—were due outstanding payments of more than $20 billion in the fall of 2011.[12]

At the same time, and solely in 2011, the Ministry of Railways had obligations to pay off more than $15.8 billion in bond principal and $6.3 billion to cover interests (*Caixin Weekly*, 2011). To do so, it needed an injection of liquidity from the Ministry of Finances and new loans from the China Development Bank in November of 2011.[13] Furthermore, favorable conditions were established to ease fund-raising difficulties. For example, the Ministry of Finance announced a preferential tax policy halving the 25 percent income tax on the coupon earnings of bonds issued by the railway ministry from 2011 to 2013 under the supervision of the National Development and Reform Commission.[14]

And there is more. As if all these problems weren't enough, other unexpected difficulties have affected Chinese HSR that could irremediably damage its profitability and public image. Two months after its February 2010 opening, the Beijing–Fuzhou high-speed rail line quietly closed because of a lack of passengers due to the enormous difference in price—approximately three times—between HSR and the conventional train (*Caixin Weekly*, 2011). This lower-than-expected demand has occurred on practically all of the inaugurated routes.

Overall, the profitability of railway transport services fell from 6 to 7 percent growth in 2000 and 2001 to negative growth in 2008 and 2009, mostly due to the increased costs derived from the introduction of high-speed rail services (Wang et al., 2012). These results were hurt not only by the enormous debt and investment realized in recent years but also by the entry into service of new HSR lines to be constructed in the rural west, which will unquestionably be running a deficit for a long time (Jin and Wang, 2011).

DEMAND AND MODAL COMPETITION

The demand for high-speed rail services in China increased quickly in the first years thanks to the entry into service of different lines. Figure 8.2 shows this rising evolution comparing the number of available miles and the number of daily passengers.

The principal attraction of HSR is unquestionably its spectacular time savings in relation to other modes of transportation, particularly the conventional train and the bus. For example, HSR reduced the travel time between Shanghai and Nanjiing from 120 to 73 minutes with its direct service. From Shanghai to Beijing, HSR reduced the time of the journey from fourteen hours to only four.

Nonetheless, the demand for HSR is below expectations. Some causes for this seem to be related to pricing and the lack of purchasing power of the average Chinese citizen. Indeed, the very high costs of HSR have been shifted onto ticket prices, and thus onto the users, which reduces passenger accessibility to this mode of transport and limits its competitiveness with other, less expensive transportation modes. Traditional intercity rail travel is estimated to cost between 2 to 3 cents per kilometer per person in China, while high-speed rail usually costs between 7 cents and 10 cents (*Caixin Weekly*, 2011).

Furthermore, in many cases the introduction of HSR has brought with it the dismantling and cancellation of conventional services with much lower ticket prices—up to three times less—than those of HSR. This policy has even been used in order to displace passengers to this new mode of trans-

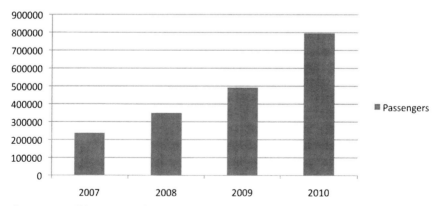

Figure 8.2.   China: Demand

portation. The result, however, has been a notable increase in the demand for collective transportation services by road. In fact, the introduction of HSR meant the reduction in capacity of some lines after the dismantling of conventional services. As an illustration of these cancellations, it is enough to examine what happened on the Wuhan–Guangzhou line. Before HSR started running in December 2009, many routes between Guangzhou and the cities of Wuchang and Hankou, including direct trains, were quietly shut down. Similarly, high-speed rail lines between Beijing and Tianjin, Shanghai and Ningbo, and Shanghai and Hangzhou replaced at least some slower trains—even those running at 155 mph (*Caixin Weekly*, 2011).

Most mobility in China is due to worker migration, especially during holidays and vacation periods, and these travelers are not likely to be able to afford high-speed rail ticket prices. Instead, they decide to travel by bus, especially on routes where conventional train services have been dismantled.[15,16] According to declarations by the Ministry of Transportation spokesman He Jianzhong, the situation has pushed many passengers, who used to ride home by slow trains because of the cheap tickets, onto long-distance buses. This extra traffic adds pressure to the road transport system during peak periods.[17]

In terms of competition with air transportation, it is notable that numerous flights and origin–destination pairs offered prior to the entry into service of HSR have been canceled. According to the magazine for airline company executives, *Airline Leader* (2011), the General Administration of Civil Aviation of China (CAAC) managing director, Li Jiaxiang, stated that some 50 percent of flights less than 310 miles in length and about 20 percent of flights between 500 and 620 miles could become unprofitable as a result of HSR competition. Sectors above that threshold were not likely to be threatened. The losses for the sector could rise to $1.5 billion in 2012—between 3 percent and 4 percent—according to the magazine.

Nevertheless, the air transport industry is breathing again after the temporary cancellation of HSR projects and the reduction of speed for existing services. This reduction of speed gives a competitive edge to air companies, which have now resumed some routes that had been lost after the entry into service of HSR. For example, the *21st Century Business Herald* reported that the suspended short-haul flights from Nanjing to Wuhan and from Zhengzhou to Xi'an will resume service. Flights between Nanjing and Wuhan were suspended entirely due to the inauguration of the Hening and Hewu high-speed rail links, whose ticket prices were much lower than taking the plane. The travel time from Wuhan to Nanjing has risen from three hours to three hours and fifty minutes.

Doubts concerning the safety of HSR and its technical standards, which arose after the corruption scandal at the heart of the Ministry of Railways, may also explain part of the market share recovered by air transportation after the accident at Wenzhou in July 2011. Lack of safety seems to be another of

Table 8.3.   Energy Use and CO_2 Emissions per Mode of Transportation in the Shi Zheng Corridor (China)

Transportation	Energy Use (Kwh or Lt./pass-km)	CO_2 Emissions (Kg/pass-km)
Car	0.042	0.10
Bus	0.016	0.04
Conventional Train	0.020	0.02
High-Speed Train	0.032	0.03
Airplane	0.067	0.17

Note: Recall that these estimates do not take into account the emissions and energy used during infrastructure construction.

the elements hurting the load factor of HSR, which on many lines is far from full capacity. The Beijing–Shanghai line, the busiest of China's high-speed rail links, can run at full capacity during holidays, but the load factor on ordinary days reaches only 70 to 80 percent at most. The load factor for the Nanjing to Wuhan line is typically only 50 percent.

ENVIRONMENT AND OTHER EXTERNALITIES

Very little information exists on the environmental effect of the introduction of HSR in China. Among the few studies published, the World Bank (2009) presents some estimates for the Shi Zheng corridor, where energy efficiency and pollution of the different transportation modes on this corridor are compared. Nonetheless, it is necessary to keep in mind that this service isn't yet in operation and that it is only an estimate. Table 8.3 shows the comparison.

The HSR project on this corridor aims to join the cities of Shijiazhuang and Zhengzhou at a cost of $6.5 billion at a speed of 217 mph, exclusively for passenger use. As one can see, while the differences between energy use and pollution between HSR and the airplane are quite significant in favor of the train, the conventional train appears as a more sustainable option once all of the necessary infrastructures are built. These results are consistent with the literature and the studies that we have drawn attention to throughout this book in other experiences where the analysis of environmental effects has been developed with greater interest.

NOTES

1. The objectives of the program were to reduce unemployment and resume economic growth by providing affordable housing, easing credit restrictions, lowering taxes, and boosting public investment in infrastructure.

2. Some previous tests had been made prior to 2007. Furthermore, since 2004, a line with Maglev technology exists between the Shanghai airport and the city's metro system, although the extension of this line is only 19 miles and thus of little significance in the entirety of the present network in which the first significant sections officially opened to the public in 2007.

3. If this requisite was applied in Spain, only six cities would be able to participate in the AVE network.

4. See article by Michael Wines and Keith Bradsher (2011), "China Rail Chief's Firing Hints at Trouble," published by the *New York Times* on February 17, 2011. Retrieved from www.nytimes.com/2011/02/18/world/asia/18rail.html?_r=1&pagewanted=all.

5. See article by Michael Forsythe, "Is China's Economy Speeding Off the Rails?," published by the *New York Times* on December 22, 2009. Retrieved from www.nytimes.com/2009/12/23/world/asia/23iht-letter.html.

6. See article by Will Freeman, "Freeman & Kroeber, 'Opinion: China's Fast Track to Development,'" published on July 2, 2010, by the *Wall Street Journal*. Retrieved from online.wsj.com/article/SB10001424052748704025304575283953879199386.html?mod=asia_opinion&utm_source=twitterfeed&utm_medium=twitter.

7. See article by Liu Meng, "Excluding Construction Investment Was Flat This Year, the Beijing-Tianjin High-Speed Rail," translated from Chinese. Published by the *Economic Observer* on September 18, 2010.

8. See article by Jeremy Warner on the financial troubles of the Chinese Ministry of Railways, "China Stops Work on all High-Speed Rail Projects," published by the *Telegraph* on July 28, 2011. Retrieved from www.telegraph.co.uk/finance/comment/jeremy-warner/8669207/Chinas-economic-miracle-may-be-about-to-come-off-the-rails.html.

9. See article by Peter Foster on China suspending HSR projects, "China Stops Work on all High Speed Rail Projects," published by the *Telegraph* on November 8, 2011. Retrieved from www.telegraph.co.uk/news/worldnews/asia/china/8694622/China-stops-work-on-all-high-speed-rail-projects.html.

10. See the article "China Off the Rails?," published by the *Economist* on March 31, 2011. Retrieved from www.economist.com/node/18488554.

11. See the article "China's High Speed Rail Projects on Hold Due to Cash Crunch," published by the *Economic Times* on October 27, 2011. Retrieved from articles.economictimes.indiatimes.com/2011-10-27/news/30328478_1_railway-projects-high-speed-railway-freight-lines.

12. See the article by Jane Lin and Shanshan Wu, "China's Railways Ministry Broke, Waiting for Bail-Out," published by the *Epoch Times*. Published on November 3, 2011. Retrieved from www.theepochtimes.com/n2/china-news/chinas-railways-ministry-broke-waiting-for-bail-out-63563.html.

13. See the article by Wen Rongping, Xi Si Zhang Xiangdong, and Hu Rongping, published by the *Economic Observer* 543 on November 7, 2011. Retrieved from www.eeo.com.cn/ens/2011/1107/215192.shtml.

14. See the article "China Railway Ministry to Sell $3 Billion in Bonds," published by the *Wall Street Journal* on October 17, 2011. Retrieved from online.wsj.com/article/SB10001424052970204346104576636190923550466.html.

15. See the article by Keith Bradsher, "China Sees Growth Engine in a Web of Fast Trains," published by the *New York Times* on February 12, 2010. Retrieved from www.nytimes.com/2010/02/13/business/global/13rail.html?pagewanted=all.

16. See the article by Michael Forsythe, "Is China's Economy Speeding Off the Rails?," published by the *New York Times* on December 22, 2009. Retrieved from www.nytimes.com/2009/12/23/world/asia/23iht-letter.html.

17. See the article by Xin Dingding, published by *China Daily* on December 1, 2011. Retrieved from www.chinadaily.com.cn/cndy/2011-01/12/content_11831362 .htm.

9

Other Experiences

Italy, Korea, and Taiwan

ITALY

The substantial economic growth that occurred in the 1950s and 1960s sparked a significant increase in mobility that was primarily channeled by way of the road. Thus, in 1950, the *Istituto par la Ricostruzione Industriale* was commissioned to build the expressway between Milan and Naples, receiving a state subsidy for 36 percent of the total cost. By 1970, after two decades of intense construction, the Italian expressway system had reached an extension of almost 2,485 miles. The increase in the offer of road infrastructure, in terms of both quantity and quality, wasn't accompanied by an equivalent improvement in rail's offer, which experienced a heavy loss of competitiveness in respect to the road. This loss was particularly significant in light of the fact that Italy's principal intermodal competition occurs between forms of ground transportation, given that the country is not attractive to domestic air traffic because of its geography and urban structure, unlike other European countries with a similarly sized population and economy.

The degradation of rail service and the growing congestion of road traffic led to the beginnings of the modernization of rail's infrastructure. Priority was given to modernizing the Florence–Rome line. This line followed a torturous and very long 195-mile route to avoid the orographical difficulties posed by a more direct route. Approval was given in late 1968 for the construction of a new line between both cities that would be 148 miles long and permit circulation at 155 mph. This line, the Florence–Rome *Direttissima*, was the precedent of high-speed rail in Italy. Work on the line began in early 1970 and was projected to last for five years. However,

129

the line didn't enter into partial service until 1977 and wasn't fully operational until 1992. While it was a significant improvement given the typical quality of the offer at the time in Italy, its technical characteristics are not comparable to those of high-speed rail, the *Rete Alta Velocità/Alta Capacità* (AV/AC).

Work on Italy's HSR network, the *Rete Alta Velocità/Alta Capacità* (AV/AC), began in 1991 with the founding of the TAV Company (Società TAV). The company was awarded a concession to build and operate the Milan–Naples and Turin–Venice lines. This concession was extended in 1992 to include the Milan–Genoa line. Società TAV is of mixed public-private ownership, with 60 percent of the capital in private hands and the remaining 40 percent belonging to the State Railways—Ferrovie dello Stato (GFDS, 2007a). The main rationale behind the introduction of HSR in Italy was the extremely low share of rail traffic in Italian mobility statistics. Even in recent years, rail journeys account for just 5 percent of all passenger transit, and trains are responsible for carrying just 12 percent of the nation's freight (GFDS, 2007b). Both figures are well below European averages. Moreover, air transportation cannot guarantee the intermediate stopover that is possible using land transportation, because of the relatively short distances between the main cities in Italy (Catalani, 2006).

Interestingly, the initial plan envisaged the construction of an HSR network that would run independently of the conventional system, as had been the case in Japan, France, and Spain. However, by 1996 this had changed toward a more integrated conception of the network, and so plans for the *Alta Velocità* were replaced with plans for the *Alta Velocità/Alta Capacità* (GFDS, 2007a). The latter sought to integrate the new HSR network with the conventional network, thus enhancing rail transportation capacity, expanding the effects of HSR, and avoiding the degradation of the conventional service in those areas between cities served by new HSR lines. However, it soon became apparent that there was a marked lack of willingness on the part of private shareholders to provide the capital required, and so, in 1998, 60 percent of this private share was acquired by Ferrovie dello Stato.

The first lines to enter into service were the Rome–Naples in 2005 and the Turin–Novara and Modena–Lavino in 2006. The last line to enter into service was the Naples–Sorrento, measuring 29 miles. Today, the Italian HSR network covers around 570 miles, including the *Diretissima* Florence–Rome, with the almost 160 miles this line has nowadays, as shown in figure 9.1. Main HSR services run between:

- Rome–Naples (129 miles): The line entered into service at different stages between 2005 and 2009. Travel time between the cities has been reduced from 105 to 65 minutes.

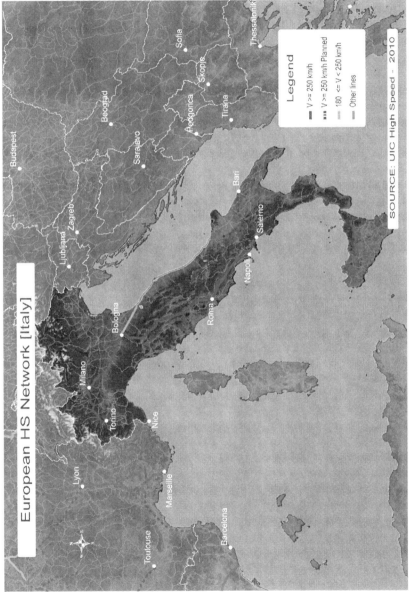

Figure 9.1.   Italy: HSR Lines. Source: UIC (International Union of Railways)

- Turin–Milan (78 miles): It entered into service at different stages between 2006 and 2009. Travel time between the cities has been reduced from 90 to 50 minutes.
- Milan–Bologna (115 miles): It entered into service in 2008. Travel time between the cities has been reduced from 102 to 60 minutes.
- Bologna–Florence (49 miles): It entered into service in 2009. Travel time between the cities has been reduced from 59 to 30 minutes.

According to data on passenger traffic provided by Ferrovie dello Stato, the number of travelers in high-speed trains (*Frecciarossa* and *Frecciargento*) was about twenty million in 2010. The real traffic obtained is lower than the initial estimates. For example, for the Milan–Bologna section, Trenitalia (the operator of the service) calculated in 2007 an estimate of 8.8 million journeys for 2010, but the real figure was around 6.5 million (Beria and Grimaldi, 2011). In the case of the Rome–Naples line, Trenitalia had calculated an estimate of 4.6 million passengers for 2010, while the real demand for that year was somewhat below three million (Beria and Grimaldi, 2011); other estimates even suggested lower figures for this section (Cascetta et al., 2011). Similar discrepancies between estimates and realities were recorded on other lines, such as the Bologna–Florence and the Turin–Milan.

The fact that almost all of the high-speed rail lines have only recently entered into service makes it more difficult than in other experiences to find studies on the impact of the new rail service on alternative modes of transportation. In the case of the Rome–Naples line, the results of a survey made in 2008 indicated that in the first years of the new HSR service, the volume of car and conventional intercity train traffic remained practically unchanged, while there was a growing use of the HSR. In all, the modal share of road travel dropped from 51 percent to 45 percent, while that of rail rose from 49 percent to 55 percent, with 7.8 percent of automobile traffic deviating to HSR (Cascetta et al., 2011).

In this sense, it is important to remember, as mentioned above, that the territorial characteristics and the urban structure of Italy cause the most significant intermodal competition to occur between the railway and the road, given the limited number of city-to-city relations in Italy with high traffic density for which the offer of air transportation is an attractive alternative. Thus, among the five domestic air routes with the most traffic in Italy in 2010, four connect the two principal cities of the peninsula (Rome and Milan) with the two principal cities of Sicily (Catania and Palermo), according to figures provided by ENAC (2011). Annual passenger traffic on these routes is 1.7 million passengers between Rome and Catania, 1.4 million between Rome and Palermo, 1.35 between Milan (Malpensa and Linate) and Catania, and 0.95 million between Milan (Malpensa and Linate) and

Palermo. The only route that surpasses these four is the Milan (Malpensa and Linate) and Rome connection, with 2.2 million passengers. According to estimates for direct traffic in HSR between Milan and Rome, the number of passengers in 2010 was around three million, which suggests a modal share of the HSR somewhat higher than that of the airplane between the two large Italian cities.

Contrary to the HSR strategy adopted in Japan, France, and Spain, the Italian HSR was conceived to provide a spread of benefits—linking up with the conventional lines—rather than concentrating them. However, this strategy caused an increase in projected costs. According to official information, the decision to shift from the high-speed strategy to that of the high speed/high capacity caused these projected costs to increase unchecked: from $13.9 billion in 1992 (1 euro= $1.30), that is $20.2 billion at 2006 prices, to $41.6 billion in 2006 (GFDS, 2007a; original figures in euros). Thus, projected costs have more than doubled in constant terms, according to official information provided by Ferrovie dello Stato, the managing state company of railway infrastructure (management of the train service is separate, and essentially in the hands of the likewise state company, Trenitalia). It should be pointed out that these figures refer to all of the lines planned in 1991, although some have yet to be realized.

More information exists for lines that have already been built and have entered into service and suggests that the estimates and official figures may have severely underestimated real costs, which furthermore have grown enormously for the lines built in the second half of the past decade. In this sense, the testimony presented by Cicconi (2011) to the European Parliament on November 16, 2011, is very revealing. This testimony provided a veritable forensic analysis of the financial costs of high-speed rail in Italy and deserves detailed examination. One of the most interesting aspects is that, on the one hand, it takes into account the official data supplied by the Ferrovie dello Stato. On the other hand, it incorporates into the analysis some accounting adjustments required by the European Union, stemming from the infringement procedure for excessive deficit in Italy, opened in 2005 and closed in 2007.

Using the information supplied in GFDS (2007a), Cicconi (2011), and Beria and Grimaldi (2011), and with the information concerning the Consumer Price Index in Italy, we have been able to create table 9.1, which presents detailed financial information for all of the high-speed rail lines in Italy that have entered into service over the last five years, with the sole exception of the short 29-mile section between Naples and Sorrento.

The cost per mile of HSR lines in Italy is much higher than those reported in other European countries such as France and Spain. On average, the cost per mile of the lines currently operating in Italy has been a little above $100 million per mile in 2011 terms. This cost per mile is much higher than

Table 9.1.   Alta Velocità/Alta Capacità Lines—Construction Costs

Main Lines	HST Lines Miles (1)	Contracted Costs in 1991 (1991 US $ Billions) (2)	Contracted Costs in 1991 (2011 US $ Billions) (3)	Projected (2006) Construction Costs (2006 US $ Billions) (4)	Projected (2006) Construction Costs (2011 US $ Billions) (5)	Real Deviation in Costs (5)/(3)	Cost per Mile (2011 US $ Million) (5)/(1)
Rome–Napoli (2006)	129	2.59	4.49	7.37	8.16	82%	63
Torino–Milan (2006)	78	1.40	2.42	10.12	11.21	363%	144
Milan–Bologna (2008)	115	1.93	3.34	8.99	9.95	198%	87
Bologna–Florence (2009)	49	1.40	2.42	7.65	8.46	250%	173

Source: (2) Cicconi (2011); (4) GFDS (2007a); CPI in Italy from INFLATION.EU Worldwide inflation data; (3) and (5), author's update.
Note: We used the average exchange rate as of the end of 2011 (1 euro = US $1.30). In parenthesis after name of line, (year when HST operation began).

that of the Florence–Rome *Diretissima*: around 2011 $45 million per mile (€20.3 million per kilometer in 2007 terms, in Cicconi, 2008).

As the data presented in table 9.1 shows, the difference in the cost per mile between the various HSR lines is very great, given that the Bologna–Florence line, for example, almost triples the cost of the Rome–Naples. A characteristic common to all of the lines is the existence of significant discrepancies between initial cost estimates and final projections. In the case of the Rome–Naples line, the final cost has doubled the initial estimates, even though the discrepancy in this case is the most moderate. In the case of the line with the highest cost per mile, the Bologna–Florence (2011 $173 million per mile), the final cost projection is more than 250 percent of the initial estimate.

The large cost discrepancies in respect to initial estimates, which have generated the highest costs per mile in Europe, have been the focus of attention and analysis in Italy, notably in a public hearing of the Italian parliament in 2007 that included information provided by Ferrovie dello Stato (GFDS, 2007a). According to the figures and estimates presented, the primary causes of the cost overruns have been:

- The contracting method of the construction projects, which were granted by direct negotiation with HSR instead of through a competition. It is estimated that if competitive procedures had been used to assign contracts, the savings per mile could have been between $9 million and $14 million in 2011 terms.
- The specificities of the projects, derived from the requisites of interconnectivity between new lines and conventional ones, as well as the hyper-urban characteristics of the Italian territory, its orographical complexity and seismic activity.
- Adaptation to environmental and landscape regulations. An average cost of $14 million to $18 million in 2011 terms per mile is attributed to these factors.

Although construction of the lines is the primary component of HSR costs in Italy, it is not the only one. In Cicconi's report (2011) presented to the European Parliament, other components accrue to the total cost: the creation of junctions or rail sections to provide access to stations in cities, whose projected costs rose to $11 billion in 2011 terms; the aerial infrastructures (power lines and signs) of all of the lines, with projected costs of somewhat more than $4 billion in 2011 terms; the interim interests from loans activated by HSR and directly borne by the state, with estimated financial charges of more than $11 billion in 2011 terms.

Upon considering all of the costs involved in the creation of the high-speed rail infrastructure of the seven projects planned and contracted in

1991, which include, in addition to the lines mentioned above, the Milan–Verona, Verona–Venice, and Terzo valico (formerly Genoa–Milan) lines, Cicconi calculates a global estimate of $130 billion in 2011 terms. A large part of this cost consists of debts hidden in the accounting of the state companies, outside of the budget. After observing "the devastating effect of the HSR model on future public finance," it is no surprise that Cicconi (2011, p. 7) ends his testimony to the European Parliament thus: "We therefore appeal to the European Parliament to ask our country to account for this glaring omission and especially to prevent the TAV (HSR) model from dragging Italy and Europe towards a catastrophe of the public accounts."

Having observed the enormous cost of the implantation of high-speed rail in Italy, and of the financial obligations imposed on the national budget, we may now turn our attention to an evaluation of the relation between its costs and benefits as described in the cost benefit analysis made by Beria and Grimaldi (2011).

This analysis takes into consideration the costs of spending on the construction of the line (without considering other additional costs), operating costs, benefits generated through savings in travel time, and environmental benefits derived from the reduction of polluting emissions (very limited in Italy due to the scarce air traffic absorbed).[1] Lastly, wider economic benefits (which are not found in the usual accounting of a CBA) are calculated to be between 10 percent and 20 percent of the project, although effects of this magnitude are more common in developing economies with less mature infrastructures. In all, therefore, this analysis underestimates the total costs of implanting HSR and overestimates its positive effects.

Through the applied CBA, Beria and Grimaldi estimate the demand necessary to justify the investment from the point of view of social benefits. Table 9.2 summarizes the principal results obtained.

Table 9.2.   *Alta Velocità/Alta Capacità* Lines—Simulated Demand and Estimated Demand Needed to Justify the Investment (Million Passengers–Mpax)

	Rome– Naples	Torino– Milan	Milan– Bologna	Bologna– Florence
Demand needed to justify the investment Mpax/year	7.9	14.2	8.9	19.4
2010 demand targeted by Trenitalia in 2007 Mpax	4.6	2.1	8.8	11.5
Demand in 2010 (estimated with +/- 10% margin) Mpax	2.6–3.2	1.2–1.5	5.9–7.2	9.8–12
Demand in 2010 / Demand needed (in %)	33% –41%	8%–11%	66%– 81%	51%– 62%

Source: Adapted from Beria and Grimaldi (2011), p. 21, table 4.

The first observation to be made about these results is that Trenitalia's estimates of the demand for 2007 were lower than the demand necessary to justify the investment. Only in the case of the Milan–Bologna line did Trenitalia's envisioned demand reach the necessary level. The situation was much worse for the remaining lines, and in the case of the Turin–Milan the demand estimated by Trenitalia was only 15 percent of what was needed to justify the investment.

The financial results of the implantation of high-speed rail in Italy have been devastating and have imposed enormous obligations on the national budget. In terms of its socioeconomic benefits, the existing estimates make clear that the level of use of high-speed rail is far below the demand necessary to justify the investment in more general terms. It should come as no surprise, therefore, that critical recommendations are now being made in respect to railway policy to establish future priorities that consider only those projects with more favorable demand and to apply aggressive cost-reduction strategies. And, in a general way, to abandon the model of high-speed rail lines, which has proven incapable of modernizing Italy's rail system in a sufficiently effective way in respect to mobility, even as it has imposed huge costs.

KOREA

The first high-speed rail services in Korea, called Korea Train Express (KTX) were inaugurated in April of 2004, although the first studies to begin the design of the network were made in 1973. The first business plan wasn't approved until 1990, and construction began in 1992. The first route chosen in the Korean experience was the Seoul–Daegu–Busan line (255 miles)—the Kyeongbu line—although only a shorter section to the intermediary city of Daegu was opened in 2004, while the rest of the conventional infrastructure was electrified up to Busan. Korea thus became the world's fifth country to have HSR services (>155 mph) of a significant distance and the second Asian country after Japan. The complete route to the port city of Busan didn't enter into service until November of 2010. In all, the project called for the construction of 138 miles and the upgrading of another 116.

Construction of a second line between Seoul and the city of Mokpo, called the Honan line (156 miles), began in 2009 and is expected to be completed between 2014 and 2017. The high-speed route to Mokpo shares the existing Seoul–Busan tracks to Osong. From there it heads southwest for 144 miles to reach Mokpo, with some sections paralleling the existing conventional Honam railway route, which takes two hours fifty-eight minutes to traverse from Seoul to Mokpo. The goal is to reduce the travel time to one hour and forty-six minutes after the complete development of the HSR infrastructure. The construction of this line will also be realized in two stages. A first stage up to Kwangju—with completion due by 2015—while the second stage will complete the route from Kwangju to Mokpo.

The primary motive behind the planning for HSR services in Korea was congestion and the need to alleviate some bottlenecks in the country's most transited expressway and conventional rail routes. This congestion and lack of capacity was considered to be partly responsible for the competitive weakness of the Korean economy, and for this reason the government expected a significant contribution to the regional and international development of the country with the entry into service of HSR. The alternative solution of increasing the capacity of the conventional train service by 15 percent was considered, but it was discarded as being a provisional solution that would soon prove insufficient. The government also believed that HSR would disperse or extend economic activity beyond the metropolitan area of Seoul, where over the past few decades most of the country's economic activity had become concentrated, as demonstrated by the fact that 84 percent of government departments are located there, along with 65 percent of the universities and 91 percent of the corporate headquarters present in South Korea (Dong-Chun Shin, 2005).

Korea is one of the world's most densely populated countries, as well as one with the most mountainous terrain. In terms of density, Korea is among the five densest countries in the world among those nations with 494 inhabitants per square mile. On the other hand, 70 percent of its territory is mountainous. Two large transportation corridors exist in the country, through which the country's economic activity and mobility flow. The first is the Seoul–Busan corridor, which unites the north of the country with the southeast, and thus 70 percent of both the population and the GDP. It is estimated that two-thirds of transportation originates and moves along this corridor.

The second corridor runs between Seoul and Mokpo (see figure 9.2), joining the political capital with the southwest of the peninsula and which expects to be the second HSR route. This route, in contrast, has less traffic given its more rural characteristics and lower activity. It is no surprise, therefore, that the first route chosen by the government was precisely the route between Seoul and Busan, given the fact that most of the country's urban development and industry is located there.

In Korea, rail infrastructures have been operated and maintained separately since 2003. This separation gave rise to two entities that have played a decisive role in the sector. On the one hand, following the semiprivatization of rail services in 2005, KORAIL—a government agency—came to control the management and operation of KTX and conventional rail services. On the other hand, KRNA (Korea Rail Network Authority) took over responsibility

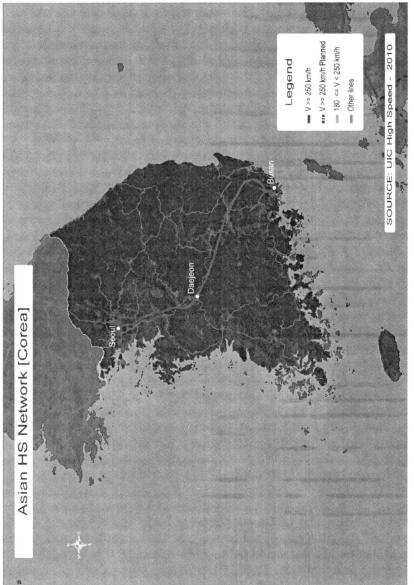

Figure 9.2. Korea: HSR Lines. Source: UIC (International Union of Railways)

for the construction and maintenance of infrastructure, thereby completing the separation process.

As in all experiences, high-speed rail made it possible to drastically reduce the travel time in comparison to travel by road or conventional rail. For the Seoul–Busan line, the HSR travel time is two hours and eighteen minutes, while by road it easily takes more than five hours, and four hours and eighteen minutes by conventional rail. In fact, one of the regional results of the KTX has precisely been the extension of the commuter belt of Seoul. With an average distance between stations of 36.6 miles, an area of influence exists within 200 miles of the city center of Seoul that takes only one hour of travel time. Three of the KTX stations of the Seoul–Busan line are even located within the metropolitan area of Seoul.

The demand in traffic when the line opened was about seventy thousand daily passengers after three months of operation. This figure is very far from the estimates made by the Korea Transport Institute in 2003. Real traffic was 46 percent of the expected traffic in 2004, and real income was only 54 percent of the expected income. The discrepancy between the real and expected traffic was not limited to the first year of operation. At present, the number of daily passengers is around 140,000, reaching in 2011 the estimate realized in 1998 for expected traffic in 2004 (Suh, Yang, and Kim, 2005). The load factor realized on the Seoul–Busan line is about 73 percent on average, although it increases to 85 percent on the weekends.

A commonly accepted explanation of this discrepancy is the economic slowdown and the impact of the financial crisis of 1997. The overestimates in demand were essentially due to the discrepancy in the assumptions made in respect to socioeconomic variables, as shown by the GDP growth rate of 6.4 percent used for the estimate of the 1996–2003 period, in contrast to the 3.8 percent real growth (Chang and Jang-Ho Lee, 2008). In addition to this, stations are hard to access, which sometimes makes them less convenient than private transportation, and the construction of the network was not completed on time. The construction of the network to Busan has met with significant delays and very little has been done to further construction on the second route to Mokpo. In all, 66 percent of the routes served by the KTX used conventional infrastructure (Lee, 2005). According to Suh, Yang, and Kim (2005), the estimates of demand were made assuming the existence of complete HSR service between Seoul and Busan, and not in the mixed operation carried out between 2004 and 2010. At any rate, the overestimation of the demand led to a public scandal that forced the government to postpone work on the Honan route. Even so, this line came to be seen as inalienable to local citizens, and politicians have competed with promises to recover the project.

The price of the KTX is usually 1.3 times the price of the conventional train, although it is lower than the price of air transportation. On the Seoul–

Daegu route, 27 percent of the journeys made by conventional train were displaced to the KTX, while 14.5 percent of bus journeys were displaced and 15 percent of those made by private transportation. This displacement is proportional to the length of the route traveled by passengers, so that for short routes the displacement is less, while for longer routes the displacement is larger. Also, 30.4 percent of the journeys between Seoul and Busan made using other forms of transportation were also displaced to the KTX, even during the period in which high-speed rail only existed up to Daegu. Figure 9.3 shows HSR's market share during the first year of service of the Seoul–Busan line according to the distance of the trajectories from Seoul. This demonstrates how market share increases with distance but falls on the longest journeys, precisely where the old infrastructure entered into service and where, therefore, HSR lost competitiveness.

As in other experiences, the greatest impact after the inauguration of high-speed rail was felt by air transportation. Korean Air and Asiana Airline, the two companies with significant operations in 2004 on the Seoul–Busan, Seoul–Daegu, Seoul–Mokpo, and Seoul–Guangju routes, anticipated the impact of the arrival of HSR on their demand and drastically reduced the frequency of their flights. For example, on the Seoul–Daegu route—which competed against full HSR service—the number of flights fell from 517 in January of 2004 to 293 in March, just prior to the entry into service of the KTX in April. In June of that same year, the number of flights was 183 (Suh, Yang, and Kim, 2005). In contrast, rail services increased with the entry into service of the KTX, even with the resulting reduction in conventional

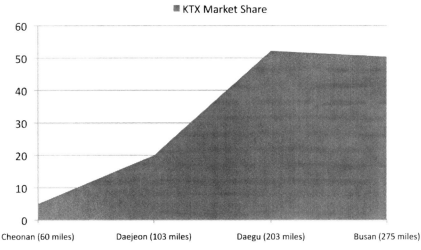

Figure 9.3. KTX Market Share. Source: Chang and Lee (2008). Modal share is measured based on daily passengers.

services. The number of seats offered increased by 33 percent (Suh, Yang, and Kim, 2005).

On the Seoul–Daegu route, the displacement of passengers to HSR reached 71.5 percent, while on the Seoul–Busan route this displacement remained at 29 percent while no direct HSR connection existed between Daegu and Busan. According to Park and Ha's figures (2006), the number of flights between Seoul and Daegu also fell 71.3 percent with the entry into service of HSR, a significant figure but still lower than the expected 85 percent.

The estimated cost of the HSR project in Korea in 2004 when the first stage was completed was $11 billion. This stage included the electrification of the entire network and the addition of new links for high-speed rail oriented toward passenger service. The second stage cost an additional $7 billion in 2010 with the inauguration of high-speed rail services to Busan. The line to Mopko involves a further estimated $10 billion (Briginshaw, 2007). Nevertheless, Dong-Chun Shin (2005), managing director of Korea's Ministry of Transportation, recognized that real costs amply surpassed these estimates, above all because of cost overruns related to expropriating land from private owners. The total cost of the project may have increased by as much as 300 percent, as the President of Korail recognized (Briginshaw, 2007). Similarly, Jeong Gwan Lee—from the Korean consulate in San Francisco—recently confirmed that the Korean government originally estimated the cost for the entire project to be about $5 billion, although the cost turned out to be four times higher.[2] The access price to the infrastructure Korail must pay, together with its own accumulated debt—some $2.5 billion—explain why this agency is losing about Won 600 billion a year—about $520 million—despite the subsidies it receives for public service. Furthermore, the agency's bond balances have roughly doubled since 2008.

To finance this project, which became the most important infrastructure project in terms of volume of spending in the history of Korea, the government contributed 35 percent of the capital, while the remaining funds came from loans, 10 percent with government backing and the remaining 55 percent from the domestic and international financial sector.

As in other experiences, the cost of building the HSR network in Korea has been greatly conditioned by the country's geographical and topographical conditions, as well as by the need to safeguard the infrastructure from earthquakes. A clear example of the complexity and cost of the work is shown by the fact that 46 percent of the HSR's tracks pass through tunnels or that the network has 86 bridges and viaducts.

The technology used by the KTX was partially imported from Europe. Specifically, the KTX used vehicles from the French company Alstom, and thus its vehicles are similar to the ones used on the French TGV network—they travel at 190 mph—along with another group of vehicles produced in

Korea, but under license from Alstom. Each train is 387 meters long, has seating for 935 passengers, and weighs 700 tons, making them among the longest and heaviest TGV-type train in use. Technological development in this industry has made it possible to create local Korean technology that aims to be exported to countries such as Brazil and the United States, with vehicles designed to travel at 217mph.

High-speed rail in South Korea is a current news topic because of its relation to the 2018 Olympic Games in Pyongyang. High-speed rail was one of the strong points of the winning proposal for the Olympic site of the Winter Games. The Korean Olympic Committee proposed a project that would make it possible to connect the international airport of Incheon with the site of the Games, about 100 miles away, in sixty-eight minutes. In doing so, they overcame the primary concern of the proposal, which was the isolation of the Olympic site. The $8.7 billion project is currently a matter of great controversy, and members of the government now anticipate that the trajectory during the Olympic Games will take ninety-three or one hundred seven minutes instead of the estimated and announced sixty-eight minutes. In fact, the Minister of Transportation has stated that such a high-speed rail project never existed. Concerns over high investment costs and doubts over how much demand there will be once the Games are over could be the decisive factors in this rectification. Although another point of view is given by Sohn Chang-hwan, the director of designing and planning venues for the Pyongyang Organizing Committee, who has stated:

We never said we would build a bullet-train track from Incheon to Pyeongchang, but the media did [. . .] the only proposed plan is connecting Wonju and Gangneung with a new express railroad [. . .] The 68 minute proposal was the best possible time that could be [. . .] We said that number to persuade the International Olympics Committee members.[3] (Sohn Chang-hwan, director of designing and planning venues for the Pyongyang Organizing Committee)

According to the government—which attributes the controversy to the national and international press—the transversal line between Wonji and Gangneoung will have a station near Pyongyang, halfway between the cities of origin and destination on the route, at a maximum speed of 155 mph but with a travel time always greater than ninety minutes.

TAIWAN

The growth of Taiwan's population and economy since the 1970s favored the use of transportation infrastructures until these reached a measure of saturation and congestion in the years prior to the financial crisis that hit the economies of Asia in 1997. In fact, the desire to build a high-speed rail network appeared in the early 1970s, although planning didn't begin until 1987 when the executive branch of the government ordered the Ministry of Transportation to carry out the first studies. The project wasn't passed in parliament until 1993.[4]

The congestion on the expressways and regional train services on the western corridor, home to 70 percent of the population, was the primary argument and motivation for considering high-speed rail as a long-term solution. Just traveling this corridor, which is less than 220 miles long, occupied around six to eight hours during peak periods. In fact, this corridor alone occupies the sixth position in world population density, if we consider it as separate from the rest of the island. In addition to these arguments, the Bureau of High-Speed Rail declared that the high-speed rail line joining the country's two largest metropolitan areas, Taipei and Kaohsiung, would contribute to balanced regional development, while it minimized the environmental and ecological impact of the transportation.

The Taiwanese high-speed rail line, exclusively for passenger use, was inaugurated in January of 2007; it is 214 miles long, with twelve planned stations, eight of which were in service by 2011. This line joins the southern metropolitan area of Kaohsiung—the island's most densely populated zone (25,467 inhabitants per square mile), home to almost three million people—and the northern area of Taipei, the political capital of the country and the most populated in absolute terms with 6.9 million inhabitants. Between these two areas, the HSR also connects the important city and surroundings of Taichung, third in terms of population with 2.6 million. Geographical characteristics consisting of large mountainous zones in the center of the island encouraged 70 percent of the twenty-three million Taiwanese to concentrate in the plains of this western corridor, and thus most of the infrastructures have also been developed here (roads, conventional railroads, high-speed rail, etc.).

HSR achieved significant reductions in travel time in respect to conventional train services and road travel. While the corridor between Taipei and Zuoying (the administrative district of Kaohsiung and last station on the line) takes almost five hours by conventional train, HSR manages to travel the same distance in an hour and a half. Compared to road travel, this time savings is even greater, given that the average road trip takes more than five hours, except on days of heavier traffic when this time can be substantially longer.

Nevertheless, HSR is not superior to air transportation in travel time on routes where there is enough distance for air services to exist. For example, the travel time by plane to Tainan lasts some fifty minutes, while by high-speed rail it takes one hour and fifty-five minutes given the lack of direct service. Something similar occurs when comparing the services that connect Taipei

Figure 9.4. Taiwan: HSR Lines. Source: UIC (International Union of Railways)

with Kaohsiung. Air service takes about an hour to fly between the island's two main airports, while HSR covers this distance in an hour and a half.

Another notable feature of the design of Taiwan's high-speed rail network is the controversial locations of the stations (see figure 9.4). While one of the advantages of HSR in respect to air traffic is the direct connection of the economic and financial centers of the cities, Taiwan decided in most cases to locate these stations on the periphery of the cities. This decision was made with the expectation that by locating HSR stations there, property values would increase and the peripheral zones of the cities would be revitalized. This goal doesn't seem to have been accomplished. The study by David Andersson, Oliver Shyr, and Johnson Fu (2010) shows how the improvement in accessibility provided by HSR doesn't affect housing prices, precisely because interurban connections and the commuting by the inhabitants of these metropolitan areas don't gain significant advantages with HSR. The price of the service likewise doesn't seem to encourage repeated use. In fact, six stations are located at least twenty minutes from the city center by private transportation. By public transportation, four of these stations are located at minimum distances of thirty minutes.

It is not surprising that 40 percent of the trips made by HSR in Taiwan are business oriented, while tourism represents 30 percent of the traffic. The third category, consisting of visits to friends and family, makes up 22 percent of the traffic. It is estimated that these passengers are displaced from other modes of transportation and that only 8 percent of the total trips are induced by the presence of HSR as a form of transportation.[5] This would seem to indicate that HSR does practically nothing that other modes of transportation already did in a reasonable way. Furthermore, the Taipei–Kaohsiang axis will find it difficult to contribute to a greater exchange of business trips in light of the fact that the industrial structure of Kaohsiang is based predominately on manufacturing—in contrast to Taipei, where services have much greater weight—and that this industry has undergone a measure of relocation to mainland China and elsewhere in Southeast Asia. This economic structure and its relations with Southeast Asia encourage business trips to be made increasingly outside of Taiwan. This perhaps explains why traffic rises on the weekends thanks to family and tourist trips.

If there is a noteworthy aspect to the Taiwanese experience, it is the use of models of public-private cooperation based on the traditional Build-Operate-and-Transfer (BOT) format. In this model, private participation assumes the investment and financial costs of construction and maintenance and operation of the infrastructure in exchange for charging users the cost of the trajectory for a period of time sufficient to recoup the investment before returning the infrastructure to the public sector at the end of the concession. The principal particularity here is the fact that the HSR project in Taiwan was one of the world's largest BOT projects in terms of volume of investment, costing around $15–18 billion.[6] The mountainous terrain, and thus the large number of necessary viaducts and tunnels, inevitably increased construction costs. Eighteen percent of the line's length passes through tunnels, while 73 percent runs on raised infrastructures, making it the world's longest elevated HSR line. Furthermore, the infrastructure had to be built taking seismic risks into consideration. All of this explains the enormous spending on infrastructure that has fallen on the financial back of the concessionary company.

The private sector's involvement, considered in 1994 under the law that allowed private financing of infrastructure projects and which the parliament passed in 1996, arose from budgetary restrictions that made it difficult for the government to be the sole investor. The state contributed land and helped in acquiring loans, as well as providing help in environmental matters and HSR's integration with other public sector services. The companies that bid for the world's largest BOT contract were the CHSR consortium (Chinese High Speed Rail Consortium)—with Japanese technology—and the THSR consortium (Taiwan High Speed Rail Consortium), which used Eurotrain European technology—with French and German technology. The latter won and thus designated its preference for the technology offered by Alstom and Siemens in 1997.[7] The winning company changed its name to Taiwan High Speed Rail Corporation (THSRC) and obtained rights over the infrastructure for a period of thirty-five years, as well as rights of exploitation of the stations and their surroundings for fifty years. It was chosen primarily because THSRC's offer, in contrast to the offer presented by CHSRC, didn't require public financing. However, and despite having designated European technology as preferential, the new corporation THSRC ended up signing a contract with the TSC (Taiwan Shinkansen Consortium) to import the Japanese *Shinkansen* technology instead of European technology, which led to a round of litigations between the company and the European technology consortium.

Despite the original business estimates,[8] the BOT of the HSR of Taiwan has become one of the clearest examples of the failure of this form of public-private cooperation on large infrastructures where demand is highly uncertain. What seemed like a relief for the Taiwanese taxpayer thanks to the private sector involvement through a BOT agreement, turned out to be veritable nightmare.

Demand is one of the most significant risks in the sector of transportation infrastructures. Indeed, it is difficult to predict demand in the short-term; for a longer period of thirty-five years—as was the case of the concession—it is simply impossible. This is why the discrepancies between planned and real traffic determine the expectations for the real profitability of these projects. While the government predicted 275,000 daily passengers in the first years and 400,000 toward the end of the period of the concession, real traffic for the first years of operation was much lower. In fact, the number of daily passengers was about 100,000 in 2010, after ticket prices were lowered beginning in March of 2008, when the number of daily passengers had numbered only 74,500. While traffic has increased, the factor of occupation has remained stable because of the increase in the frequency of the service. According to the study by Yung-Hsiang Cheng (2010), this factor of lower-than-expected occupation—46 percent in 2010 according to Jokull Johannesson and Yu Kien-hong (2010)—indicates that revenues are still unable to cover the financial, variable, and depreciation costs of assets and infrastructure.

The first explanation for this discrepancy, and thus for the optimism of the predictions, is that the estimates were made prior to the 1997 financial crisis. Although the estimates were later modified, the figures continue to be much higher than the reality, with estimates of between 150,000 and 200,000 daily passengers.

The second explanation apparently lies in the government's desire to obtain better offers in the bidding for the concession. Greater demand would make the project into a much more attractive business and could thus guarantee greater private participation and less public commitment in terms of guarantees and facilities provided by the public sector. This appears to be the opinion of Nita Ing, who was president of the Taiwan High Speed Rail Corporation for eleven years, as she states in an interview published in the *Commonwealth Magazine* N° 431 on September 24, 2009:

> A man whose relationship with the high speed railway is relatively close—I won't say his name—participated in the project and says that the government indeed inflated the estimates to make the railway more attractive to investors. It's not as if we just became aware of this today, so we can't say we were deceived, and bringing this up now will not help the situation. All we can say is that we were too naive at the time. (Nita Ing, former president of the Taiwan High Speed Rail Corporation)

With this discrepancy in traffic and the enormous loans required to finance the project—which furthermore generated significant cost overruns—the project faces great difficulty in becoming profitable over the thirty-five years of the concession. The estimates made by Yung-Hsiang Cheng (2010) indicate that the net revenues in value present in 2001 would only be positive in the final years of the concession. Unable to wait for the future evolution of the project's profitability, the government of Taiwan was forced to rescue Taiwan High Speed Rail Corporation (THSRC) in 2009 and take control of the management board, naming a new president and increasing its presence in this body to reflect its 36 percent stake in the company. The motive for the rescue—which was not a takeover—was that THSRC had already lost $2.13 billion in the first two years of operating the network, as well as two-thirds of its capitalization through accumulated losses. The company needed $2.5 billion in new credit to remain afloat, but the enormous losses of the company and an outstanding debt of more than $10 billion made it difficult to reach an agreement with creditors. With the company teetering on bankruptcy, caused by the discrepancy in traffic and enormous financial and repayment costs, the government was forced to absorb its losses and increasingly assume the corporation's debt load, as well as to guarantee the new loans. State-controlled banks offering lower interest rates and longer repayment periods made most of these loans. Thus, the company was able to acquire refinancing for $12 billion through the largest syndicated loan in the history of Taiwan.

In fact, this wasn't the first time the project was in need of government aid. The government's participation in financing the project, both directly and indirectly, may have reached 84 percent, according to declarations by Taiwanese deputies in the financial committee of the parliament in 2002,[9] which contradicts the commitment to the absence of public financing in the offer made by the winning bidder. This first public intervention made it possible to surmount the lack of guarantees by the national banks for the necessary international loans. Just the contribution to the corporation of land and capital cost government coffers $3.3 billion and $1.2 billion, respectively.

With the public rescue of 2009 it was possible to refinance the outstanding debts and reform the accounting of repayments and capital depreciations to favor the company's financial survival.

Despite this financial disaster, high-speed rail services will continue to function. The president of the government, Wu Den-yih made clear in 2009 that services will continue given that their cancellation would have a serious impact on the nation.

High-speed rail in Taiwan makes it possible to travel the 214 miles from one end of the route to the other in only ninety minutes, with only one stop. When this service stops at all of the stations on the line, the travel time rises to two hours. HSR began its services with a frequency of nineteen daily round-trip journeys, but this frequency progressively increased until reaching 140 daily services in 2008.

The competitiveness of HSR in respect to other modes of transportation has also been studied in Taiwan. As the frequency of HSR service has risen, air transportation services on routes prior to the arrival of HSR have declined. With the entry into service of the high-speed train, it is estimated that the factor of occupation for air services of the four major domestic airlines fell from 24 percent to 13 percent.[10]

Alternative modes of land transportation have also suffered the impact of the arrival of HSR, although in a mixed way. On the one hand, interurban bus services, with passengers very sensitive to ticket prices, saw their market share fall approximately 10 percent on the longest routes, such as the Taipei–Kaohsiung (from 34.5 percent to 24.7 percent) and the Taipei–Tainan (from 60.1 percent to 51.9 percent). Conventional rail with stations in the center of the principal cities also lost passengers on these routes, falling from a share of 9.7 percent to 5.3 percent on the Taipei–Kaohsiung line. On the Taipei–Tainan line, however, the decline was less, dropping from a share of 7.3 percent to 6.4 percent.

On the same routes, air transportation has also seen its market share fall. On the Taipei–Kaohsiung route, the drop has been from 24 percent to 13 percent after the opening of high-speed rail service. In the case of the Taipei–Tainan route, the fall has been much less, given that the travel time of the route is much more attractive for air transportation because of the lack of direct HSR service. Its market share fell from 11.4 percent to 7.7 percent. On shorter routes, such as the Taipei–Taichung route (103 miles), the reduction of market share for the bus and conventional rail services has been all but insignificant, the bus's market share falling from 31 percent to 29 percent, and the train from 9.4 percent to 8.6 percent. The HSR's lesser comparative advantage and its high monetary cost explain these differences for medium- and long-distance routes.

Figures 9.5–9.7 show the immediate impact of HSR on the different competing modes. The figures indicate the market share of the various modes on each route, ordered from greater to lesser distance.[11]

On the other hand, the direct route between Taipei and Zuoying—the administrative district of Kaohsiung—suffers a disadvantage in respect to air transportation of about fifty minutes of in-vehicle travel time, although considering the door-to-door travel time, this difference turns out to be insignificant.

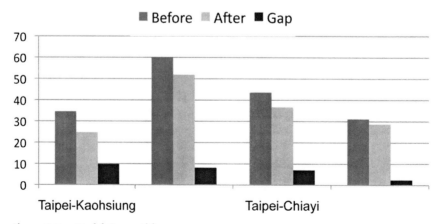

Figure 9.5. Modal Competition

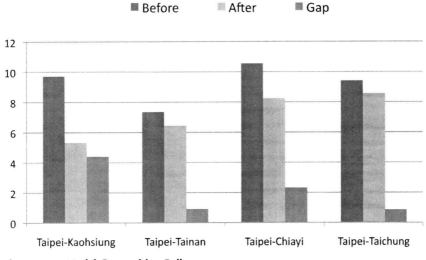

Figure 9.6.   **Modal Competition Railways**

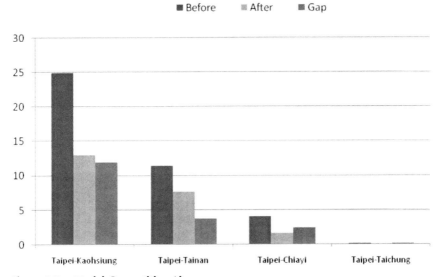

Figure 9.7.   **Modal Competition Air**

The airlines reacted by canceling the various routes that ceased to be profitable—such as the Taipei–Taichung route flown by Mandarin Airlines—reducing the frequency of their services and reducing prices, which have approached prices offered by HSR. The seriousness of the competition posed by HSR even led to an agreement of cooperation between the four main airlines (Mandarin Airlines, TransAsia, Far Eastern Air Transport, and

Uni Airways) to permit any passenger with a reservation for a flight between Taipei and Kaohsiung to be able to use any of the airlines.

The Taiwan experience has been based on importing technology. Although on the one hand, its uses the technology of the Japanese *Shinkansen*—the trains are a variant of the 700 Series *Shinkansen* and travel at a maximum speed of 186 mph—the system of traffic management is European (TGV and ICE). In fact, the choice of this technology was the subject of controversy and heated debate. As mentioned above, at first, the government of Taiwan chose as preferential the European technology promoted by Alstom and Siemens in 1997. Nevertheless, it ended up choosing the Japanese technology in 1999, apparently for its price, technology, financing, and safety attributes. The press, however, tended to interpret the change in decision as a matter of foreign policy strategy by the Taiwanese government, particularly after the trip made to Japan by the president of Taiwan, Lee Teng-hui, before the decision was made. The president's opinions, reflected in a book published in 1999, seem to validate the journalists who held this view, given that the president highlighted the political advantages associated with the Japanese choice.[12] The European consortium didn't back down, however, and initiated legal action at various international levels until reaching an agreement with the Taiwanese government for damages of around $89 million, interests included.

NOTES

1. The environmental benefits estimated from the shift from air are estimated to be of US $325 million overall in forty years. The estimation does not take into account the environmental costs resulting from the construction of the HSR lines.

2. Statements reported in an article by Cheryl Jennings (2011), published online on November 15, 2011, in ABC7 News, abclocal.go.com/kgo/story?section=news/assignment_7&id=8433340.

3. Statements reported in the article by Duncan Mackay (2012), "Pyeongchang 2018 in controversy over high-speed rail link" published on January 4, 2012, in www.insidethegames.biz. Article downloaded on January 18 at www.insidethegames.biz/olympics/winter-olympics/2018/15393-pyeongchang-2018-in-controversy-over-high-speed-rail-link.

4. Although planning didn't begin until that year, a measure of informal planning began to develop in the Ministry of Transportation in 1980.

5. Ministry of Transportation and Communications (2007), "Investigation of passenger transfer preferences on HSR transfer transportation mode, survey report" (in Chinese, cited in Yung Hsiang Cheng, 2010). Estimates of induced traffic.

6. To contextualize the enormous cost of the project, some estimates published by the media indicated that the cost per Taiwanese rose to $650.

7. Major players in the CHSR consortium included the Kuomintang-controlled China Development Corp., Cathay Life Insurance Co., China Steel Corp., Huang

Kuo Corp., and Tuntex Corp. The foreign partner in the group was Japan High-Speed Rail. The THSR consortium included Continental Engineering Corp., Pacific Electric Wire and Cable Co., Fubon Insurance Co., Evergreen Marine Corp., and Teco Electric and Machinery Co. GEC Alstom of France and Siemens of Germany were the foreign partners in the bid.

8. Taiwan High Speed Rail Corportation said it expected to be profitable by its second year and to break even twelve months after its first commercial operation. It expected to manage returns from the investments sixteen years after its construction. AFX News Limited. (2006). *Taiwan High Speed Rail Sees Operating Profit in Second Year of Operation.* Available: www.forbbbes.com/feeds/afx/2006/11/30/afx3215855.html

9. Declarations by Norman Yin in the financial committee on April 3, 2002. See article by Joyce Huang (April 4, 2002), "Derailment of train project feared," *Taipei Times,* retrieved October 3, 2010.

10. See the study by Yung-Hsiang Cheng (2010) for more information about the impact of the entry into service of HSR in respect to other modes of transportation.

11. The data necessary for the construction of these figures and which make it possible to compare the impact of the inauguration of HSR are found in Yung-Hsiang Cheng (2010).

12. Lee Teng-hui. *Taiwan de zhuzhang.* Yuan liu chu ban shi ye gu fen you xian gong si; Chu ban edition (1999).

III

AN EVALUATION OF
HIGH-SPEED RAIL

10

Lessons from International Experiences

This journey across countries and continents to examine the different HSR experiences provides some important lessons that should not be ignored when considering future extensions of high-speed rail, in the United States and elsewhere.

Using the case studies that appear in this book, this chapter aims to discern the key elements that can determine the degree of desirability of a massive investment project such as the HSR, and the response or results arising from international experiences. The elements relate to the key aspects of an HSR project as presented in chapter 3. The purpose of this chapter is to provide a set of lessons grounded in the evidence to date in order to make possible an informed debate on each of these key elements in the United States. Such an approach is intended to provide the reader with knowledge of what can and cannot be expected from an HSR project according a set of conditions and limitations that definitely affect the sense of its social contribution.

To achieve this, we follow the same structure as in chapter 3, in order to show the lessons from international experiences in terms of the motives and objectives of the projects; the design structure and functionality of the network; investment and profitability; economic, regional, and mobility impacts—including intermodal competition—and environmental aspects, based on the limited analysis made of this technology.

OBJECTIVES AND MOTIVATION

In light of international experience, HSR projects seem to make most sense when they seek to solve capacity restrictions, lightening congestion on certain corridors, and when facilitating industrial connections by enhancing accessibility for freight transportation. The linking up with other corridors to promote regional equity or to foster regional development only seems to result in the economic failure of the project. In fact, the extension of HSR networks to more remote and less densely populated areas has caused major financial problems for developers and management companies, who are consequently forced to cover huge deficits with operating income earned on the few profitable routes, if these exist at all in their networks. Despite this, HSR has not made any significant impact on regional development in these rural areas. Examples of this sequence can be found in virtually all network experiences, although not all of them have taken objectives of efficiency into consideration, not even at the start of their initial projects.

We may consider two large groups to exist in which efficiency has indeed played an important role. On the one hand, those that sought to alleviate the mobility of passengers on dense routes (Japan, France, Korea) so that modernization could allow these rail routes to compete with other modes of transportation; and on the other, those countries that used railway modernization as the ideal strategy to encourage freight transportation, either by providing for its high-speed transport and the connection of industrial centers with primary ports (Germany), or by displacing passengers to other, separate infrastructures, thereby freeing up greater capacity for freight traffic (China).

For all these reasons, the use of HSR technology in the United States should seek to solve significant problems of passenger rail congestion or lack of passenger rail capacity. The enormous investment costs, as well as the habitual incurring of debt and associated financial costs, can only be justified by huge time savings for a very high volume of users or freight, in such a way that the competitiveness of the territories increases with the addition of this new mode of transportation in respect to existing alternative modes. The most satisfying experiences have precisely been those that have achieved large time savings on very dense routes and where HSR has very marked competitive advantages in respect to the other modes of transportation with which it competes. Even so, only two clearly profitable routes exist in the world, the Tokyo–Osaka and the Paris–Lyon. A larger number of lines cover their operating costs and make an annual profit, although without recouping the investment on infrastructure.

A third motive behind the development of HSR in some experiences, such as the Italian one, is the competitive advantage railway seems to enjoy over its rivals because of the country's geographic characteristics and urban structure. This is the case for medium distances in which travel by road is slow and the plane doesn't achieve an efficient service or one superior to high-speed rail. In fact, there are only a limited number of city-to-city relations in Italy with high traffic density for which the offer of air transportation is an attractive alternative. Italy hoped to encourage a spread of benefits rather than concentrate them. The large distances that separate the primary hubs of population concentration in the United States, which furthermore enjoy high density in air traffic, do not seem to correspond to the Italian pattern.

Still within the context of general motivations, it is interesting to note, after a review of the experiences, that political objectives do not appear to have been a main driver of HSR development, with the significant exception of Spain. However, politics does seem to have influenced the structure of the network, the number and location of stations, and the extension of the networks to less populated rural zones. In Spain, "HSR political supply" from the national government has been fostered by huge foreign subsidies for construction from the European Union. In addition to this, "HSR political demand" from regional and local governments has been encouraged by the fact that the full costs of construction have been borne by the central government budget (with the help of those foreign subsidies). This might explain the ambitious plans for HSR extension in Spain, jointly with the arguments of national construction by way of the infrastructures defended in Bel (2011). On the other hand, the Japanese political structure—it's also the same in Spain—permits a measure of overrepresentation of rural territories, which decisively influenced the extension of HSR to less populated zones and thus to loss-making routes with the argument of promoting regional development. For a long time, rural districts were allocated more seats per resident than urban areas in the Japanese electoral system (Baker and Scheiner, 2007). The same occurs in the Spanish electoral system (Márquez and Ramírez, 1998). However, electoral systems do not favor rural and less populated areas in France (Criddle, 1992), Germany (Manow, 2007), and Italy (Ortona, Ottone, and Ponzano, 2005). Because of this, political incentives for central governments to extend the HSR network to rural and less populated areas are higher in Spain and Japan than they are in France, Germany, and Italy. Likewise, pressure from local politicians demanding the extension of HSR networks may be more effective in Spain and Japan for the same reason. The frequently used argument of territorial equality and regional development in these experiences encourages local demands and makes it difficult to define the limits of the extension of the network. Clearly, nobody wants to remain on the sidelines of prosperity, if, as governments argue, this is apparently associated with HSR.

Nonetheless, in other experiences, such as in Germany, we have found the influence of the political game in the definition of the route or the number and location of stations. In fact, political relations between different territories and the distribution of authority in decentralized countries often determine the design of their infrastructures, including HSR.

We do not think this is likely to happen in the United States to the same degree: First, in respect to the extension of networks to rural zones with low population density, because no foreign subsidies are available in this case, as occurred in the case of Spain. Second, the US federal government is offering only partial funding of construction costs, while the remaining costs have to be borne by states (and eventually local) governments. Still some degree of "political demand" can be expected from local governments as long as they are not required to confront large expenditures, as shown by the activism of the mayors of Los Angeles, Chicago, Orlando, and Albany in USCM (2010). Even so, once a project is proposed and even approved, local demands are likely to appear that aim to influence the path and design of the potential HSR route. If the argument used for the extension of the route is that of regional development, above and beyond questions of efficiency in the transportation, it is to be expected that no territory or local or regional political representative will want to be left out of such a windfall. However, we expect public debate to grow on the cost-benefit implications of HSR in the United States, particularly in a time of strong fiscal restrictions such as the present.

STRUCTURE, DESIGN, AND FUNCTIONS

Perhaps the first major decision to make is whether to run a joint passenger/freight network. Some countries have chosen to build high-speed lines exclusively for passenger services; others have chosen to share the upgraded tracks with freight transport even though this means renouncing higher speeds and accepting higher costs so as to promote industrial connections. As few economic impacts are directly attributable to passenger HSR, it seems reasonable to include freight transportation, especially in the United States where a much higher share of freight is transported by rail than in Europe and Japan. However, we must be cautious regarding the suitability of joint operation of passenger and freight traffic in the United States, because rail network and institutional structure for freight transportation in the United States is very different from those countries reviewed above. In the United States, the freight network has traditionally been under private ownership.[1] However, if HSR projects are supported only by passenger traffic, they will produce little—if not irrelevant—impacts on most areas served, unless HSR projects consider the private lines for freight. The international experience shows us that this passenger orientation can make sense as a separate infrastructure when it frees up freight train services, as was the goal of the development of Chinese HSR, or when the volume of passengers to transport is very high, as is the case in Japan.

Lower construction costs have been reported in those projects that have combined conventional rail with dedicated HSR tracks to reflect the level of traffic on a corridor or in order to access downtown areas. The rationale underpinning this strategy is the avoidance of the high costs of land expropriation that make it particularly expensive to build a dedicated railway through a city. Using conventional railways for this purpose alleviates the cost burden considerably. The investment cost rises, on the other hand, with the intensive use of viaducts and tunnels, which furthermore will be more necessary for routes that permit freight transportation.

In respect to this last point, the primary lesson here is the one affecting the network design and the decisions regarding which routes to implement. Routes have to be established between the most highly populated centers so as to ensure satisfactory occupancy rates and to guarantee that the service can break even, particularly in light of high construction and operation costs. This is the case in France, where HSR lines are centered on Paris to reflect the country's strong political, economic, and demographic centralization. Given the decentralized, regional structure of the United States, with its different mega-regions, a more decentralized network connecting these hubs would seem to make better sense. This is the case of the decentralized networks of Germany and China. The Spanish experience, in contrast, follows a design of centralization much more similar to the French design, with a degree of centralization around Madrid that finds little support from the patterns of mobility and economic activity in Spain, which has worrying consequences for the financial sustainability of the network.

On the other hand, the design should connect poles of large population concentration with the fewest number of stations. These stations are only desirable when they incorporate a large volume of passengers into the network and thereby justify the reduction in the speed of the HSR service, regardless of political pressures from the different territories.

A further point to bear in mind is the fact that European and Japanese downtown areas are denser than their American counterparts. For this reason, American HSR projects will not reap the benefits of one of the main comparative advantages of HSR, namely, city-center connection. We have seen that the location of the HSR station can be crucial to achieving a comparative advantage over air transportation. Thanks to HSR links, commuting from airports can be avoided, as can road congestion at the entrance to big cities. In the American case, however, it is necessary to travel from residential areas to the downtown area, which makes better local transportation connections necessary or more park-and-ride services.

Finally, it should be pointed out that HSR stations located outside the downtown district and without adequate multimodal connections are usually unsuccessful. Particularly the choice of a location far from the center and in underdeveloped zones chosen with the aim of making use of the investment in HSR to encourage growth there has failed over and over again in a range of experiences. Furthermore, connection difficulties with the city center sharply weaken HSR's competitiveness with other modes of transportation.

INVESTMENTS AND PROFITABILITY

The development of an HSR network entails huge construction and operation costs. The construction of high-speed rail is probably the largest spending project on infrastructures ever realized in each one of the described experiences. Data collected on the cost of the main routes in service or planned are of a magnitude hardly comparable to any other infrastructure. This is why justification for such an effort and the expected social return are so important. This investment is made in most cases through budgetary resources and a high use of debt. By doing so, the effort is deferred in time in the hope that the operation of the service will evolve satisfactorily in the middle and long term. Nonetheless, as we have indicated, only two routes are profitable and have recouped their investment.

The key decision at the outset, as discussed above, concerns the complementariness of carrying passengers and freight. Complementariness with freight transport increases costs, since the track gradients have to be more carefully controlled, and usually implies a greater use of tunnels. However, making freight carriage compatible with that of passengers can boost industrial productivity and increase connectivity between industrial areas and airports, ports, and logistic areas.

Various costs need to be taken into account when considering the additional expenditure incurred from building HSR lines. Land expropriation costs increase the initial investment substantially, and this is a key factor when HSR lines enter densely populated areas and downtown districts. In cases where the station has been located far from the center to reduce such investment and to develop other zones, the choice has eroded the competitiveness of HSR as a transportation mode, resulting in a significant trade-off in the public choice regarding HSR design.

From the strict perspective of costs, some countries such as France chose to use conventional lines to access their major cities, given that construction and expropriation costs would have been exorbitant, which produces a cost savings in exchange for a reduction in speed.

Similarly, the use of bridges and tunnels notably increases construction costs, which is why an oleography of the territory is essential to determine the necessary amount of the investment. Another key factor is the maximum velocity of the chosen design, given that marginal costs increase considerably with each unitary increase of speed.

Cost overruns are also one of the most common features, as shown by numerous examples, and run high in almost all instances; administrations should be fully aware that eventual construction costs might far outstrip initial expectations. A review of the various experiences demonstrates that cost overruns are a constant that enormously damage the financial expectations of the projects and the viability of their managers, who have frequently been choked by excessive debt and associated financial costs. These cost overruns appear to arise from four different sources. First, from the contracting method based on bilateral negotiations without public competitions. Second, from the specificities of the projects in relation to interconnection with existing lines, and the orographical complexity and seismic activity of the territory. In fact, the risk of earthquakes has caused huge cost increases for safety reasons in the Asian experiences, a matter that should also be considered in relation to projects located on the West Coast of the United States. Thirdly, from the environmental adaptation of the projects and regulations concerning the landscape. In the German case, significant concern for HSR's impact on the environment has also been a reason for cost overruns. Finally, from the influence and intervention of different political actors with often contradictory interests.

One issue that certainly should not be ignored is the political pressures that are brought to bear and which can lead to incremental costs and decreasing benefits. These political pressures, mentioned previously in relation to objectives and motivations, might emerge from the supply side—with governments placing greater emphasis on political interests than on satisfying transport needs—or from the demand side, with local and regional governments that might exert pressures for an HSR station, even if this runs contrary to sound transportation rationale. All of these factors can combine to raise construction costs and lower the average commercial speed. The economic and financial results of the project will suffer from the side of costs and investment but can also be weakened from the demand side, and thus in respect to revenue, if the political influence on the route and stations undermine the development of HSR as an efficient means of transportation. Such influence damages high-speed rail's competitiveness in respect to alternative modes of travel. For this reason, it is important not to let technical decisions concerning the structure and design of the network incorporate elements of political demand and offer, but rather for these decisions to be based on a strict concept of efficiency in the sole pursuit of goals of an integrated transportation policy that does not stand in the way of the development of other modes. To this end, the potential volume of a route and the efficiency of existing modes are decisive in justifying the enormous investment.

According to estimates calculated by de Rus and Nombela (2007, p. 21), investment in HSR is difficult to justify when the expected first-year demand is below eight to ten million passengers for a line of 312.5 miles, a distance at which HSR's competitive advantage over road and air transport is clear.[2] In line with this criteria, the European Commission stated in 2008 that "only under exceptional circumstances (a combination of low construction costs plus high time savings) could a new HSR line be justified with a level of patronage below six million passengers per annum in the opening year; with typical construction costs and time savings, a minimum figure of nine million passengers per annum is likely to be needed" (European Commission, 2008, p. 84).[3] The economic rationale for new HSR infrastructure depends heavily then on the expected volume of demand. Thus, building an HST line should only be considered in the case of links with high demand expectations for rail travel, i.e., routes connecting densely populated metropolitan areas, with severe problems of road congestion, and a deficient air connection. In this regard, the economic rationale for the four HSR lines that have been given priority in the United States is by no means clear.

This economic framework casts doubts on the use of Public-Private Partnerships (PPPs) in HSR projects. This is clearly illustrated by the Italian and the Taiwanese cases. In Italy, the HSR was originally conceived as a PPP but was later nationalized owing to a shortage of additional private investments. In Taiwan, HSR was the world's largest Build-Operate-and-Transfer concession in terms of volume of investment. Unfortunately, the Taiwan experience will be used in manuals and case studies in graduate courses around the world due to its devastating financial failure, which required government backing and intervention to save it from bankruptcy. The difficulties encountered in recouping costs and the need for higher subsidies have increased government's role in HSR, which originally began as private or public-private initiatives with promises of steering clear of public investment. Nonetheless, the state has repeatedly assumed the risks of both construction and demand.

Not only public-private projects, however, have produced worrying results from the financial point of view. Another of the most spectacular cases is China, particularly the financial disaster of its Ministry of Railways. The state enterprise that has most energetically extended its high-speed rail network in recent years and which boasts of being the world leader in terms of the length of its network, is on the verge of bankruptcy, even while it continues to be used as a reference and benchmark by politicians and governments in the West who are impressed by the Chinese extension of HSR. Spain, which is currently adjusting its national budget at around €40 billion, has spent this same sum of euros on an HSR network whose very small volumes of passengers will make public aid absolutely necessary, placing enormous weight on taxpayers.

In conclusion, HSR is a massive project from the point of view of investment that involves an enormous debt load for public finances. The strategic decisions made concerning its design—route, functionality, stations, tunnels, viaducts, speed, complementariness with conventional lines, contracting methods, environmental regulations, etc.—directly and decisively affect the amount of the investment. For this reason, it is necessary for this design to adapt to existing patterns of mobility, connecting only those hubs with significant market potential and in cases where HSR has enough competitive advantages over other modes of transportation. The mobilization of such enormous resources can only be considered for a design centered on the return of this investment and with a limited cost overrun. Even with private participation and investment, the public sector is usually called upon to rescue managing companies that make poor predictions of demand or costs. For this reason, whether the projects are public or public-private, the social and financial profitability of the projects should be considered as the primary goal.

DEMAND AND MODAL COMPETITION

Despite the enormous success of HSR on some specific corridors, particularly in the initial lines of the pioneering countries, we have verified in our review that one of the constant features of the most recent HSR experiences is overestimation of demand. Striking cases have been commented on in the experiences of China, Taiwan, Korea, Spain, etc. It is common to find a demand for the first year of operation around half that of the demand predicted in the financial economic plans often used to justify the introduction of HSR technology. This overestimation can be due either to errors in prediction, or else to the strategic desire of governments—particularly in cases where private financing is required—to defend the economic viability of their decisions and investments. This lower-than-expected demand has been particularly affected by the economic crisis, which has modified the macro variables used in the previously made predictions.

Only on the densest routes have we seen that HSR demand has been high since its beginning and has significantly increased in the initial years. In fact, it is common to find increases in demand in the first two years of HSR because of its novelty and the need for a period of time to pass for its complete development on any of the existing routes. Nevertheless, in numerous experiences, we have seen that demand has a difficult time reaching the expected levels, apart from those cases where the congestion of conventional services limited the development of traffic density on the corridor. Such was the case with the initial Japanese and French routes. Even so, other experiences based on the increase of capacity on congested routes have contributed much lower than expected volumes of passengers, as was the case with the first Korean route, which only achieved 46 percent of the expected traffic. In all of these experiences, the introduction of HSR provided an efficient mode of transportation on a corridor with important problems of capacity. In the other experiences not tied to motivations of efficiency, this demand has developed in a much less satisfactory way.

In all cases, we have seen that the principal advantage and strongpoint of HSR is its spectacular time savings in respect to conventional train services. Despite the fact that this saving is gained through the enormous mobilization of resources, it means a significant competitive advantage and thus an improvement in the productivity of railway transportation. In fact, HSR provides a highly reliable, fast service with average delays of only a very few minutes. It can furthermore offer considerable advantages in terms of comfort, can allow passengers to use their electronic devices while in transit, and subjects them to less rigorous security restrictions and controls than in air transportation.

Its competitive advantage in terms of time is less evident when compared to air transportation. In fact, the conditions that determine this competitiveness are based on the distance of the route, the average velocity—affected by the route and the stations—and the price. HSR offers similar door-to-door timings in comparison with air transportation on routes of around 400 miles. Its comparative advantage would seem to lie on routes that range from between 100 to 500 miles. In terms of time, the limit is set at around three hours of HSR travel. Over shorter distances, HSR finds it difficult to compete with road transportation, while over longer distances air transportation takes the upper hand.

Nonetheless, it is necessary to keep in mind that the important thing in intermodal competition is not only the "in vehicle" time but also the door-to-door time, as we have noted. For this reason, the location of stations and the connectivity of these stations with city centers is a decisive aspect of HSR competitiveness.

Price is another determining factor. We have seen how in some experiences, such as the Chinese, the difference in price between conventional rail services and HSR has displaced passengers with low purchasing power away from the railway to the road—bus lines—instead of feeding HSR, which implies a clearly inequitable impact and a limitation for the load factor of the services. In fact, in most of the experiences, we have seen how the incorporation of HSR has led to the dismantling of conventional services, which means the substitution not only of a slower mode but also a less expensive one. The most successful experiences, such as the Japanese, have adapted the restructuring of conventional services so that these function as feeders to the primary hubs of the HSR network, which demonstrates an integral design of transportation policy in Japan that aims to take advantage of its complementariness. An integrated approach as well as a multimodal one seems to be the spirit that exists behind the design of the German network, which hopes to complement air transportation rather than compete against it, with the inclusion of the principal airports within its HSR network. The aim by doing so is to complement long-distance trips by air transportation with short and medium-distance trips by HSR.

On the other hand, the difference in price between HSR and air transportation does not follow a clear pattern, although lower prices are more commonly found in HSR, especially if these receive government subsidies or don't need to recover the investment costs of the infrastructure. Nevertheless, prices can be very similar for routes where competition is stronger. For this reason, low-cost airlines that exploit routes with high traffic density seem to compete better against HSR. In contrast, for long routes where HSR loses competitiveness in time, air transportation is more successful.

The modal distribution of traffic has been affected by the introduction of HSR in all of the cases studied, having the greatest impact on the airline industry. Immediately following the inauguration of HSR service, and even before HSR enters into service, it is common to find a drastic reduction of frequencies, as well as the cancellation of various routes that had been served by air transportation. In all of the experiences, a significant drop has been observed in the market share held by air transport after the arrival of HSR. Similarly, road transportation has suffered from competition from HSR, albeit to a lesser extent. Logically, this reduction in market share of the airlines has been perceived only on routes of distances of less than 500 miles. Problems in HSR services or the competitive pressure generated by low-cost airlines provide the industry with breathing space in the face of HSR's arrival. In fact, the change of business models in the sector of regular airlines with the emergence of low-cost models that exploit economies of density in point-to-point services began in the 1990s in the United States but didn't reach Europe and the rest of the world in a significant way until the 2000s. For this reason, the significant impacts assumed by the industry were very important in the experiences prior to the change in the air transportation sector and particularly its liberalization. At present, the strong presence of airlines with these characteristics limits HSR's capacity to capture traffic in contrast to the records obtained in the pioneering HSR experiences.

In most cases, therefore, HSR obtains traffic that was already transported by an alternative mode, while its capacity to induce new demand is modest and limited. For a country such as the United States, with a strong presence of air transportation, a negative impact for short routes of less than 500 miles is to be expected. However, the large air corridors in the United States are located at much greater distances, and it will thus be very difficult for HSR to attract passengers. In other corridors, the presence of low-cost airlines will make it difficult for HSR to achieve a significant market share.

Finally, the location of stations in relation to the population concentrations of large cities, as well as their number—which affects the speed of the route—will have an important effect in determining the capacity of HSR to compete with air transportation. In experiences where the population is more concentrated in city centers, HSR will enjoy greater accessibility and, therefore, have a competitive edge over air transportation, normally located far from these centers. However, in countries with a low population concentration in these centers, such as in the United States, HSR ceases to enjoy this advantage of location and accessibility.

ECONOMIC AND REGIONAL IMPACTS

It is consistently reported that HSR does not generate any new activities, nor does it attract new firms and investment but rather helps to consolidate and promote ongoing processes as well as to facilitate intra-organizational journeys for those firms and institutions for whom mobility is essential. In fact, we have seen that HSR is capable, above all, of displacing passengers from other modes of transportation but generates little new demand. For this reason, it is essential that it offer a significant productivity gain to those passengers switching from an alternative mode of transportation to HSR.

It is perhaps worth pointing out that only those cities with a significant weight of services in their economic structure appear to benefit from HSTs. In other words agricultural and industrial activities are indifferent to HSR stops. Evidence of this lack of economic impact is the little attention given to HSR railway stations by firms in their location decisions, even those of service companies, as we have seen even in successful experiences such as the French one.

In fact, for regions and cities whose economic conditions compare unfavorably with those of their neighbors, a connection to the HSR line may even result in economic activities being drained away and an overall negative impact (Givoni, 2006; Van den Berg and Pol 1998; Thompson 1994). Medium-size cities may well suffer the most as a result of the economic attraction of the more dynamic, bigger cities. Indeed, Haynes (1997) points out that growth is sometimes at the expense of other centers of concentration. Several reports and the reviewed experiences show how the centralization of activities happens in big hubs, especially in those belonging to the services sector.

Some of the studies that have defended the positive impact of HSR have done so on routes fully justified by the high volume of traffic and the need to solve structural problems of congestion. The clearest example is the HSR line joining the cities of Cologne and Frankfurt in Germany. This route appears to generate a positive impact, according to the already mentioned article by Ashlfeld and Feddersen (2010), by decongesting a very densely transited route, which has favored the development of its GDP and improved accessibility to peripheral territories. However, the impact occurred with HSR's arrival, and at present the economic growth of the area of study seems to have returned to its long-term pattern.

Besides business journeys, tourism is the first sector to show an immediate effect following the inauguration of an HSR line. Indeed, the number of tourists in cities linked to the network tends to increase thanks to this alternative mode of transport. However, the number of overnight stays falls due to easier same-day travel, which also has a marked impact on business trips. Therefore, HSR impacts on the tourist industry by promoting the number of leisure travelers to connected cities, but at the same time it reduces the number of nights spent in hotels. Finally, the reports reviewed also show that HSR had only marginal impacts on population and housing growth. At any rate, there are numerous and important methodological limitations in the studies that have evaluated the impact of HSR on population growth.

Demand pressure for receiving HSR projects, however, still arises from the territory, affecting the network's design, cost, and mobility impacts. In fact, in Japan and Spain, economic expectations led to political pressure for HSR stations, while in France officials were immune to this. In Germany, we have seen how politics have influenced the number and location of stations. As we have explained, the political and electoral system could explain these differences.

ENVIRONMENTAL ADVANTAGES

There has yet to be a detailed, systematic evaluation of the impact of an expanding HST network on the reduction in CO_2 emissions at either an aggregate or country level. However, some information is available on the environmental effects of HSR, particularly as regards its energy consumption and emissions, although some of the experiences are difficult to compare.

For example, according to estimates conducted by van Essen et al. (2003), energy consumed per MJ/seat-mile by air transport is 240 percent higher than that attributable to HSR. However, the energy consumed by HSR is 12.8 percent higher than a petrol-driven car when traveling on the expressway, 55.9 percent higher than a diesel-driven car on the expressway, and 140.9 percent higher than an intercity train. Similarly, the recent paper by Lukaszewicz and Andersson (2006) finds a 32 percent difference between conventional and high-speed rail using KWh/seat-km as a measure. Other estimates (van Wee, van den Brink, and Nijland, 2003) conclude that while energy use and emissions for HSR are much higher than for conventional trains, they are relatively similar to those for cars and buses.

The studies made for Japan, the country with the longest HSR experience, shows that energy consumption per passenger-mile is a quarter less than that of air transportation, and a sixth less than that of automobiles (Matsumoto, 2007). Its emissions are a fifth part of the emissions produced by the airplane and an eighth part of those generated by cars. These savings are at least partially compensated for by the increase in traffic associated with HSR, given that the availability of seat-miles tends to rise with HSR in respect to the situation prior to its introduction.

While the studies seem clear in respect to the environmental advantage of HSR in relation to air transportation, the relation to the conventional train is less clear, although the studies that correct for passenger-miles or seat-miles tend to find a measure of advantage for HSR in respect to the conventional train. In the most favorable analysis for HSR for Spain—conducted by García-Alvarez (2007)—HSTs and conventional trains were reported as producing similar emissions on two of the lines analyzed, while the conventional train was much more efficient on the remaining line. The distance of the route is decisive in this result, given that energy consumption and emission of gases are greatly affected by the vehicle's acceleration and deceleration.

Clearly, the overall impact of HSR on energy consumption is heavily dependent on the source of its traffic—whether it is newly generated or attracted from previously existing modes (and, in the case of road transportation, on whether it replaces cars or buses). The environmental benefit will unquestionably depend primarily on the degree to which it is capable of substituting journeys, above all, the most polluting journeys, which come from air transportation. In contrast, if it primarily displaces passengers from the conventional train, which is dismantled with the arrival of HSR, the environmental impact of the operation will be much more debatable and even negative.

In fact, recent literature is beginning to indicate that HSR is not a particularly useful tool for fighting CO_2 emissions, at least when compared to the modernization of conventional rail services, which can travel at high speeds without the intensive energy consumption or polluting gas emissions linked to HSR.

Above and beyond this, the main concern is the construction of infrastructure. Building a new and separate HSR line involves significant CO_2 emissions that environmental HSR analyses do not take into account (together with the environmental impact caused by land use, noise, and visual disruption, among others), as well as a larger use of energy than during HSR's operation (which can be as much as fifteen times higher, according to Ebeling, 2005). In fact, Kageson (2009, p. 25) concludes, after presenting evidence comparing the environmental impact of different transport modes, that the reduction of CO_2 through HSR construction, "is small and it may take decades for it to compensate for the emissions caused by construction [. . .] Indeed, it will take too long for traffic to offset the emissions caused by building the line. Under these circumstances it may be better to upgrade an existing line to accommodate for somewhat higher speeds as this would minimize emissions from construction and cut emissions from train traffic compared to HSR."

Along these same lines we find the contribution by Chester and Horvath (2010), quoted in chapter 1 in the section relating to HSR in California. Their life-cycle analysis shows how HSR presents very high emissions when the construction period is taken into consideration, even higher in some pollutants, such as sulfur dioxide (SO_2). These authors conclude that the payback of energy utilization and greenhouse gases with average loading assumptions would occur after twenty-eight years for energy utilization and seventy-one for greenhouse gases in California.

Adopting Maglev technologies instead of the standard high-speed rail technology most used in the world would imply an even more intense use of energy and CO_2 emissions per passenger-mile, some four times higher than the standard high-speed train in its operation—and without including its construction.

The principal source of electricity generation also implies a greater or lesser ecological impact in terms of emissions, as does the distance traveled by the HST. For short distances, the energy use at the acceleration (start) and deceleration (end) of HSR journeys weakens its advantage in energy consumption, while on long routes this greater consumption is diluted by improved consumption on the journey.

Another frequently recurring externality in HSR experiences is the barrier and noise effect. These environmental problems need additional regulation and specific technical actions to lessen their negative effects, which impede public acceptance of HSR as it passes through urban zones.

Among the international experiences, the German case has placed great emphasis on the environmental aspects and consequences of HSR. This interest has made the processes of planning, design, and construction more complex, generating cost overruns in some projects. One of the strategies used to limit environmental impact was to follow the route of German expressways almost in parallel, which in the United States could imply the use of the corridors used by interstate highways.

Finally, HSR is a highly safe mode of transportation but is clearly not immune to accidents. Some of these have been particularly serious, such as the recent accident in July of 2011 in China in which forty people died. The very high speed and doubts over the quality of the equipment and infrastructure are the primary factors determining the probability of HSR accidents occurring. This has motivated—along with the financial problems and corruption—the rethinking of the extension of the high-speed

Table 10.1. Summary of Lessons Offered by International Experiences

	Summary of Lessons
Motivation and Objectives	HSR has to be devoted to solve congestion in corridors between large populated cities. Political or administrative objectives and extending lines for regional equity and development lead to the economic failure of the project.
Structure, Design, and Functions	In spite of the characteristics of the American rail structure, the international experience shows that passenger-oriented HSR has a minimum economic impact on the territory served, unless it solves congestion problems providing huge time savings. Freight oriented HSR is more expensive but might produce higher productivity impacts. Lower construction cost is associated with combining HSR and conventional rail, particularly in the entrance to big cities. Routes have to be established according to demand (commercial basis) and should reproduce mobility patterns. Adequate multimodal connections are needed—transportation modes must be designed using an integral strategy. The lower the number the stations, the most competitive is HSR. Also, the location of stations must be well connected to population centers. Conventional services should feed HSR hubs, and therefore coordination across services is essential. HSR must do something new or much better than competitive modes to make it worthwhile.
Investment and Profitability	The development of an HSR network entails huge construction and operation costs (especially important land expropriation cost, bridges, and tunnels). In most experiences, it becomes the largest infrastructure project in terms of investment in each national history. The key decision that affects cost concerns complementarities (passenger/freight) and the extent of combination with existing conventional rail. Political pressures (connection and station costs) can increase HSR cost and constrains its profitability due to opportunism or private interests from both politicians and bureaucrats. Also environmental regulations and, of course, the topography of territory and seismic activity. Only two routes in the world are profitable. Some others recoup operating costs and get operating benefits though do not recover infrastructure investment. In most cases, there are significant overruns. Investment is executed without cross subsidies from profitable routes, if any. The extension of the network to rural areas without demand produces financial crisis and debt crisis that require funds and rescue by the state. Private participation experiences are very unsatisfactory, and taxpayers usually cover in the end cost and demand risks.

Demand and Modal Competition	Provide significant travel time savings when compared to conventional rail services, but similar door-to-door timings are reported for air transportation on routes of around 400 miles. Demand usually increases in the first two years. However, lower-than-predicted demand is not unusual in recent projects, affecting financial expectations of developers and managers. Modal distribution is affected when HSR starts operation, with greatest impact on the airline industry for routes below 500 miles. Low-cost carriers are able to compete with HSR, limiting the ability of HSR to gain market share. Conventional services are usually dismantled, and prices for interurban services increase.
Economic and Regional Effects	HSR does not generate any new activities, nor does it attract new firms and investment, but rather it helps to consolidate and promote ongoing processes as well as to facilitate intra-organizational journeys for which mobility is essential. Regions and cities whose economic conditions compare unfavorably with those of their neighbors, a connection to the HSR may even result in economic activities being drained away and an overall negative impact. Medium-size cities may well be the ones to suffer most due to the centralization of activities in large nodes. Tourism and the services sector are the only activities favored, while no effects are reported for industrial and agricultural. We only expect economic impacts when congestion is relieved or time savings are spread to a large volume of passengers and freight.
Environmental Impacts	Energy consumption and CO_2 emissions are lower for HSR than for air transportation. However, mixed results are reported in the rest of modes. For instance, they are also larger for HSR than for conventional rail per seat-mile. In fact, it is necessary to wait more than three decades to compensate energy and pollution generated during construction.

rail network in China. While the risk can never be zero, HSR offers a very high level of safety (see table 10.1).

NOTES

1. Except for the transitory period in which Consolidated Rail Corporation, commonly known as Conrail, was operating under government ownership; Conrail was created in 1976 to take over the potentially profitable lines of bankrupt carriers and was privatized in 1987.

2. De Rus and Nombela's computations take into account actual construction, rolling stock, maintenance and operating costs of European HSR lines, average values of time, potential travel time savings, and a 5 percent discount rate.

3. This is the minimum level of demand from which a positive economic net present value could be expected when new capacity does not provide additional benefits beyond time savings from diverted and generated demand. This exercise implies several assumptions on demand growth, value of time, and traffic diversion generated.

11

Conclusion

Desires, Beliefs, and Reality

The technological revolution of the railway has been accompanied by enormous myths and beliefs about its contribution to society and the economy. High-speed rail is unquestionably a technological advance that has become a symbol of modernity. However, the review of the international experiences made in this book shows that the conditions necessary for this infrastructure and its transportation services to have a positive impact, economically and socially, are enormously restrictive. Thanks to a highly successful start, with the inauguration of service on corridors with enormous traffic densities and clear problems of congestion and lack of capacity, HSR quickly became a success and gained worldwide recognition. With this, HSR became a desirable technology situated on the technological frontier of ground transportation.

The success of the pioneering experiences in Japan and France had a strongly contagious effect that led to the copying of the HSR model in different countries over the following decades, without due consideration, in some countries, of the suitability and appropriateness of HSR in relation to the particular characteristics of these countries' mobility and existing transportation system. In this book, we have seen how a lack of consideration of what HSR can or cannot offer in reality, or a view based on myths and beliefs that are out of sync with the reality of functioning HSR projects, has been the source of huge financial debacles and the failure of HSR as a transportation strategy. Understanding that HSR is not an appropriate strategy in all places and at all times, and thus to accept the differences of each country in terms of mobility and fiscal capacity, is essential if one wishes to avoid making an error that will compromise the public treasury for decades, with the resulting burden placed on the taxpayer. For this reason, it seems necessary on many occasions to have the courage—and the prudence—to renounce the "modernity" offered by HSR.

This book has aimed to provide the reader with information on the main issues that policymakers must think about when considering the possibility of adopting HSR technology for their countries. A number of obvious lessons can be drawn from the cases reviewed here. The first is the need to understand whether or not demographic and mobility characteristics allow HSR to be a highly competitive mode of transportation in respect to other modes. To be so, HSR must be able to do something new, or fundamentally much better than the other modes. This means it can provide large time savings that can be spread out or shared among a large volume of passengers. It is necessary, therefore, for the project to take into consideration the specific characteristics of the urban patterns and economic structure of the country, including its traffic patterns, because of the overriding importance of a country's mobility characteristics. Countries that have ignored or given little importance to the characteristics of their mobility or city structure and have been obsessed with the goal of modernizing their network through HSR will suffer (or already suffer) serious financial problems. Some are already suffering. Others will do so very soon.

This is so because the cost of HSR is immense. The second lesson here is related to the investment necessary for carrying out an HSR project. In most experiences—if not all—the implementation of HSR has been the project with the largest volume of investment in transportation infrastructure in the history of each country. This demonstrates that HSR is not just any project but rather one whose importance to and burden on public finances is highly significant and can condition them severely. This makes it necessary for its contribution to justify the enormous collective effort that it always imposes on the government, which is to say, on taxpayers, given that taxpayers are the final guarantors of an infrastructure as strategic and highly expensive as HSR.

For all these reasons, cost considerations are of central importance when making choices concerning HSR projects and their implementation. The fixed costs of HSR investment are huge and cost overruns notoriously high. In addition, political factors (on the supply as well as on the demand side) can contribute to further increasing costs. This political pressure can be important where rural districts are favored by the electoral system in terms of parliamentary seats per inhabitants. However, benevolent politicians could also accommodate the project to balance it between citizen (potential user) needs and the taxpayer's welfare, but this requires the absence of private interests in the design of their policy. Also, the execution of efficient projects requires bureaucrats and policymakers who are free from the influence of private interests.

With such a high cost, the potential demand for HSR services must be exceptionally high, as it was in the pioneering experiences, in order to make investment in HSR socially profitable. This means its main targets must be those corridors that link densely populated metropolitan areas, which suffer severe congestion problems and deficient air links. These constraints also hinder the use of PPPs, and governments must be prepared to intervene in constructing their HSR networks. In fact, another lesson is that PPPs in relation to HSR have failed and do not seem to be the right path for obtaining financing for an HSR project. The enormous risks in demand and construction seem to be the primary reasons for this failure—unexpected cost overruns and lower-than-predicted demands—which usually must be shouldered by taxpayers.

Another lesson we must highlight is that in almost all experiences networks have been extended—in most cases because of the success of the first routes—to less populated regions with lower potential demand. In doing so, the profitability of the network has been weakened even further, subsidies have increased, and in many experiences even the manager or developer of the network has suffered severe financing and debt crises. In these cases, the myth of economic prosperity and territorial development associated with HSR has acted as a catalyst for territorial demands and territorial pressure to influence the HSR projects.

Most of the studies analyzed, however, seem to indicate that HSR, particularly when oriented to passenger service, contributes practically nothing to these territories, especially if problems of congestion or lack of capacity in the face of a mobility demand limited by capacity prior to HSR are not solved. Only in the services sector—in some specific cases, such as tourism, although also with mixed results and very dependent on the already existing attraction of an area—does HSR seem to have contributed benefits. Nonetheless, the myths about the attraction of businesses and thus about the locating of economic activity or improvements in productivity, do not seem to be upheld by the real data and results in those experiences that have been more or less evaluated, even in the pioneering experiences.

It is necessary to emphasize, however, that HSR is not neutral in the distribution of economic activity and population between hubs of different sizes. Most of the studies have found a relocation of activity favorable to the large hubs. Thus, another myth associated with HSR, the notion that this infrastructure distributes activity to less developed zones, turns out to be false as activity becomes concentrated in the strongest hubs with the most economic activity. HSR, therefore, is not an instrument for spreading out and sharing activity in a territory but rather operates in the opposite way.

Finally, we cannot end these conclusions without commenting on one of the most significant myths that always accompanies HSR, and which is very present in the current debate on HSR in the United States. Is HSR an environmentally friendly form of transportation? While HSR is more environmentally efficient than air transportation and the use of private car with low occupancy (not so with respect to bus transport), it is responsible for more CO_2 emissions and energy consumption than conventional intercity trains when corrections are made for use or for the offer provided (passenger-miles or seat-miles). Thus, the source of the trips drawn by HSR from other modes of transportation is essential to determine its environmental impact. A strong attraction of journeys that previously traveled by air will favor its environmental impact, while a simple displacement of passengers from conventional rail to high-speed rail will have a negative impact on the environment. In the first case, the substitution of traffic by HSR in relation to air traffic will primarily depend on the distance of the route. According to all experiences, the airline industry is most impacted by the arrival of HSR but only for routes of less than about 450 miles. Beyond this distance, air transportation is indifferent to the introduction of HSR. Below this distance, furthermore, low-cost companies exist on routes with very dense traffic, and—based on their price advantage—they seem to be able to compete successfully with HSR, which determines the limits of the capacity of attraction of HSR in respect to air traffic on these routes.

The second result, which demonstrates the greater efficiency of improved conventional rail, has led many academics to advise using modern conventional rail instead of HSR. Doing so permits high speeds (renouncing the highest speeds of HSR), but energy consumption and emissions are much lower. In contrast, we have demonstrated how in most countries after the arrival of HSR these services have been dismantled, and only in some experiences they play a role as feeders to the primary HSR hubs.

HSR is not a very useful environmental policy. But not only for its lower efficiency compared to conventional rail, or by the fact that this efficiency depends on the way in which HSR is removing passengers. But also because many analyses and evaluations usually ignore two fundamental aspects of HSR projects. On the one hand, consideration is made of the comparative advantage of HSR thanks to its technological improvements, without taking into account that the other transportation modes are also improving their technologies to make them more efficient and more favorable to the environment. To ignore this is to favor the impact of HSR over other modes, as if these were stagnating in their technological development. Secondly, however, and much more importantly, the environmental debate of HSR has for a long time ignored the life-cycle focus, particularly ignoring the period of construction of the infrastructure. During the construction phase of HSR, the volume of emissions emitted and energy consumption is enormous and very difficult to recover in scenarios of average energy and emission savings made during the useful life span of HSR. Only with very high densities of demand, in addition to a very high degree of substitution of the airplane, is this possible and—at any rate—at a very high economic cost.

This work aims to distinguish between the realities and beliefs or myths associated with HSR, in order to provide the necessary information and assessment about what has happened in the world with HSR. This should enrich the debate on what can and cannot be expected from the introduction of HSR in countries that are currently debating their model of ground transportation.

Just as we began this concluding chapter, it is important to emphasize that HSR is a technological advance; a great idea, very convenient to passengers because of its speed, comfort, and reliability. Nonetheless, it is extraordinarily expensive and thus implies a huge opportunity cost. It is also a decisive social choice. To be able to take a position regarding this social choice, it is necessary to keep in mind, as shown throughout this book, that HSR will make contributions to the territory under extremely restrictive conditions that can only be satisfied by very exceptional corridors in the world. For this reason, countries without these characteristics would do well to renounce this symbol of modernity, adequately provide for the social effort implied by its implementation, and safeguard their public finances. Definitively, it is a question of being reasonable when the moment arrives to consider these very modern and sophisticated projects, which, however, are very likely to end up becoming a nightmare for taxpayers, present and future.

Bibliography

ADB (Asian Development Bank). *Best Practices for Private Sector Investment in Railways.* Asian Development Bank, 2006.

ADIF (Administrador de Infraestructuras Ferroviarias). *Memoria Económica. Ejercicio 2010.* Madrid: Adif, 2011.

Airline Leader. "Airlines Acknowledge Threat of High Speed Rail." *Airline Leader* (May 7, 2011): 13.

Albalate, Daniel, and Germà Bel. "Cuando la economía no importa: Auge y esplendor de la Alta Velocidad en España." *Revista de Economía Aplicada* 19, no. 55 (2011): 171–90.

———. "High Speed Rail: Lessons for Policy Makers from Experiences Abroad." *Public Administration Review* (forthcoming).

Amos, Paul, Dick Bullock, and Jitendra Sondhi. *High-Speed Rail: The Fast Track to Economic Development?* Washington, DC: The World Bank, 2010.

Andersson, David Emmanuel, Johnson Fu, and Oliver F. Shyr. "Does High Speed Rail Accessibility Influence Residential Property Prices? Hedonic Estimates from Southern Taiwan." *Journal of Transport Geography* 18, no. 1 (2010): 166–74.

Aoki, Eiichi, Mitsuhido Imashiro, Shinichi Kato, and Yasuo Wakuda. *A History of Japanese Railways 1872–1999.* Tokyo: East Japan Railway Culture Foundation, 2000.

Arduin, Jean-Pierre. "Las líneas de Alta Velocidad y el acondicionamiento del territorio." *Obras Públicas* 22 (1991): 22–23.

Arduin, Jean-Pierre, and Jincheng Ni. "French TGV network development." *Japan Railway & Transport Review* 40 (2005): 22–28.

Ashfeld, Gabriel, and Arne Feddersen. "From Periphery to Core: Economic Adjustments to High Speed Rail." Working paper MPRA (Munich Personal RePEc Archive), September 2010.

Baker, Andy, and Ethan Scheiner. "Electoral System Effects and Ruling Party Dominance in Japan: A Counterfactual Simulation Based on Adaptive Parties." *Electoral Studies* 26, no. 2 (2007): 477–91.

Bazin, Sylvie, Christophe Beckerich, and Marie Delaplace. "Analyse prospective des impacts de la Ligne à Grande Vitesse Est-européenne dans l'agglomération rémoise et en région Champagne-Ardenne." Report final de recherche pour le Conseil Régional Champagne-Ardenne, Université de Reims Champagne-Ardenne, 2006.

Bel, Germà. *La demanda de transporte en España: Competencia intermodal sobre el ferrocarril interurbano.* Madrid: Instituto de Estudios del Transporte y las Comunicaciones (IETC), 1994.

———. "Política de transporte: ¿Más recursos o mejor gestión?" *Economistas,* no. 111 (2007): 279–84.

———. "Las infraestructuras y los servicios de transporte." In *La Ley de Economía Sostenible y las reformas estructurales. 25 propuestas,* edited by Manuel Bagués, Jesús Fernández-Villaverde, and Luís Garicano, 102–7. Madrid: FEDEA, 2010.

———. "La racionalización de las infraestructuras de transporte en España." *Cuadernos Económicos de ICE* 80 (2010): 211–28.

———. "Infrastructure and Nation Building: The Regulation and Financing of Network Transportation Infrastructures in Spain (1720–2010)." *Business History* 53, no. 5 (2011): 688–705.

———. *Infrastructure and the Political Economy of Nation Building in Spain, 1720–2010.* London: Sussex Academic Press, 2012.

Beria, Paolo, and Raffaele Grimaldi. "An Early Evaluation of Italian High Speed Projects." *Trimestrale del Laboratorio Territorio Mobilità e Ambiente* 4, no. 3 (2011): 15–28. Dipartimento di Pianificazione e Scienza del Territorio Università degli Studi di Napoli Federico II.

Bonnafous, A. "The Regional Impact of the TGV." *Transportation* 14, no. 2 (1987): 127–37.

Briginshaw, David. "KTX Takes the Lead in Korea." *International Railway Journal* 47, no. 1 (2007): 21–23.

Brownstone, David, Mark Hansen, and Samer Madanat. "Review of 'Bay Area/California High-Speed Rail Ridership and Revenue Forecasting Study.'" UC Berkeley, Institute of Transportation Studies. Research Report UCB-ITS-RR-2010-1, 2010. www.its.berkeley.edu/publications/UCB/2010/RR/UCB-ITS-RR-2010-1.pdf.

Brux, G. "Neubaustrecke Köln-Rhein/Main Fertiggestellt (New High-Speed Rail Line Cologne-Rhine/Main Area Completed)." *Eisenbahningenieur* 53, no. 2 (2002): 28–33.

Caixin Weekly. "Fast Trains to Trouble." *China Economics and Finance* 28 (April 4, 2011).

Campagne, Pierre-Yves. "Du rapport Nora (1969) au rapport Haenel (1994)." *Revue générale des chemins de fer,* Janvier (2004): 15–21.

Campos, Javier, and Ginés de Rus. "Some Stylized Facts about High-Speed Rail: A Review of HSR Experiences around the World." *Transport Policy* 16, no. 1 (2009): 19–28.

CARRD. "The California High Speed Rail Project: What Does It Cost and Why Does It Matter?" Californians Advocating Responsible Rail Design (February 4, 2011). www.calhsr.com/wp-content/uploads/2011/02/CARRD-Capital-Cost-Estimate-February-2011-v1.11.pdf.

Cascetta, Ennio, Andrea Papola, Francesca Pagliara, and Vittorio Marzano. "Analysis of Mobility Impacts of the High Speed Rome–Naples Rail Link using within Day Dynamic Mode Service Choice Models." *Journal of Transport Geography* 19, no. 4 (2011): 635–43.

Catalani, Mauro. "The Impact of the High Speed System on the Naples–Rome Railway Link." Proceedings of the European Transport Conference 2006. Strasbourg (France), September 18–20, 2006.

Chang, Justin S., and Jang-Ho Lee. "Accessibility Analysis of Korean High-Speed Rail: A Case Study of the Seoul Metropolitan Area." *Transport Reviews* 28, no. 1 (2008): 87–103.

Cheng, Yung-Hsiang. "High-Speed Rail in Taiwan: New Experience and Issues for Future Development." *Transport Policy* 17 (2010): 51–63.

Chester, Mikhail, and Arpad Horvath. "Life-Cycle Assessment of High-Speed Rail: The Case of California." *Environmental Research Letters* 5, no. 014003 (2010): 1–8.

CHSRA. *Report to the Legislature.* Sacramento, CA: California High-Speed Rail Authority, December 2009. www.cahighspeedrail.ca.gov/images/chsr/20091223222521_CHSRA_Busines_Plan_Dec_2009.pdf.

CHSRA. *California High-Speed Rail Program Draft 2012 Business Plan.* Sacramento, CA: California High-Speed Rail Authority, November 2011. www.cahighspeedrail.ca.gov/assets/0/152/302/c7912c84-0180-4ded-b27e-d8e6aab2a9a1.pdf.

Cicconi, Ivan. *I costi per l'alta velocità in Italia sono mediamente il 500% più elevati di quelli francesi, spagnoli e giapponesi.* Firenze: Comune di Firenze, 2008.

———. "The High Speed Black Box." Testimony presented before the European Parliament. Strasbourg, November 16, 2011.

Clever, Reinhard, and Mark Hansen. "Interaction of Air and High Speed Rail in Japan." *Transportation Research Record: Journal of the Transportation Research Board* 2043 (2008): 1–12.

Cour des Comptes. "Le projet 'TGV Méditerranée." In *Rapport public annuel* 227–51. Paris: Cour des Comptes, 2004. www.ccomptes.fr/fr/CC/documents/RPA/Tgv-Mediterranee.pdf.

Criddle, Byron. "Electoral System in France." *Parliamentary Affairs* 45, no. 1 (1992): 108–16.

Daluwatte, Sihil, and Ando Asao. "Transportation and Regional Agglomeration in Japan; through a Long Term Simulation Model 1920-85." *Journal of Advanced Transportation* 29, no. 2 (1995): 213–33.

De Rus, Ginés. "Crisis económica y déficit público: financiación, priorización y sostenibilidad de las infraestructuras." Presented in UIMP-Santander, June 28, 2010.

De Rus, Ginés, and Vicente Inglada. "Análisis coste-beneficio del tren de alta velocidad en España." *Revista de Economía Aplicada* 1, no. 3 (1993): 27–48.

———. "Cost-Benefit Analysis of the High-Speed Train in Spain." *Annals of Regional Science* 31, no. 2 (1997): 175–88.

De Rus, Ginés, and Chris Nash. "In What Circumstances Is Investment in HSR Worthwhile?" University of Leeds: ITS WP 590, 2007.

De Rus, Ginés, and Gustavo Nombela. "Is Investment in High Speed Rail Socially Profitable?" *Journal of Transport Economics and Policy* 41, no. 1 (2007): 3–23.

De Rus, Ginés, and Concepción Román. "Análisis económico de la línea de alta velocidad Madrid-Barcelona." *Revista de Economía Aplicada* 14, no. 42 (2006): 35–79.

Dobruszkes, Frédéric. "High-Speed Rail and Air Transport Competition in Western Europe: A Supply-Oriented Perspective." *Transport Policy* 18 (2011): 870–79.

Dong-Chun, Shin. "Recent Experience of and Prospects for High-Speed Rail in Korea: Implications of a Transport System and Regional Development from a Global Perspective." Institute of Urban and Regional Development University of California, Berkeley, Working Paper 2005–02 (2005).

DOT. "Vision for High-Speed Rail in America." Washington, DC: US Department of Transportation, April 2009.

Dunn, James, and Anthony Perl. "Policy Networks and Industrial Revitalization: High Speed Rail Initiatives in France and Germany." *Journal of Public Policy* 14, no. 3 (1994): 311–43.

Ebeling, Klaus. "High Speed Railways in Germany." *Japan Railway and Transport Review* 40 (2005): 36–44.

Ellwanger, Gunther, and Martin Wilckens. "Hochgeschwindigkeitsverkehr gewinnt an Fahrt (High-speed traffic booms)." *Internationales Verkehrswesen* 45, no. 5 (1993): 284–90.

ENAC. *Dati di traffico 2010*. Rome: Ente Nazionale per l'Aviazione Civile, 2011.

Enthoven, Alain C., William C. Grindley, and William H. Warren. *The Financial Risks of California's Proposed High-Speed Rail Project*, 2010. www.cc-hsr.org/assets/pdf/CHSR-Financial_Risks-101210-D.pdf.

Ericson, Steven J. *The Sound of the Whistle: Railroads and the State in Meiji Japan*. Cambridge, MA: Harvard University Press, 1996.

European Commission. *Interaction between High Speed and Air Passenger Transport—Interim Report*. Interim Report on the Action COST 318, April. Brussels: EC, 1996.

European Commission. *Guide to Cost-Benefit Analysis of Investment Projects*. Brussels: European Commission, 2008.

Flyvbjerg, Bent. "Survival of the Unfittest: Why the Worst Infrastructure Gets Built—and What We Can Do About It." *Oxford Review of Economic Policy* 25, no. 3 (2009): 344–67.

Fogel, Robert W. *Railroads and American Economic Growth: Essays in Econometric History*. Baltimore, MD: Johns Hopkins Press, 1964.

FRA. "Vision for High-Speed Rail in America. High-Speed Rail Strategic Plan." *The American Recovery and Reinvestment Act*. Washington, DC: US Department of Transportation, April 16, 2009.

García-Alvarez, Alberto. "Consumo de energía y emisiones del tren de alta velocidad en comparación con otros modos de transporte." *Anales de Mecánica y Electricidad* 84, no. 5 (2007): 26–34. Revised and expanded in *Vía Libre*, January 2008.

GFDS. *Rete AV/AC. Analisi dei costi*. Rome: Grupo Ferrovie dello Stato, 2007a.

GFDS. *Piano Industriale 2007–2011*. Rome: Grupo Ferrovie dello Stato, 2007b.

Givoni, Moshe. "Development and Impact of the Modern High-speed Train: A Review." *Transport Reviews* 26, no. 5 (2006): 593–611.

Gómez Mendoza, Antonio. "Del ferrocarril al AVE. ¿Los mismos errores históricos?" *Clio. Revista de Historia* 45 (2005): 44–49.

Gutierrez Puebla, Javier. "El tren de alta velocidad y sus efectos espaciales." *Investigaciones Regionales* 5 (2004): 199–221.

Groth, David E. "Biting the Bullet: The Politics of Grass-Roots Protest in Contemporary Japan." Unpublished PhD thesis, Stanford, CA: Stanford University, 1986.

———. "Media and Political Protest: The Bullet Train Movements." In *Media and Politics in Japan* edited by Pharr and Krauss 213–41. Honolulu: University of Hawaii Press, 1996.

Hawkins, Nigel. *High Speed Fail. Assessing the case for High Speed 2.* London: Adam Smith Institute, 2011.

Haynes, Kingsley E. "Labor Markets and Regional Transportation Improvements; The Case of High-Speed Trains: An Introduction and Review." *The Annals of Regional Science* 31, no. 1 (1997): 57–76.

Hays, Jeffrey. "Shinkansen and Maglev Magnetic Trains." 2009, last updated October 2011. factsanddetails.com/japan.php?itemid=852&catid=23&subcatid=153.

Heinisch, R. "High Speed Trains in Germany." *Rail International* 23 (1992): 23–24.

Hirota, Ryosuke. "Japon: L'effet Shinkansen." *Transports* 310 (1985): 678–79.

Hood, Christopher P. *Shinkansen: From Bullet Train to Symbol of Modern Japan.* London: Routledge, 2006.

———. "The Shinkansen Local Impact," *Social Science Japan Journal* 13, no. 2 (2010): 211–25.

Hosokawa, Bill. *Old Man Thunder: Father of the Bullet Train to Symbol of Modern Japan.* London: Routledge, 1997.

Huang, Teng, and Joseph M. Sussman. "Financing Methods for High-Speed Rail with Application to Portugal." ESD Working Paper Series 2009-09, 2011.

Imashiro, Mitsuhide. "Changes in Japan's Transport Market and Privatization." *Japan Railway and Transport Review* 13 (1997): 50–53.

ITF (International Transpont Forum). *Trends in the Transport Sector 1970–2007.* OECD-ITF, 2009.

Jaensch, Eberhard. "Railway Infrastructure and the Development of High-Speed Rail in Germany." *Railway Technical Review: The International Journal for Rail Engineers, Operators and Scientists,* no. 2 (2005): 3–11.

Jin, F., and Y. Wang. "Assessment of the Mid- to Long-Term Transport Network Plans in China." Presentation at *Annual Conference of Chinese Association of Geographers,* Wulmuqi, China (2011): 24–25.

Kageson, Per. "Environmental Aspects of Inter-City Passenger Transport." OECD-ITF. Discussion Paper, 2009-28.

Kamel, Karima, and Richard Mattewman. "The Non-Transport Impacts of High Speed Trains on Regional Economic Development: A Review of the Literature." Working Paper. Kent: Locate in Kent, 2008.

Kasai, Yoshiyuki. *Japanese National Railways—Its Break-up and Privatization.* Folkestone: Global Oriental, 2003.

Kien-hong, Peter Yu, and Jokull Johannesson. "Near-Bankruptcy of the Taiwan High Speed Rail Corportaion: What Went Wrong?" *International Journal of Business and Management* 5, no. 12 (2010): 14–22.

Klein, Olivier. "Le TGV-Atlantique et les évolutions de la mobilité : entre crise et concurrence." *Les Cahiers Scientifiques des Transports* 32 (1997): 57–83.

Klein, Olivier, and Gérard Claisse. *Le TGV-Atlantique: entre récession et concurrence. Evolution de la mobilité et mise en service du TGV-Atlantique: analyse des enquêtes réalisées en septembre 1989 et septembre 1993.* Lyon: Laboratoire d'Economie des Transports, 1997.

Kondoh, Haruo. "Political Economy of Public Capital Formation in Japan." *Public Policy Review* 4, no. 1 (2008): 77–110.

Leavitt, Daniel, Peter Cheng, Erin Vaca, and Peter Hall. "Potential for Improved Intercity Passenger Rail Service in California: Study of Corridors." University of California at Berkeley, Institute of Urban and Regional Development, WP 612, 1994.

Lee, Yong Sang. "Achievements of KTX Project for Past Year and Improvement Measures." Presented at the 5th World congress and Exhibition on High Speed Rail held in Milan, November 7–9, 2005.

Levinson, David, Jean Michel Mathieu, David Gillen, and Adib Kanafani. "The Full Cost of High-Speed Rail: An Engineering Approach." *Annals of Regional Science* 31, no. 2 (1997): 189–215.

López Pita, Andrés. *Alta velocidad en el ferrocarril.* Barcelona: Universitat Politécnica de Catalunya, 2010.

Lukaszewicz, Piotr, and Evert Andersson. *Energy consumption and related air pollution for Scandinavian electric passenger trains.* Report KTH/AVE 2006:46. Stockholm: KTH Rail Group, Royal Institute of Technology, 2006.

Mannone, Valérie. "L'impact régional du TGV Sud-Est." Ph.D thesis, Université de Provence, Aix-en-Provence, 1995.

———. "Gares TGV et nouvelles dynamiques urbaines en centre ville: le cas des villes desservies par le TGV Sud-Est." *Cahiers Scientifiques du Transport* 31 (1997): 71–97.

Mannone, Valérie and Umr Telemme. "Gares TGV et nouvelles dynamiques urbaines en entre ville: Le cas des villes desservies par le TGV Sud-Est." *Les Cahiers Scientifiques des Transports* 31 (1997): 71–97.

Manow, Philip. "Electoral Rules and Legislative Turnover: Evidence from Germany's Mixed Electoral System." *West European Politics* 30, no. 1 (2007): 195–207.

Márquez, M. L., and V. Ramírez. "The Spanish Electoral System: Proportionality and Governability." *Annals of Operations Research* 84, no. 1 (1998): 45–59.

Masson, Sophie and Romain Petiot. "Can the High Speed Rail Reinforce Tourism Attractiveness? The Case of High Speed Rail between Perpignan (France) and Barcelona (Spain)." *Technovation* 29 (2009): 611–17.

Matsumoto, Hiroki. "Testimony before the of the House of Representatives." Transportation and Infrastructure Commitee in the Hearing of International High Speed Rail Systems that took place on April 19, 2007.

Ministry of Transportation and Communications. *Investigation of passenger transfer preferences on HSR transfer transportation mode, survey report,* 2007 (In Chinese, cited by Yung-Hsiang Cheng, 2010).

Nakamura, H., and T, Ueda. "The Impacts of the Shinkansen on Regional Development." Proceedings of Fifth World Conference on Transport Research (Japan: Yokohama) 3 (1989): 95–109.

Noda, Yumiko. "Shinkansen Speeds Ahead," in PWC, *Gridlines* (2011): 15–21.

Ollivro, Jean. *TGV et fonctions supérieures dans les régions Bretagne et Pays de la Loire.* Rennes: Université de Rennes II, 1997.

Ortona, Guido, Stefania Ottone, and Ferruccio Ponzano. *A Simulative Assessment of the Italian Electoral System.* Department of Public Policy and Public Choice—Polis. Università del Piemonte Orientale "Amedeo Avogadro." Working paper n. 60 (2005).

O'Toole, Randal. "High-Speed Rail: The Wrong Road for America." *Policy Analysis* (Washington, DC: The Cato Institute), no. 625, October 31, 2008.

———. "The High Cost of High-Speed Rail." Austin (TX): Texas Public Policy Foundation, Center for Economic Freedom, 2009.

Park, Yonghwa, and Hun-Koo Ha. "Analysis of the Impact of High-Speed Railroad Service on Air Transport Demand." *Transportation Research Part E* 42, no. 1 (2006): 95–104.

Peterman, David Randall, John Frittelli, and William J. Mallett. *High Speed Rail (HSR) in the United States.* Washington, DC: Congressional Research Service, 7-5700, 2009.

Plaud, Alain. "The New High Speed Lines and Regional Planning in Japan." *Transportation Research Board,* no. 9 (1977): 387–93.

Rong, Zhang, and Dominique Bouf. "How Can Competition be Introduced into Chinese Railways?" *Transport Policy* 12 (2005): 345–52.

SACTRA. *Transport and the Economy: Full Report.* London: UK Department for Transport, Standing Advisory Committee for Trunk Road Assessment, 1999.

Sasaki, Komei, Tadahiro Ohashi,, and Asao Ando. "High-Speed Rail Transit Impact on Regional Systems: Does the Shinkansen Contribute to Dispersion?" *The Annals of Regional Science* 31 (1997): 77–98.

Schwieterman, Joseph P., and Justin Scheidt. "Survey of Current High-Speed Rail Planning Efforts in the United States." *Transportation Research Record* 1995 (2007): 27–34.

Smith, Julian. "High-Speed Rail: Why, When and How the Signals Line Up." In PWC, *Gridlines* (2011): 2–11.

Suh, Sunduck, Keun-yul Yang, and Jeon Hyun Kim. "Effects of Korean Train Express (KTX) Operation on the National Transport System." *Proceedings of the eastern Asia society for transportation studies* 5 (2005): 175–89.

Takagi, Kiyoharu. "Development of High Speed Railways in China." *Japan Railway & Transport Review* 57 (2011): 36–41.

Takashima, Shuichi. "Railway Operators in Japan 3: Tohoku and Niigata Region." *Japan Railway & Transport Review,* no. 29 (2001): 40–49.

Taniguchi, Mamoru."High Speed Rail in Japan: A Review and Evaluation of the Shinkansen Train." University of California Working Paper UCTC, no. 103, 1992.

Thompson, Louis S. "High Speed Rail in the United States—Why Isn't There More?" *Japan Railway & Transport Review* 3 (1994): 32–39.

UKDfT. *High Speed Rail: Investing in Britain's Future—Decisions and Next Steps.* London: UK Department for Transport, 2012.

Uriol Salcedo, José I. *Historia de los caminos de España. Vol. II Siglos XIX y XX.* Madrid: Editorial AC, 1992.

USCM. "The Economic Impact of High-Speed Rail on Cities and their Metropolitan Areas." Washington DC: The United States Conference of Mayors, 2010. www.infrastructureusa.org/wp-content/uploads/2010/06/usmayors-hsr.pdf.

Van den Berg, Leo, and Peter Pol. *The European High-Speed Train-Network and Urban Development.* Aldershot: Ashgate, 1998.

Van Essen, Huib, Olivier Bello, Jos Dings, and Robert van den Brink. *To Shift or not to Shift, that's the Question. The Environmental Performance of the Principal Modes of Freight and Passenger Transport in the Policymaking Process.* Delft: CE Delft, 2003.

Van Rozycky, Christian, Heinz Koeser, and Henning Schwarz. "Ecology Profile of the German High-Speed Rail Passenger Transport System, ICE." *The International Journal of Life Cycle Assessment* 8, no. 2 (2003): 83–91.

Van Wee, Bert, Robert van den Brink, and Hans Nijland. "Environmental Impacts of High-Speed Rail Links in Cost-Benefit Analyses: A Case Study of the Dutch Zuider Zee Line." *Transportation Research D* 8, no. 4 (2003): 299–314.

Vickerman, Roger. "High-Speed Rail in Europe: Experience and Issues for Future Development." *Annals of Regional Science* 31, no. 1 (1997): 21–38.

Wang, James, Chaohe Rong, Jiang Xu, and Sui Wai Oscar Or. "The Funding of Hierarchical Railway Development in China." *Research in Transportation Economics* 35, no. 1 (2012): 26–33.

Whitelegg, John. *Transport for a sustainable future: The Case for Europe.* London: Belhaven, 1993.

World Bank. *Tracks from the Past, Transport for the Future: China's Railway Industry 1990–2008 and Its Future Plans and Possibilities.* Report from the World Bank's Program of Lending, Analytical and Advisory Services to the Railway Sector in China, no. 56415 (2009).

Yamaguchi, Katsuhiro, and Kiyoshi Yamasaki. "High-Speed Inter-City Transport System in Japan: Past, Present and the Future." Joint Transport Research Centre, International Transport Forum (OECD). Discussion paper 2009-17, 2009.

Zhong, Chiyuan, Germà Bel, and Mildred Warner. "High-Speed Rail Accessibility: What can California learn from Spain?" Working paper, Cornell University: Department of City and Regional Planning, 2012.

Index

ADB. *See* Asian Development Bank

Adif. *See* Administrador de Infraestructuras Ferroviarias

Administrador de Infraestructuras Ferroviarias (Adif), 98, 101–3

Airline Leader, 125

airlines, 18, 31, 48, 50–51, 89, 92, 149, 151–52, 167

air traffic, 27, 61, 129, 136, 146, 159, 178

air transportation, 21, 23, 26–27, 32, 38, 42, 46, 48, 50, 53–54, 57, 59, 81, 89, 95, 100, 107, 109, 125, 130, 132, 140–41, 144, 149–50, 159, 161, 166–68, 170, 173, 178

Albalate, Daniel, iii, v, 99, 193

Alta Velocidad Española (AVE), vii, 95, 96, 98–110, 111n3, 114, 127n2

Andersson, David Emmanuel, 146

Andersson, Evert, 17, 32, 169

Ando, Asao, 53

Aoki, Eiichi, 37

Arduin, Jean-Piere, 28, 64–65, 68

Ashlfeld, Gabriel, 83, 90, 169

Asian Development Bank (ADB), 52

AVE. *See* Alta Velocidad Española

Bazin, Sylvie, 69, 70–73

Bel, Germà, iii, v, 8, 20, 95–96, 99, 111n1, 159, 193

Beria, Paolo, 132–33, 136

Bonnafous, A., 28, 68, 76n3, 109

BOT. *See* Build-Operate-and-Transfer

Bouf, Dominique, 114, 116

Briginshaw, David, 142

Brownstone, David, 16

Brux, G., 81

Build-Operate-and-Transfer (BOT), 146–47

Caixin Weekly, 120, 122–25

Californians Advocating Responsible Rail Design (CARRD), 16

California High-Speed Rail (California HSR), 14–18

California High-Speed Rail Authority (CHSRA), 16, 18, 19n4

California HSR. *See* California High-Speed Rail

Campagne, Pierre-Yves, 63

Campos, Javier, 25, 91

CARRD. *See* Californians Advocating Responsible Rail Design

Cascetta, Ennio, 132

Catalani, Mauro, 23, 130
CBA. *See* Cost-Benefit Analysis
centralization, 28, 39–40, 52, 62, 68, 82, 101–2, 161, 168, 173
Chang, Justin S., 140–41
Cheng, Yung-Hsiang, 148, 152n5, 153
Chester, Mikhail, 18–19, 171
China, vii, xiv, 3–4, 42, 86, 96, 98, 110, 113–18, 120–26, 127nn4–17, 128, 146, 152n7, 158, 161, 164–65, 171, 174
CHSRA. *See* California High-Speed Rail Authority
Cicconi, Ivan, 133–35, 136
Claisse, Gérard, 67, 69, 71, 77
Clever, Reinhard, 43, 48
conventional network. *See* conventional service
conventional service, 59, 74, 83, 115, 130
Cost-Benefit Analysis (CBA), 45, 98, 102, 136
Cour des Compotes, 64, 183

Daluwatte, Sihil, 53
Delaplace, Marie, 181
Department of Transportation (DOT), 14, 17, 19, 29
De Rus, Ginés, 14, 25, 91, 98, 101, 103–4, 164, 174n2
Dobruszkes, Frédéric, 89
DOT. *See* Department of Transportation
Dunn, James, 57, 79, 87

Ebeling, Klaus, 85, 90–91, 170
The Economist, 7, 122, 127
Ellwanger, Gunther, 87, 89
ENAC. *See* Ente Nazionale per l'Aviazione Ceivile
energy consumption, 17, 18, 32, 53–54, 91, 169–71, 173, 178
energy use, 126, 169, 171
Ente Nazionale per l'Aviazione Ceivile (ENAC), 132
Enthoven, Alain, 16, 19n6
environment, xiii–xv, 17–19, 21, 29–32, 53–54, 74, 80, 83, 87, 91–92, 104, 109, 110, 126, 135–36, 144, 147, 152n1, 157, 163, 165, 169–73, 178
environmental. *See* environment
Ericson, Steven, 37
Europe, xi, xiii, 3, 4, 13, 16–17, 35, 105, 135–36, 142, 160, 167
European Commission, 25, 27, 61, 88, 99, 104, 111n4, 164

Feddersen, Arne, 83, 90, 169
Florida HSR, 12, 17
Flyvbjerg, Bent, 8
Fogel, Robert W., xi
France, vii, xii–xiv, 3–5, 7, 14, 19, 22, 24, 27–28, 57–71, 74–77, 81–82, 86, 88, 91, 96, 99–102, 114, 116, 130, 133, 153, 158, 159, 161–62, 169, 175
Fu, Johnson, 162

García-Alvarez, Alberto, 109, 111, 170
Germany, vii, xii, xiv, 3–5, 7, 14, 19, 22, 25, 59, 62, 79–81, 83–87, 89–93, 96, 99–102, 116, 153, 158–59, 161, 168–69
GFDS. *See* Grupo Ferrovie dello Stato
Givoni, Moshe, 28, 190, 168
Gómez Mendoza, Antonio, 110
Grimaldi, Rafaele, 132–33, 136
Grindley, William C., 16, 19n6
Groth, David E., 45
Grupo Ferrovie dello Stato (GFDS), 130, 133–35

Ha, Hun-Koo, 142
Hansen, Mark, 16, 43, 48
Haynes, Kingsley E., 28, 51, 86, 168
Hays, Jeffrey, 42
Heinisch, R., 86
Hirota, Ryosuke, 51–52
Hood, Christopher P., 37, 45, 51, 53
Horvath, Arpad, 18–19, 171
Hosokawa, Bill, 37
Huang, Teng, 51, 152–53

ICE. *See* Inter City Express
Imashiro, Mitsuhido, 52

Inglada, Vicente, 98, 101, 103–4
Inter City Express (ICE), 82, 86, 88, 91,
    152
International Transport Forum (ITF),
    191
Italy, vii, xii, xiv, 3-5, 14, 23, 25, 81,
    96, 99–102, 116, 129–37, 159,
    164
ITF. *See* International Transport Forum

Jaensch, Eberhard, 81, 88
Japan, 43–45, 48, 51–55, 59, 66, 68,
    81–82, 86, 88, 96, 99, 100–101,
    114, 130, 133, 137, 152, 153, 158–
    60, 166, 169–70, 175
Johannesson, Jokull, 148

Kageson, Per, 29, 109, 170
Kamel, Karima, 51
Kasai, Yoshiyuki, 37, 54
Kien-hong, Yu, 148
Klein, Oliver, 67, 69, 71, 77n4
Kondoh, Haruo, 43, 185
Korea, vii, xiv, 3–4, 63, 95, 129, 137–
    40, 142–43, 158, 165
Korea Train Express (KTX), 95, 137,
    138, 140–42
KTX. *See* Korea Train Express

Leavitt, Daniel, 15
Lee, Jang-Ho, 140–41
Lee, Yong Sang, 140
Levinson, David, 15
López Pita, Andrés, 107
Lukaszewicz, Piotr, 17, 32, 169

Madanat, Samer, 16
Maglev, 42, 54, 86, 118–19, 127n1,
    171
Mannone, Valérie, 44, 67–69, 71
market share, 39, 50, 54–55, 89, 105,
    125, 141, 150, 167, 173
Masson, Sophie, 76
Matsumoto, Hiroki, 50, 53, 170
Mattewman, Richard, 51
Ministry of Transportation and
    Communications, 152

Nakamura, H., 51
Nash, Chris, 14, 25
Ni, Jincheng, 64–65
Nijland, Hans, 17, 32, 169
Noda, Yumiko, xii
noise, 29, 54, 91, 170–71
Nombela, Gustavo, 25, 164, 174n2

OECD. *See* Organisation for Economic
    Co-operation and Development
Ohashi, Tadahiro, 53
Ohio HSR, 17
Ollivro, Jean, 77n4
opportunity cost, xiv, 26, 31, 104, 111,
    179
Organisation for Economic Co-
    operation and Development
    (OECD), 96
O'Toole, Randall, 13, 16–18, 52

Park, Yonghwa, 142
Perl, Antony, 57, 79, 87
Peterman, David Randall, 43
Petiot, Romain, 76
Plaud, Alain, 53
Pol, Peter, 44, 109, 168
PPP. *See* Public–Private-Partnership
privatization, xii, 36, 44, 52, 55, 138,
    191
productivity, 22, 26–27, 29, 31, 104,
    113, 115, 162, 166, 168, 172, 177
profitability, xii, 17, 23, 42, 44, 63–64,
    75–76, 86, 98, 101, 120, 123, 147–
    48, 157, 162, 165, 172, 177
Public-Private-Partnership (PPP), xii,
    164, 177

Rete Alta Velocità / Alta Capacità (Rete
    AV/AC), 130
Rete AV/AC. *See* Rete Alta Velocità /
    Alta Capacità
Román, Concepción, 98, 104
Rong, Zhang, 114, 116

SACTRA. *See* Standing Advisory
    Committee for Trunk Road
    Assessment

Sasaki, Komei, 53
Scheidt, Justin, 19n1
Schwieterman, Joseph P., 19n1
Shinkansen, vii, xi, 12, 19, 35–37, 39–40, 42–56, 66, 96, 147, 152
Shyr, Oliver F., 162
Spain, vii, xii–xiv, 3–4, 7–8, 14, 19, 23, 25, 27, 63, 65, 81, 86, 95–102, 104–5, 107, 109–111, 116, 127n3, 130, 133, 159–61, 164–65, 169–70, 191
Standing Advisory Committee for Trunk Road Assessment (SACTRA), 15
Suh, Sunduck, 140–42
Sussman, Joseph M., 51

Taiwan, vii, xii, xiv, 3–5, 42, 129, 145–49, 152, 153n8, 164–65
Takagi, Kiyoharu, 115
Takashima, Shuichi, 43
Taniguchi, Mamoru, 43, 45
taxpayers, xiii, xv, 7, 164, 172, 176–77, 179
technological. *See* technology
technology, xi, 14, 17–18, 29, 32, 42, 51, 54–56, 62–63, 81, 86, 88, 101, 111, 114, 118, 127, 142–43, 147, 152, 157–58, 165, 171, 175–76, 178–79
TGV. *See* Train à Grande Vitesse
Thompson, Louis S., 168
Telemme, Umr, 67, 186
tourism, 28–29, 31, 53, 71, 73, 75–76, 146, 169, 173, 177
Train à Grande Vitesse (TGV), vii, 28, 57–59, 61–76, 77n4, 88, 142–43, 152

The UK. *See* The United Kingdom
UK Department of Transport (UKDfT), 7
UKDfT. *See* UK Department of Transport
The United Kingdom (UK), iii, iv, xiii, 3–5, 7, 42, 61, 63
The United States (US), iv, vii, ix, xi, xiii, xiv, 7–11, 13–15, 17–19, 29, 63, 113, 143, 157, 158–61, 163–64, 167–68, 171, 178, 192
The United States Conference of Mayors (USCM), 14–15, 160
Uriol Salcedo, José, 110
The US. *See* The United States
USCM. *See* The United States Conference of Mayors

Van den Berg, Leo, 44, 109, 168
Van den Brink, Robert, 17, 32, 169
Van Essen, Huib, 32, 169
Van Wee, Bert, 17, 32, 169
Vickerman, Roger, 32, 58, 61, 63–64, 66–67, 87, 101

Wang, James, 114, 116, 118, 121, 123–24
Warner, Mildred, ix, 8
Warren, William H., 16, 19n6
Whitelegg, John, 32, 87
Wilckens, Martin, 87, 89
Wisconsin HSR, 17

Yamaguchi, Katsuhiro, 44
Yamasaki, Kiyoshi, 44
Yang, Keun-yul, 140–42

Zhong, Chiyuan, ix, 8

About the Authors

Daniel Albalate holds a MSc in economics from University College of London, and a PhD in economics from the Universitat de Barcelona (UB). He is assistant professor of economics at UB where he coordinates the Pasqual Maragall's Chair of Economy and Territory. His research interests include public sector reform and infrastructure and transportation policy. He has published fifteen articles in international academic journals. In 2010, Albalate received the William E. and Frederick C. Mosher Award for the best *Public Administration Review* article by an academician in 2010. In 2011 he was selected as a finalist in the Young Researcher of the Year Award from the International Transport Forum (OEDC). Has also collaborated as consultant for regional and local governments in Spain, as well as for road safety foundations.

Germà Bel holds a MSc in economics from the University of Chicago, and a PhD in economics from the Universitat de Barcelona. He is professor of economics at UB, where he is the director of the Pasqual Maragall's Chair of Economy and Territory. He has been visiting professor at Cornell University, visiting scholar at Harvard University and at the European University Institute. His research interests include public sector reform, privatization, infrastructure and transportation policy, and local services. Bel has published sixty articles in international academic journals, and several books on infrastructure and local services. In 2010 he received the Mosher Award for the best *Public Administration Review* article by an academician in 2009. In 2011 he received the award for the best 2010 academic article by the US Academy of Management (Public and Nonprofit Division). Bel was advisor to the Spanish government, and member of the Spanish Parliament from 2000 to 2004.

CPSIA information can be obtained at www.ICGtesting.com
Printed in the USA
BVOW021223060612

291797BV00003B/2/P